SINDH REVISITED

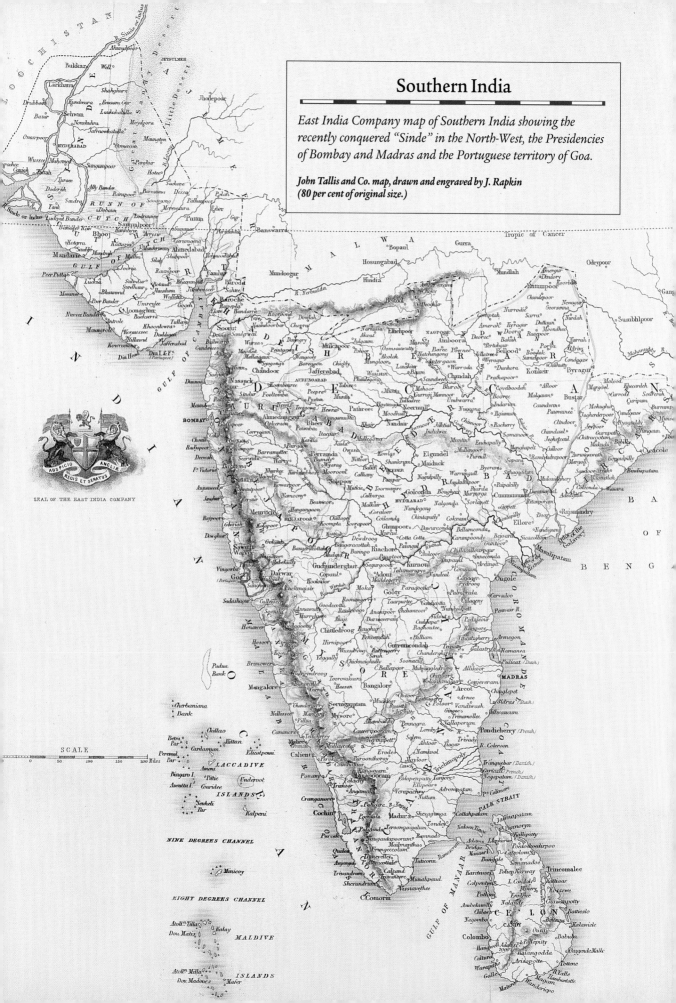

SINDH REVISITED
A JOURNEY IN THE FOOTSTEPS OF
CAPTAIN SIR RICHARD FRANCIS BURTON
1842-1849: The India Years

CHRISTOPHER ONDAATJE

HarperCollins*Publishers*Ltd

First edition: 1996

Canadian Cataloguing in Publication Data

Ondaatje, Christopher

      Sindh revisited : a journey in the footsteps of Captain Sir Richard Francis Burton : 1842–1849, the India years

ISBN 0-00-255436-4

1. Burton, Richard Francis, Sir, 1821–1890.   2. Burton, Richard Francis, Sir, 1821–1890 — Journeys — India.   3. Ondaatje, Christopher — Journeys — India.   4. India — Description and travel.   I. Title.

DS414.2.053 1996   915.404'315'092   C95-932443-7

96 97 98 99 ML 10 9 8 7 6 5 4 3 2 1

Book design by Jackie Young/ink
Printing and binding by Metropole Litho, Quebec, Canada
Film separations by Batten Graphics, Toronto
Production by Paula Chabanais & Associates
Printed and bound in Canada

Bombay's Apollo Bunder, facing the Arabian Sea.

For Charles Ritchie (1906-1995)
Diplomat, adventurer, author and friend

Sindhi women work in the fields, their clothes colourful against the light-green foliage or the dry brown earth.

Contents

Hindu girl carrying sticks in the outskirts of Sindh.

ACKNOWLEDGEMENTS

This book, and the journey that is at the heart of it, would have been impossible without Haroon Siddiqui. From the first, he helped me to turn the concept of following Richard Burton in India into a plan. I have relied on his knowledge, his encouragement, his interview techniques and his many detailed research memos on the things we encountered in our journey. He helped me to go where Burton had gone, to see what Burton had seen and to express what I had found.

In India and Pakistan, I had the efficient and friendly assistance of a bevy of people, each of whom offered not only expertise but also hospitality. Chief among these is Abdul Hamid Akhund, secretary, Department of Culture and Tourism, in Sindh. For his guidance, his energetic travels on our behalf and his thoughtful planning of many of our forays into Sindh, I am deeply grateful.

A number of people helped me turn the journey into a book. I thank Rosemary Aubert for her meticulous research and editorial assistance in the early stages, Margaret Allen for her skilful structuring of the narrative and editing of the final drafts and Joyce Fox for her tireless work in the physical preparation of the manuscript.

I also owe a debt to the biographers of Burton whose work inspired, informed and shaped my own: Edward Rice, Frank McLynn, Fawn Brodie, Byron Farwell, Georgiana Stisted and, especially, Isabel Burton.

Finally, I must thank my wife, Valda, who dutifully listened to my dream of chasing after Richard Burton in India, who waited calmly for my return and who, perhaps like Isabel Burton herself, never lost patience with my travels nor interest in my tales.

The eye again noted a people different from their Indian neighbours. Their characteristic is a peculiar blending of the pure Iranian form and tint with those of the southern Aryans. Their features are regular; their hair, unlike the lank Turanian locks of the Great Peninsula, though coarse, is magnificent in colour and quantity.

SIR RICHARD F. BURTON, 1876,
Sind Revisited

The Sindh today displays an amazing kaleidoscope of people, who look Indian, Mongol, European and even Arab.

Prologue

He knew the Lizzard Song of the Sansis, and the Hálli-Hukh dance ... had mastered the thieves' patter of the chángars, *had taken a Eusufzai horse-thief alone near Attock; and had stood under the sounding board of a border mosque and conducted services in the manner of a Sunni Mollah.... [He] put on the disguise that appealed to him at the moment, stepped down into the brown crowd, and was swallowed up for a while...*

RUDYARD KIPLING, ***Kim***
1901

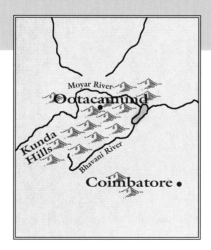

Prologue

I was dwarfed by the fading opulence that surrounded me. The remnants of an imperial past. It was my past, and it was not. Beyond the walls of the club, the jungle waited as it has always waited. Not to reclaim me, though it could, but to reclaim this land of India from those who colonized it long ago. I was in the Wellington Club near Ootacamund, high in the Nilgiri Hills in the south.

Outside in the heavy dark, the air threatened rain. There was a sinister feeling to the atmosphere — a feeling of mystery, perhaps even doom. I was alone; the club was empty, the night watchman nowhere to be seen. Perhaps he had taken off to one of the local bars in the town up the hill. The doors of the club were wide open. It was very quiet; nothing moved.

Except me. I was energetic with busy purpose — writing. My pen flew over the page. There was so much to write about. My trip was almost over. It had been long and tiring, but rich in insights. I simply had to get it all down. So much about Burton; about the East; about the narrow, constrictive Victorian world he fled from in the early 1840s and the 10,000-year-old civilization he fled to.

The discovery of an exotic, seductive civilization entirely different from one's own can profoundly alter one's outlook — Burton's and my own. In trying to follow in Burton's footsteps in India, I had experienced two journeys: the journey of my mind through years of research, and the physical journey over thousands of miles. Two journeys — one truth.

Hanging on the wall in front of me, high above where I sat, was the skin of a black leopard. Sinister, snarling; evoking images of an evil, enigmatic, curious, self-destructive, solitary, elusive figure. But dead now. Contained, captured and tamed. As I looked at it, I thought of the traveller and poet Wilfrid Blunt's first-hand description of Richard Burton:

> *His dress and appearance were those suggesting a released*
> *convict ... a rusty black coat with a crumpled black silk stock, his*
> *throat destitute of collar, a costume which his muscular frame and*
> *immense chest made singularly and incongruously hideous, above*

In the Laxmi Vilas Palace armoury, Baroda.

Previous page: Crowded street scene during the urs *in Sehwan.*

it a countenance the most sinister I have ever seen, dark, cruel, treacherous, with eyes like a wild beast's. He reminded me of a black leopard, caged, but unforgiving....

I was in my mid-thirties when I first heard about the nineteenth-century explorer Sir Richard Francis Burton. My fledgling publishing company was then only three years old, and I was flailing about trying to buy publishing rights, reprint rights, or even paperback rights of biographies that interested me, in both the United States and England. The subsidiary rights agent for W.W. Norton and Company in New York gave me a copy of Fawn Brodie's magnificent *The Devil Drives: A Life of Sir Richard Burton*.

Isabel Burton in 1869.

The book changed my life — or at least it changed my ambition. At that time, I was also deeply involved in an adventure of my own in the world of finance, with its many ups and downs, risks and intrigues, achievements and frustrations. A jungle, in a way, but one that needed different mental abilities and different powers of concentration from those of a Burton-type adventurer.

Fawn Brodie's book really opened my eyes to a world of adventure, and introduced me to one of the most baffling characters and heroes of any era. I went on to read everything I could get my hands on about Burton and by Burton. I read the biographies many times. I saw the films. The more I read, and the more I saw, the more I was fascinated.

It has now been twenty-five years.

The more I read and the more I understood Burton, the more clearly I saw that there were huge gaps in what had been written about this amazing discoverer — even in the most acclaimed studies. It was not mere geographical discovery that held Burton, but also the greater search for what lies hidden in the depths of man — those things that are perhaps ultimately unknowable.

All the biographies of Sir Richard Burton have added something. From Byron Farwell to Fawn Brodie, from Edward Rice to Frank McLynn (and before that Hitchman, Hastings, Wright, Dearden, Bereovici and Richards); and, of course, the earliest biographies by Isabel Burton and Burton's niece Georgiana Stisted. Each work has a different slant and comes to a different conclusion, and each author did his or her biography for a completely different reason.

All of them tried to capture Burton's life in its entirety. But it is impossible to capture this astonishing life in a few hundred pages or even a few volumes. Despite the best intentions and the most careful scholarship, there are enormous gaps in all the authors' research — except perhaps for that of Isabel Burton. As his wife, she knew everything, though she would write only what she wanted to write to protect her husband and, I believe, herself. Only Isabel made the effort to go to the places Richard Burton went. Only she made any effort to share the experiences Burton involved himself in. She was very much a part of his life, and very much an alter ego; but she couldn't do *everything* he did, wasn't allowed to go *everywhere* he went. She could only hover around the perimeter of his discoveries and daring.

John Hanning Speke.

To me there was always something missing in writings about Burton — something that no amount of digging into the records could provide. As my research proceeded, the old saying about understanding how a man lives by walking a mile in his shoes came back to me. If I *really* wanted to fill the gap in my understanding of Richard Burton, perhaps I would have to do something that, to my knowledge, had never been done before: follow in his footsteps. It wouldn't be for a mile, though. It would have to be for thousands of miles!

Burton is known primarily for his search for the source of the Nile; indeed, my first ambition was to walk the entire route that Burton and Speke walked between 1858 and 1863, even to the source of this mighty river. In preparation, I studied everything about Burton's Nile journey, and everything by Burton on the subject. But when all this research was complete, I came to a disappointing conclusion. Burton's African journey, for all its gruelling difficulty and frustration, was mostly a physical journey. I became convinced that re-creating it wouldn't really give me the key to the most fascinating personality of the Victorian era.

I went back to the books, maps, articles — even pictures — until I finally realized that many critically important clues to understanding Burton lay in India and the seven years he spent there from 1842 to 1849 — a period that very few of his biographers had explored in any depth. Burton was in India when he was between the ages of twenty-one and twenty-eight. These are critical years in a person's development, and although Burton had many adventures after 1849, I believe it was his exposure to India's ancient yet living civilization that opened his mind and changed his life forever.

What was it he discovered? What was it about India that changed Richard Burton from a rebellious, wayward youth into a man of courage, imagination, wisdom and personal power?

I determined to set out and discover Richard Burton's India. Everything that Burton did was influenced by what he found in India. He started writing in India, and the attitudes and values he held by 1849 were those he would hold in maturity. Frank McLynn, the author of *Burton: Snow upon the Desert*, was right when he noted that anyone who tries to understand Burton must examine closely the multitudinous impressions of these important years.

Haroon Siddiqui — editor, linguist and invaluable travelling companion.

Why had no one done it? Perhaps because many of the answers cannot be found in libraries, documents, interviews, armchair discussions or other people's biographies, articles and films. The answers lie in the Indian subculture itself. You must cross the barriers that Burton crossed, putting his own world aside in order to understand the people, the religions and most of all the meaning of life in a totally different world.

The ability to become absorbed by another culture was his true discovery, and the process of doing so was his true adventure. In that process lay the answer to the riddle of Burton. I knew with certainty that I must go in search of Burton and bring the truth back without disguise.

With equal certainty I knew that this was not an adventure I could go on alone. About Burton I knew much. About contemporary India and Pakistan I knew a good deal less. Of the languages that had unlocked the secrets of India for Burton I knew very little. Knowledge of English alone would not allow me to conduct my researches in India, and especially in the Sindh. I didn't have a full understanding of religion, particularly Islam, nor did I have a complete understanding of the Indian subculture.

That was where Haroon Siddiqui came in. A Muslim originally from India, Haroon Siddiqui is editor of the Editorial Page of Canada's largest newspaper, the *Toronto Star*. Obviously, the idea of taking Haroon Siddiqui with me to India and the Sindh was a good one. An eminently qualified editor and journalist, he had the added advantages of his profound understanding of Islam, as well as of India's other dominant religions, Hinduism and Sikhism, plus fluency in Urdu and Hindi and some knowledge of Persian and Arabic.

After months of sharing in my research, Haroon had become just as fascinated as I was with the extraordinary figure of Richard Burton. He already knew about Burton's ill-fated mission in search of the source of the Nile before I told him about my project, but he knew little about the Burton years between 1842 and 1849, the years in India. Since then, we had discussed all the recent biographies, Isabel Burton's biography and some of Burton's works — particularly those on India. We'd had countless discussions about the complex cultures of India.

It didn't take me long to decide that I wanted Haroon along with me on my journey. But how was I to convince him? I began by asking his advice time and time again — on everything: on my interpretations and my readings, on how best to do the journey. Getting Haroon was like stalking a leopard. I had to make him want to come with me, had to make the journey seem fun and worthwhile, had to make the adventure a journalistic quest. In the end, both of us were looking for the answer to the same question: What role did India really play in shaping the life of this extraordinary Victorian adventurer?

Now I sat in the shadows of the club. I had done the journey, and had found answers to many questions.

The lights of the Wellington Club were flickering and burning low: the generator was probably on the blink. I had a torch to find my way in the darkness to my cabin outside the main club building. But I was still writing, my thoughts full of Burton.

I glanced up. The skin of the black leopard hanging above me on the wall seemed to move in the thickening shadows. As if life had somehow been breathed into it.

Introduction

There is almost a tortured magnificence in this huge head; tragic and painful, with its mouth that aches with desire; with those dilated nostrils that drink in I know not what strange perfumes.

ARTHUR SYMONS
"Neglected and Mysterious Genius"
Forum, 1922

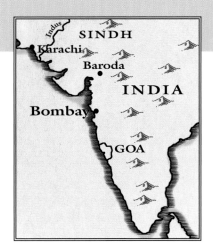

1

INTRODUCTION

The basic facts of Richard Francis Burton's life can be outlined in a few paragraphs.

He was born in Hertfordshire, England, on March 19, 1821. His father, Colonel Joseph Netterville Burton, was Irish; his mother, English. Richard became accustomed to a vagabond life when he was very young. His father's professional situation was precarious, which necessitated constant moving among England and the countries of the Continent. The need for economy and the search for a cure for the colonel's asthma aggravated the peripatetic quality of the family's existence. Richard was the eldest son; he had a brother, Edward, and a sister, Maria. His education was sporadic, but from an early age he set out to learn all he could about swords and guns. Duelling, riding, smoking, gambling and experiments with various forms of wildness — if not debauchery — propelled him through a precocious adolescence, at the end of which he entered Trinity College, Oxford. He showed an immediate obsession with the acquisition of languages, especially Arabic. He taught himself, and invented a system that he claimed would enable him to master any language in only two months. His remarkable linguistic ability, however, was not looked on as proof that he was engaging in the sort of scholarship acceptable at Oxford. His pranks did him even less good. In frustration on the part of everyone concerned, he was sent down.

As would happen often in his long, eventful life, the loss of one opportunity signalled the beginning of another. Richard Burton now joined the famous British East India Company, which had its own military — Victorian

1863 portrait of the 42-year-old Richard Burton, by Wilhelm August Rudolf Lehmann.
Once owned by Isabel Burton, the painting is now in the collection of the author.
Photo: Christie's Images.

Previous page:
... tall mud houses with windowless mud walls, flat mud roofs, and many Bad-girs or mud ventilators. The mud (Kahgil), hereabouts used as adobe or sun-dried brick, and the plaster that binds it, are river-clay (silt and warp) ... throughout Sind, perhaps I may say Central Asia, this morose looking mud is the favourite material because it keeps out the heat and cold.

SIR RICHARD F. BURTON, 1876,
Sind Revisited

England's "other" army.

Using his ever-growing linguistic skills, he steeped himself in Hindustani before setting off for Bombay as an ensign — the lowest rank of commissioned infantry officer — in June of 1842. For him, India held an immediate appeal. For one thing, India had many languages, and it was then the policy of the East India Company to encourage its members to learn some of them. Burton soon mastered Persian, Punjabi, Pashto, Sindhi, Marathi and eventually, over the next few years, many more dialects. Not just a new country but a whole new way of life opened before the eager ensign. Over the next seven years, Burton greedily took in all he could find: delving into tantric Brahmanic rituals; converting to Sikhism and then Islam; enjoying Eastern erotica; keeping native mistresses; learning wrestling and Indian sword and lance thrusts. And writing. Once he began, he kept on writing for the rest of his life. He even gave in to the first stirrings of a lifelong love of disguise. In order to learn about falconry from tribal hillmen, he went in the guise of a Baloch. And he posed as a Muslin merchant, learning the secrets of those with whom he mingled.

Burton's army career turned out to be controversial for a number of reasons. He served under General Charles Napier, whose conquest of the province of Sindh was considered by some to have been accomplished with guile and needless violence, instead of in honourable battle. It has also never been entirely clear whether the soldiers of the East Indian Army were really spies in a "Great Game" of espionage between England and Russia. Burton's own army career ended dramatically and left a mystery in its wake. He parted company with the East Indian Army because a report he had written on the boy brothels of Karachi came to the attention of General Napier's successor and was considered to be disgraceful because it was so accurate as to suggest participation on the part of the reporter. No one has ever found these "Karachi Papers," though my travels gave me a new idea as to what might have happened to them.

Burton's departure from the army left him with feelings of self-disappointment that threatened to destroy him — but not for long. After a brief period of recuperation, he went on to further adventures around the world. He entered Mecca in disguise (1853); he was wounded in Somaliland; he sought the source of the Nile on two separate eventful journeys (1855 and 1857-58); and in 1860 he crossed America to visit the Mormons in Salt Lake City. Immediately after his marriage, he was posted to Fernando Po (1861), then to Santos in 1865 and Damascus (1869). He was sent to Trieste in 1872, where he remained until his death twelve years later.

Passionate curiosity shaped his entire life. "Discovery is mostly my mania," he wrote. Before embarking on a turbulent diplomatic career, he set out with demonic restlessness to solve the geographical puzzles that had eluded other Victorian adventurers. His quest in disguise to enter the holy cities of Mecca and Medina was an extraordinary risk. Descriptions of this venture in his sensitive biographical treatise, *Personal Narrative of a Pilgrimage*

Richard Burton, circa *1875.*

to El-Medinah and Meccah, are full of a sense of danger, wonder and intrigue. He was the first white man to penetrate the equally forbidden Muslim city of Harar in Somaliland, another potentially fatal journey, as death awaited any infidel caught in these holy places.

The dramatic, highly publicized and ill-fated mission with John Hanning Speke to discover the source of the Nile involved amazing courage and stamina. Burton's discovery of Lake Tanganyika (the source of the Congo) was a significant achievement, but a dispute cost him the great exploration *coup* of the nineteenth century. His bad decision not to accompany Speke on a trek to check out the rumour of a "great sea" meant that Speke was alone when he discovered Lake Victoria, the source of the Nile. The bitter public argument that ensued ended only with Speke's death — probably by suicide.

Burton's life after India saw a myriad of accomplishments. Fawn Brodie wrote, "He shines therefore in three constellations of gifted men. He is among the first rank of British explorers, together with David Livingstone, Henry Stanley, Samuel Baker and John Hanning Speke. He was one of that group of gifted British scientists, many of them 'amateurs' — Charles Darwin, Francis Galton, Charles Lyell, James Frazer, Flinders Petrie, Arthur Evans, A.H. Sayce, and Thomas Huxley — who pushed back the frontiers of man's knowledge of man in an explosion of enthusiastic discovery. And thirdly, he was a literary figure of great distinction."

Burton called himself an anthropologist, considered at one time writing a biography of Satan and often boasted that he had committed every possible sin. In his many exotic translations and notes he attempted to explain the mysteries of Eastern sexual eroticism to the West. His curiosity and his zeal for discovery knew no bounds, and he documented everything.

In later years, Burton's diplomatic career grew increasingly tenuous and turbulent. But his anthropological search for whatever was unusual persisted.

His marriage in 1861 to the faithful and staunchly Catholic Isabel Arundell created a partnership often misunderstood by those who observed the relationship. During their long married life, Isabel accompanied Richard on his many diplomatic postings, which ended finally in Trieste (then in Austria, now in Italy). There, for nearly two decades, they lived a quiet life, marked now and then by sudden dramas — one of which was Richard's scandalous and immensely successful translation of the *Arabian Nights*. He also made a return trip to the Sindh in 1876, this time accompanied by Isabel, and published his reactions in *Sind Revisited*.

It is almost impossible to write of Burton in India without writing about Isabel. By bringing her along on his return to the Sindh, he made her an essential part of his Indian adventure. Whatever India had meant to Burton before his return, it would always be part of his life with Isabel afterwards. Her biography describes this trip in minute detail. She claims to have been little more than a stenographer, simply recording what her husband told her to write, but her visit to the Sindh with him made her much more. She became a true partner in the great adventure — a fellow traveller.

"Reader! I have paid, I have packed and I have suffered. I am waiting to join his Caravan. I am waiting for a welcome sound — the tinkling of his camel-bell."

Immediately after Burton's death, Isabel destroyed her husband's final manuscript, *The Scented Garden*, which many think may have been one of the most disturbingly erotic works of this anthropologist, mystic and sensualist. It is likely she did so in part to protect her own reputation as a proper Victorian lady. She was Burton's editor, and her notes would have been on every page of this most "improper" piece of erotica, proving her intimate knowledge of material "unfit" for a lady's eyes. She also burned his intimate diaries and journals: "I burnt sheet after sheet until the whole of the volumes were consumed." Although this fateful act may have protected Isabel's position as Burton's official — and most credible — biographer, it nevertheless remains one of the most savage acts of destruction perpetrated on the literary world.

*"One soul in two bodies..."
Richard and Isabel Burton's
unique grave in Mortlake.*

Isabel also had her husband anointed in the final sacrament of the Catholic church. And finally, his body (which, it was discovered, bore countless healed scars of religious flagellation) was laid to rest in a tomb made to resemble an Arab's tent. Burton had once told Isabel that he did not want to be cremated but would like to lie in an Arab tent. She obliged by commissioning an extraordinary mausoleum. The amazed visitor to Mortlake Catholic Cemetery in suburban London saw an unmistakable tribute to Islam: great blocks of marble, carved and chiselled into the form of an Arab tent complete with fringe and a golden, nine-pointed star at the top. A rope of camel-bells across the door rang poignantly whenever the northern breezes caught it. When Isabel's life ended, she was buried next to her husband in his Eastern-style resting place. Hardly anyone goes there anymore. The door to the mausoleum has now caved in, but the structure retains its oriental flavour. "One soul in two bodies in life or death, never long apart." This is what the Gypsy fortune-teller, Hagar, had once told Isabel would be her lot. And it was.

These are the bare facts of Richard Burton's exceptional life. Over the century since his death, the outline has been fleshed out by scholarship, speculation and pure surmise. Everything I had read about Burton seems to have been borne out by my discoveries, except one thing. I had learned that there are those who feel Burton's reputation is overblown. This is clearly wrong.

I am much more inclined to agree with those who believe that Burton's accomplishments in the fields of anthropology, linguistics, exploration and the study of the Orient are among the greatest of the nineteenth century. He was even a medicine man!

As an author, he touched on an extraordinary range of subjects. His many books covered falconry, geography, the tenets of local religions, military tools and techniques, superstitions and myths, sexual practices, imperial imperatives....

He was one of thousands who served as agents of British colonialism in India; he may have been one of an élite who served as spies. Yet, as my travels showed me, his real contribution in India was not to Britain, but to the Sindh. Although many Englishmen had written about the Sindh, Burton went much deeper than all of them. He played a significant part in the progress and revitalization of the Sindhi language in literature. His contributions to an understanding of the culture of Sindh surpass those of any other Westerner.

Dilapidated first edition title page of Burton's The Book of The Thousand Nights and a Night, *1885. In the palace library in Baroda.*

Though estimates vary as to how many languages he eventually mastered, it is safe to say that he could converse in most of them with the same flair and ease he brought to his mother tongue. In his travels, in India and elsewhere, it was his pride to be taken for a native, and it was his cleverness in all the "extras" of language, such as gesture, intonation and stance, that made this possible.

Burton was a great raconteur but wrote very little about himself, perhaps because of the Victorian aversion to the sort of unbridled self-disclosure that is so popular in the autobiographical writing of our own age.

In many ways, Burton was not a good writer. He could be strident and intolerant. He adopted the prevailing Victorian prejudices against non-whites and Jews. His frank, uncensored writing on pederasty, aphrodisiacs, transvestism and other sexual matters outraged the prudish Victorians — and still shocks some readers today.

And he put everything in. He was undisciplined in his writing, which was probably a fault, though we are fortunate that he did. Today, much of his work would have been deleted and lost forever, like his burned manuscripts and diaries. It is lucky that we have it the way he wrote it with all its blemishes. For him, writing was not only a medium to document his findings, but also a way of crystallizing — even justifying — his adventures, such as his many months of wandering the Sindh. He recorded most of his experiences, even at those times when he was plagued by chronic exhaustion and sick-

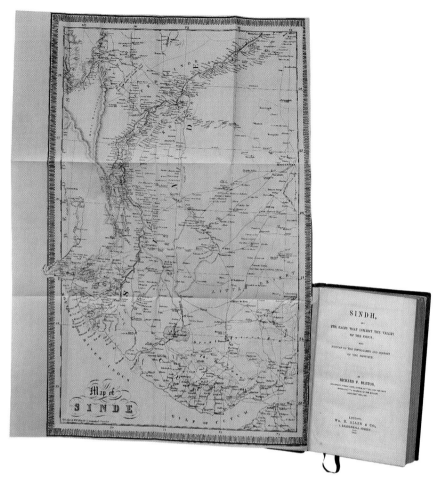

W.H. Allen 1851 fold-out map used in Richard Burton's Sindh, and the Races That Inhabit the Valley of the Indus.

ness. Thank God for his compulsion. Without it, his world would have been lost to us.

Four books came out of his seven-year sojourn in India: *Goa, and the Blue Mountains*; *Scinde; or, the Unhappy Valley*; *Sindh, and the Races That Inhabit the Valley of the Indus*; *Falconry in the Valley of the Indus*.

I now have first editions of all of Burton's books of the India years. The first to be published, the book on Goa (Richard Bentley, 1851), was not a good book, although it was certainly a good start. It is virtually a transcription of his diaries during the six months he spent on sick leave in Goa and the Nilgiri Hills. Even in this rather weak book, however, there is great material on the Todas and polyandry.

Scinde; or, the Unhappy Valley was also published by Richard Bentley in 1851, as was *Sindh, and the Races....* The latter, perhaps Burton's most brilliant anthropological work, is still used in the Sindh as a lexicon on the manners, mores and culture of the tribes that remain in the valley of the Indus River. It is a comprehensive book, and shows for the first time Burton's rare talent as an imaginative scholar of ethnology.

Falconry in the Valley of the Indus was published the next year in London (Van Voorst, 1852). A description of hunting with falcons in the Sindh, the book portrays some of the characters Burton was beginning to meet in his travels and shows him to be an acute observer. It also provides him with a platform from which to criticize the critics of his work. It is a small, rare and coveted book, and one of my most valued possessions.

Burton's writings about Sufism, the mystical offshoot of Islam, are the first by a Westerner with inside knowledge writing for the general public. His great sympathy for the Arab race centred on its religion.

Burton was always curious about religion. He moved from Protestantism to Catholicism, then to an exploration of Brahman Hinduism, Sikhism, Sufism and, finally, the world of Islam, always an important element in Sindhi culture. His love of Islam lasted for the rest of his days. Even so, in his observance of Islam, as in all other aspects of his life, Burton may not have been fully committed. Whether he was really a Muslim was one of the questions I would have to try to answer.

No portrait of Richard Burton would be complete without the observation that his was a profoundly contradictory nature. He was a scholar, but also an adventurer. His interest in sex was legendary, and there are those who think that it was, at one point, an obsession. Yet, though he explored sexual vistas unthinkable to most Victorians, after he married he remained faithful to his wife during a long and sometimes difficult marriage. Despite his great zest for life, he suffered frequently from depression and had a strong tendency towards self-destruction. When he arrived in India, he was disliked immediately by his fellow officers of the Bombay Native Infantry and was much happier in the company of the local people. He soon became known as the "White Nigger," not a promising start to his career. He was also, at times, addicted to drugs, the use of cannabis and opium becoming habitual to him. He experimented with *khat*, which has a priapic effect, and for a time, when he was middle-aged, is thought to have become an alcoholic.

Despite the contradictions, however, Burton never ceased to impress. He was striking physically and overpowering intellectually. He was broad-chested and wiry, and six feet tall in a century when such stature was far rarer than it is today. He was said to have "Gypsy" eyes. He was as handsome, dark and mysterious-looking as the popular Byronic heroes of the age. In later life, he manfully bore the scarred face of one who had done battle with Somali marauders and taken a blow from one of their spears. He was not the typical Victorian, though he came to his maturity at the same time as the British Empire did.

Burton was born in 1821 and died in 1890, a critical span in the history of England. What was that country like in the early 1840s when he left to seek a new life in a far different place?

Well, for one thing, Britain was entering a period of unprecedented prosperity — and was increasingly gripped by a stifling propriety that seemed to develop with its sudden affluence.

By the 1840s, British imperialism was in its heyday, driven by the desire to sustain and advance the mother country's economic empowerment. The goal of the British East India Company was to secure the prosperity of England without depleting its resources. Thus the East was seen primarily as a commercial property to be exploited as thoroughly as possible.

It had not always been so. In English thought in earlier decades, especially from 1800 to 1820 (the age of Byron, Keats and Shelley), the East was seen as the centre not of commercial gain, but of a kind of mystical, spiritual gain. It was this earlier, Romantic view that Richard Burton took with him to India.

Though his military service might have been expected to dim the allure of the strange and exotic, Burton's Romantic inclinations persisted. Like the writers of the British Romantic period, he remained fascinated by the mysteries of the East.

The best work I have encountered on the connection between Burton and the English Romantics is the remarkable study by Nigel Leask, *British Romantic Writers and the East*. Leask points out that each Romantic writer sought his own rewards from his involvement with the East. "For Byron the allure of the East was in the nature of a fatal attraction, a deadly cure for aristocratic spleen. For Shelley, it beckoned as an uncluttered site for the fulfilment of frustrated dreams of liberty.... For DeQuincey ... the stimulant turned out to be a narcotic...."

The narcotic was, of course, opium; and the opium trade came to represent the most shameful exploitation of the East that Britain engaged in.

During the Victorian Age, from the 1840s onwards, there was little questioning of imperialism, and the business ethic prevailed. British nineteenth-century imperialism had changed. In the Romantic era, it had been capable of recognizing and to an extent respecting the native culture of conquered lands. Then it became much more aggressive in exporting its own culture. Burton, however, remained a Romantic all his life in retaining his high regard for native culture.

I would really like to say that Burton was a Romantic writer, and to compare him with Byron, Keats and Shelley. But he wasn't, though he was deeply influenced by them. Byron, Keats and Shelley were all mature writers, even though all died young. They left a vast treasure of Romantic poetry. They were brilliant, enormously creative writers. Burton was not a creative writer. On the contrary, he was a frustrated writer despite the enormous wealth of material he produced. He was a draughtsman rather than an artist, a historian rather than a storyteller. Burton's creativity lay in his curiosity and his frustration, and in his frantic determination to record the findings and preoccupations of his inquiring mind. Byron and Shelley were social philosophers, and, in their very different ways, Keats, Byron and Shelley took aim against injustice, cruelty and ugliness, while pursuing the ideals of beauty, truth and love. Burton can hardly be termed a social philosopher, and as an officer of the British East India Company he was to some extent implicated in the injustice, cruelty and ugliness meted out by the British and the Company in the seven years he spent in India.

The main effect of Romanticism on Burton would have been through its affirmation of personal freedom. Leask points out that in India Burton enjoyed a sexual freedom that Byron could only have dreamed of. In India, Burton didn't just write about the Romantic life. He *lived* it.

Later, though, in fact probably for the rest of his life, he would not be so bold. When he went to India and "lived" the *Arabian Nights*, he was a Romantic. When he published them decades later, he was a Victorian.

When this "romantic" young man arrived in India in 1842, what kind of country did he find?

He found himself right at home in the multilingual, multi-ethnic and multicultural milieu of a country with a long tradition of religious pluralism and sexual tolerance, able to let religion and sex exist side by side, to the point where some Hindus would publicly worship the lingam (the penis-shaped symbol of the Hindu god of fertility), the Muslim Sufi saint would see no dichotomy in taking a tithe from the local prostitute, and the Brahman priest would not apologize for enjoying the *devadasis*, women who dedicated themselves to serving not just a temple but its clergy, copulating right under the noses of their many idols.

Sexual emancipation and an eclectic approach to religion were not surprising in a civilization that was thousands of years old, one that had produced the *Kama Sutra* and the carved erotica of the Ajanta and Ellora caves. It was also a civilization that had given birth to Hinduism, Buddhism, Jainism and Sikhism; that had welcomed Christians to its shores as far back as A.D. 72; and that had sheltered two persecuted minorities from Persia and the Middle East — the Zoroastrians and the Jews.

In the 700 years preceding Burton's arrival, the land had been ruled by a Muslim minority that had invaded from the north. The most glorious of the Muslim dynasties had been that of the Mughals, whose 200-year rule was marked by an unparalleled renaissance in art, architecture, music, poetry and philosophy, and who left behind such varied wonders as the art of miniature painting and the grand Taj Mahal. It was, however, a Mughal king, Akbar the Great, a contemporary of England's Queen Elizabeth I, who unwittingly paved the way for India's domination by the British by failing to perceive the threat inherent in the quiet arrival of merchant ships of the East India Company at the beginning of the seventeenth century. In the autumn of 1599, 101 London merchants had formed that unique business enterprise and won a charter, within a year, from the Queen. Soon after, their ships were returning laden with India's "black gold" — pepper and other spices — which they sold for a hefty profit in London. In 1608, Akbar's successor, Jehangir, granted the company a trading post on the west coast, at the obscure Arabian sea port of Surat. The post was moved in 1661 to Bombay, which had been ceded by the Portuguese to Charles II of England when he married Catherine of Braganza. By 1690, the company had established two posts on the east coast, one (dubbed Fort William) at Hooglee, by the Bay of Bengal, and another (Fort St. George) 800 miles south at Madras. After facing down initial competition from the French East India Company, as well as the Dutch and the Danes, the British merchants were advantageously situated to exploit the power vacuum that followed the death in 1707 of the fourth Mughal ruler, the Emperor Aurangzeb. It was the beginning of the end for the Mughal Empire. An invasion in 1737 by the Persian Nadir Shah left Delhi bleeding and India broken into semi-autonomous principalities controlled by Sikhs, Jats, Rajputs, Marathas and Muslims — a territory ripe for further British penetration.

With guile, determination and ruthlessness, the British spread their tentacles into the Indian subcontinent. They ousted their main rivals — the French and the Portuguese — and gained control of the powerful local states and kingdoms of Bengal and Mysore. The British East India Company grew into a monster monolith, and by the beginning of the nineteenth century, the British were poised to make their final and most powerful foray into the northwest territories — the areas of Sindh, Baluchistan, Punjab and the Northwest Frontier — the four provinces that comprise modern Pakistan.

The East India Company's army was stationed strategically in various princely states, and India became the biggest and most precious jewel in Queen Victoria's crown. She grew fond of her brown subjects, enjoyed curries, spoke a little Hindustani, hired a Hindu as her chief clerk at Buckingham Palace and another as her personal attendant, adopted the son of a legendary Sikh warrior from Punjab and would reprimand her officials for anti-Indian

Nineteenth-century etching showing a view of Bombay and the fort.

comments. Yet those representing her interests in India became increasingly racist and authoritarian as they cocooned themselves in the colonial splendour of their clubs and gymkhanas, enjoying their *chota* (small) and *barra* (large) pegs, served by a phalanx of native male servants. Their isolation from Indian life was sustained by the steady arrival of shiploads of spinsters from London, hunting for husbands, and settling down to a life of comfort they could never have attained in England. These "narrow and provincial women," Somerset Maugham wrote, "for the most part came from modest homes in the country and found themselves in spacious quarters with a number of servants to do their bidding. It went to their heads."

The India that Burton found was one in which the British were becoming increasingly isolated and haughty. Unlike many of his compatriots, however, he arrived in Bombay speaking Hindustani a little better than his sovereign and, like her, open to the ways of India and the Indians.

Involved in a lengthy war in Afghanistan, the British had actively sought recruits; but before Burton reached Bombay, the Afghan war was over, the English forces having suffered crushing defeat at the hands of the Afghans.

The British had already defeated the Marathas and established their power and influence over the important city of Delhi. They now turned their attention to the northwest area of the subcontinent where, following the brutal battle of Miani in 1843, they formally annexed the territories of the amirs of Hyderabad, Khairpur and Mirpur. After the two Sikh Wars of 1845-46 and 1848-49, they were also able to annex the Punjab. The British thus gained access to Afghanistan through the northern Khyber Pass and the western Bolan Pass, succeeding at last in achieving their military objectives in this strategically important northern territory.

Although Burton was only a lowly ensign, he quickly acquired a role in this military and political strategy. His exceptional linguistic skills made him useful as a translator, a surveyor in the farthest reaches of the Indus valley, and also, perhaps, as a spy. He was well suited to the tasks set him, and the independent nature of the work allowed him time and space to do what to him rapidly became the most important part of his life in the army: submerging himself in the ancient civilization he was discovering, documenting its mysteries and writing about his discoveries.

Burton's official army duties included serving as an assistant on the Sindh survey, headed by Captain Scott, the nephew of Sir Walter Scott. There is some argument to the effect that the survey was a front for the "Great Game" — spying — although ostensibly the British were merely measuring distances and water flow. While employed on the survey, Burton became an expert at disguise, disappearing to live among the tribes, sometimes passing as a Pathan, a Persian or a Jat. Mirza Abdullah, his own creation, was his favourite "cover": a half-Arab, half-Persian peddler, by day a street vendor, by night capable of astonishing intrigues.

It was in the course of such adventures that Burton met, in transit, a woman whom he afterward referred to as "the Persian Girl." Who was this

General Charles Napier, enigmatic victor in the battle of Miani, 1843.

Persian beauty? Was Burton's passion for her love? Temptation? Pure fantasy? Did she represent a major choice between staying English or going native? Or did she die — possibly for paying attention to *him* — before he could come to any decision about her? Was this Burton's greatest and only love? His niece Georgiana Stisted in her biography of Burton says that he could never again speak of this love without overwhelming grief. But Georgiana did not like Isabel, Burton's wife, and may have been trying to imply that Isabel had a rival for Burton's affections.

Whatever the truth about his feelings for the Persian Girl, it was not love but sex that led to Burton's downfall in India. He had been assigned as Napier's official interpreter. This had often meant confidential missions carried out in disguise, including the investigation of the male brothels of Karachi. The result was the "Karachi Papers," in which he pointed out that in some Karachi brothels boys and eunuchs — not women — were for hire. Apparently, however, Burton did not stop there, but provided graphic descriptions. Napier supposedly kept the report confidential, only to have it discovered by his successor, who used it to discredit Burton and stifle his army career. The report has never been seen since.

The assignment that General Napier gave young Burton may have been satisfying to his insatiable anthropological curiosity, and both he and Napier may have thought it of great value. However, his later biographers have seen Burton's involvement as a descent into vice and an unspeakable breach of the honour of an officer and a gentleman.

Burton's report on the brothels was intended as a private document between him and Napier. When it became public, it was fatal for his army career. It meant that seven years of brilliant initiative had led precisely nowhere. "The dwarfish demon called Interest had, as usual, won the fight," Burton wrote bitterly. Not his interest, but the interest of authority. The stage was set for his further rebellion. In fact, for a lifetime of it.

Burton left India in 1849. Eight years later, in 1857, social and political unrest came to a head in the Indian Mutiny, which was followed by the transfer of the East India Company's administrative powers to the India Office in London.

After nearly one hundred years of further unrest, in 1947 the separate Muslim state of Pakistan was created. It consisted of two separate areas: West Pakistan — made up of Baluchistan, the Northwest Frontier, West Punjab and Sindh; and East Pakistan — formed from East Bengal. The question of who should control Kashmir is still hotly debated. Pakistan is a new country, and its most difficult challenge has been that of unifying its diverse population groups, divided by geography, race and extremes of wealth and poverty. The harmonizing influence of the common religion has not been able to overcome demands for regional autonomy and increased democracy. The 1970 electoral victory in East Pakistan of the Awami League, which demanded regional autonomy, led to East Pakistan's secession as Bangladesh.

The Sindh that Burton knew and loved in the mid-nineteenth century was a very different place from the Sindh and the Pakistan of today. Sindhis remain a proud people, however, very conscious of their history and culture. In order to follow in Burton's footsteps, I would need — as he did — to gain their trust.

I now knew almost all the places where Burton's wanderings in nineteenth-century India had taken him. I also knew some of the questions I wanted to follow up.

Was this most famous of East India Company employees a British secret agent doing the dirty work of Victoria's empire? Or was he simply a brilliant, pioneering, amateur ethnographer, anthropologist and orientalist? Was he really sympathetic to Islam, or just a clever agnostic striking convenient religious poses to win the confidence of the natives? Was he bisexual or just a good reporter when he recorded the homosexual activities of Karachi's infamous brothels? Was he a racist, as some of his writings suggest, or did he respect the integrity and the culture and traditions of Britain's colonial subjects in India, as other evidence indicates?

The intellectual, philosophical and psychological journey in search of answers to these questions had begun a long time before. Now the physical journey was about to begin.

Armed with my research, my knowledge, my questions, my sympathy and my determination, I set off.

To Bombay — and the rediscovery of an old world.

Bombay

Fifty years ago Mombadevi Town presented a marvellous contrast to the present Queen of Western India. In those days passengers had to land in wretched shore-boats at the Apollo Bunder, and the dirt and squalor that greeted their eyes was well nigh indescribable. As to the poor cadets, under the slovenly rule of the Court of Directors, the scantiest arrangements were made for their comfort.

GEORGIANA M. STISTED
The True Life of Capt. Sir Richard F. Burton,
1896

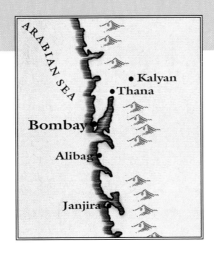

2

Bombay

I arrived in Bombay very late — practically midnight, in fact. It was a bumpy plane ride over the Himalayas, from Kathmandu in Nepal to Delhi. I changed U.S.$200 into Indian rupees at the local bank in the Delhi airport and got a whole pile of bills — which I didn't bother to count. Stuffing them into various pockets (surely inflation was not that bad!), as well as into my camera bag, I got a three-wheel taxi drive to the domestic airport from where I could catch my flight to Bombay. It was a long wait — fortunately for me, as it turned out. After hanging around for nearly an hour in the Executive Lounge under a fan that was barely moving, I heard my name called on the airport loudspeaker. "Would Mr. Christopher Ondaatje please report to the security office immediately." I listened again. The message was repeated: "Would Mr. Christopher Ondaatje please go immediately to the security counter." Picking up my camera bag, I hurried through the bustling crowd, passed through the X-ray check counter and reported to the security officer. My passport was demanded, then any other identification showing my signature, after which a sheepish-looking bank official told me that I had been accidentally short-changed by the bank. With much bowing and scraping, and many apologies, the official gave me another huge pile of notes — the equivalent of U.S.$100. I was glad to have the money, but what was I to do with all these notes?

And so, with about 6,400 rupees in small notes — which I ended up carrying in a plastic bag — I made my way back to the X-ray security checkpoint, shoved cameras, equipment, rupees, plastic bag and so on through X-ray examination and went back to cooling myself in the Executive Lounge under the listless electric fan.

After about another hour, my flight was announced, and I made my way through yet another security check and boarded the plane for Bombay. An Indian Airlines flight, very crowded, but very comfortable, and — surprisingly — on time.

Temple priest in Valkeshwar guarding the lingam nestled in the shadow of nag, *a cobra that encircles the phallic god.*

Previous page: The Haji Ali Shrine juts out 200 yards into Bombay harbour. A long line of devotees makes its way daily along the narrow pathway that connects it to the shore.

Bombay, finally, at 11:00 p.m. After a long wait for my bags, I finally made it out into the hot, humid night air.

Again the wonderful tropical smell of an Eastern city! Busy, bustling, very alive. People and small cars all over the place. On the other side of the railing, the smiling face of Mahnoor Yar Khan, the sister-in-law of Haroon Siddiqui. This was a pleasant surprise. I had been wondering how I was going to get from the airport to the Royal Bombay Yacht Club where Haroon and I would be staying. Her presence made things a lot easier and immediately solved the language problem.

Staff member at the Royal Bombay Yacht Club, once the centre of all British social activity in Bombay.

Only my excitement kept me from giving in to exhaustion as we sped towards the suburbs of Bombay. Despite the lateness of the hour, many people were out in their cars. From the outskirts, we drove through the main city, and finally to the Royal Bombay Yacht Club, the enormous colonial establishment overlooking the old pier called the Apollo Bunder. My first thought on seeing the club was, "What a run-down wreck!" To think that it had once been the centre of all social activity, British anyway, in Bombay. One consolation, though — it was only yards away from the arch known as the Gateway to India, and from the spot where Captain Sir Richard Francis Burton, then a young subaltern, had first arrived.

The next morning I awoke to the sound of car horns, dogs barking, people chattering three floors down in the street below my window and the hum of the electric fan above me. Moments later, as I put the light on, my room boy entered, smiling boldly, bringing a pot of scalding tea. "Tea, Sir?"

Ah, it was good to be back in the tropics again.

He drew the curtains. Across the street were gardens and the Apollo Bunder (official name: Wellington Pier). The sun was rising. It was almost 7:00 a.m. What a wonderful sight — a huge red ball bathing the vast Bombay Harbour in a tangerine light. A few smog clouds hung over the bay. Crows were everywhere, making an awful racket, outdoing even the honking of the cars. This is where it all began — out here below me on this promenade facing the Arabian Sea, where the British landed so long ago.

I went down to have breakfast. Haroon Siddiqui and Mahnoor Yar Khan, a writer, film director and activist (as I was to learn later), were there before me. We had fried eggs and strong coffee and planned the day. It was like

A view over the Arabian Sea from the Malabar Hills.

46

preparing to climb Mount Everest. So much to do, so much to learn. How could we possibly accomplish it all? We laughed at ourselves: loaded down with books and schedules, itineraries, dates, instructions. We had briefed ourselves to the limit: comments by and about Burton, and all kinds of theories and speculations.

The gigantic Royal Bombay Yacht Club building seen from Apollo Bunder.

"Okay," we all agreed, "let's start at the beginning. Explore Bombay. All the houses, hotels, temples. All the markets, bazaars and shrines. Everywhere that Burton went, and everything that Burton wrote about. The British legacy.

"And the interviews!" Our goal was to interview anyone who knew anything about Burton and about the British in India.

A car and driver waited for us at the entrance to the club. And so, with the eagerness of true explorers, we ventured out in search of the British Empire more than 150 years late.

Britain's long involvement in India permanently coloured the history of both countries. The British left monuments to this involvement everywhere in their buildings — an enormous array of structures of every shape and size, all testifying to the pride and commercial energy that fuelled British imperialism. We were stepping into an India that, despite the lapse of time, still harboured much architectural evidence of the imperial attitude.

Into the heat, into the bustling traffic, into the crowds — pushing and shoving — into the world of today, looking for the world of yesterday. We found ourselves in front of Watson's Hotel, where Isabel and Richard Burton stayed in 1876 on their return to India. It is still there, only a thousand yards away from the docks and the Royal Bombay Yacht Club, but no longer a hotel. A six-storey structure built in 1867, the hotel was the first iron-framed building to be constructed in Bombay, with railings imported from England. It was once a grand building, but is now very run down and ringed by small vendors and boutiques. Cheap, modern signs at street level obscure the original iron railings around the parapets, balconies and windows. The contrast between the present and its more prosperous past was almost painful to think about. I wondered which room Richard and Isabel Burton had stayed in. Did they overlook the street? Since then, the crowds, the human jungle, have moved in, infiltrating the past, disguising it, trying to obliterate it. But it is still there.

Though we had only just begun, we already felt overwhelmed. Bombay is a huge city, and even our focused excursion could have netted hundreds of

Into the heat, into the bustling traffic, into the crowds—pushing and shoving—into the world of today, looking for the world of yesterday.

buildings for us to study. But, pursuing Burton's footsteps, we went onward — and upward — climbing 100 steps in the hot morning sun towards the Babulnath Temple in the Malabar Hills — prime Bombay real estate on a raised peninsula jutting out into the Arabian Sea. We took in the magnificent view over Bombay Harbour. The three-kilometre-long "necklace" encircling the harbour displays a variety of architecture. Highrises and low-rises and many historical British buildings all overlook the port and the vast expanse of the sea.

Watson's Hotel in Bombay.

Babulnath is really quite a small temple, carved in marble and alabaster. Intricate, elaborate renderings of the Hindu gods Shiva, Parvati and Ganesh embellish the place, and there are animal images, too: jungle scenes, scenes of elephants and birds. Perhaps they tell some story from Hindu mythology. It was not permitted to take photographs, but I did — one of a man deep in prayer. Inside the temple we saw something I had read about: a lingam god of fertility. Again I took a forbidden picture — the stone object was twelve inches in diameter and sixteen inches high. A Brahman priest poured milk over the lingam, which is really symbolic of an enormous penis.

Vultures were flying over the temple, and I guessed that somewhere in the vicinity there was a Tower of Silence, the place of the dead for the minority Parsees (Persians), followers of the ancient Iranian religion of Zoroastrianism. They came to India in the tenth century, fleeing persecution, and are now a thriving business community. Their age-old custom and ancient hygienics dictate leaving the dead on a platform high above the ground, exposed to the elements — and to vultures.

Almost a mile away from the Babulnath Temple, we found Valkeshwar, one of a series of small temples surrounding a bathing *ghat*, and what was once a Brahman village settlement on the side of a hill. At one point, the Portuguese destroyed this temple, but it was rebuilt by a wealthy Hindu. Here we saw the lingam nestled in the shadow of *nag*, a cobra, encircling and guarding the phallic god. As I surreptitiously photographed a priest praying to the lingam, I remembered the story of how Burton was not allowed entrance into this temple unless he could recite a holy *mantra*, which he did in flawless Sanskrit. The impressed priest welcomed him right in: "You are a better Brahman than I." It's the same temple Burton brought Isabel to in 1876.

The *ghat*, very similar to a Roman bath, attracts the faithful, including transvestites and *fakirs* (religious devotees who live by begging). They all pray

Hindu worshipper praying at the Babulnath Temple.

by the water and bathe in it, achieving purification — an important religious ritual for Hindus, who go by the hundreds of thousands every year to the holy Ganges to bathe and to wash away their sins. The *ghat* serves the same purpose on a smaller scale.

Our next stop was the Mahalaxmi Temple, overlooking the Arabian Sea, reached via a narrow, winding avenue, through crowds of vendors, *sadhus* (sages or holy men), women with baskets — some holding live cobras, some holding flowers. We saw men with conch horns, but noted that more devotees were women than men. All who come to the temple must bring offerings for the gods. Shops and boutiques were selling shawls, coconuts, flowers, oils, shoes, food, trinkets. I noticed a sign — in English — saying "Beware of Pickpockets." It was amazing to see the religious symbol of the cobra used to make money, to earn another rupee. We learned that the women had done the fasting (*upvas* in Sanskrit) for their husbands, saving them the trouble. We learned, too, that today's crowds were bigger than usual because of the approaching Maha Shivaratri Festival, honouring the god Shiva. The sun was hot now, and there was a heightened intensity in the jostling, pressing crowd as we departed.

We returned from the temple along the narrow avenue, past the *ghat*.

From my very first hours in Bombay, I was struck — as Burton was — by the juxtaposition of Hindu and Muslim life. Way below us in the harbour, down the Malabar Hill and almost under the shadow of the Mahalaxmi Temple, we saw the Haji Ali Shrine. It was unmistakable, a very prominent feature of the view. A line of pilgrims moved slowly out onto the island in the bay to visit the

The ghat, *very similar to a Roman bath, attracts the faithful, who pray by the water and bathe in it for purification.*

tomb of this eighteenth-century Muslim saint who renounced the world after performing his Haj at Mecca. The shrine juts out 200 yards into the sea and is connected to the shore by a narrow pathway, along which we could see the constant movement of the long line of devotees.

Struck by the now familiar feeling of moving into not only a new world, but a multiplicity of worlds, we drove through the red light district, behind Bhindi Bazaar, visited and written about by Burton. Here, right in the middle of a bustling commercial district, is an area openly offering commerce in flesh. Women advertise themselves on the street. As we drove through slowly, taking a few pictures, the women covered their faces. On this first day, coming as it did after the visits to the temples, the flesh bazaar was a startling eye-opener.

We walked slowly through Bhindi Bazaar itself, in the heart of old Bombay, where millions of rupees' worth of goods are traded hourly by wholesale merchants. Probably the most densely crowded part of Bombay, this was as much a hive of activity when Burton visited it as it is today. I couldn't help speculating on how the young Burton must have felt when he was suddenly thrust into this mêlée. In small, dirty alleyways, clogged with a jostling crowd, male and female customers bargained with vendors whose carts and boutiques displayed vegetables, clothes, leather goods, perfumes, Indian beauty aids such as *kohl* (the oldest form of eyeliner), henna for hair and wigs. In his Sindh days, Burton used a wig as a disguise. Also henna, and probably *kohl*, too.

Later I learned that this area is also frequented by India's Ismaili Muslims — followers of the Aga Khan — who have their *jamat khana* (gathering place) here.

Everywhere I looked, my attention was grabbed. I noticed a high tower, read that it had been built with donations from "Messrs. Molloo Brothers of Zanzibar" — which seemed impossibly exotic. I also saw a group of women in black wearing the *burqa* (veil and outer garment), covering their bodies but not their faces, unlike their conservative Muslim sisters elsewhere who cloak themselves from head to toe. The sun was very hot and I had no hat, so I bought a black shawl and put it over my head. I was far less a curiosity with my head covering as we kept up to the swirling motion everywhere. I must have been the only pale face in the crowd! Suddenly I was experiencing the power of a "disguise" — and I began to see its appeal for Burton.

Back to the Royal Bombay Yacht Club for lunch. It felt good to get out of the crowds and into the shade, and to have a few moments away from the bustling pandemonium. It was already clear to me that the journey was going to be physically challenging. I knew I'd have to get my muscles going again.

Over lunch we talked about Jan Morris's description of the genteel loveliness of the yacht club in its heyday. In *Stones of Empire*, she said: "This was one of the very first buildings the newcomer saw upon his arrival in India ... with its long lines of al fresco tables beside the water, at which parasol'd ladies and topi'd gentlemen sat taking their tea in the afternoon sun...."

We also discussed some of what we had learned about Richard Burton's

Bombay. European involvement in the area began when the Portuguese arrived here in 1509, ten years after Vasco da Gama's "discovery" of India. The Sultan of Gujarat, hoping to satisfy the invaders and keep them from further acquisition, ceded Bombay to the Portuguese in 1534. The Portuguese built a fort, the remnants of which can still be seen. Not long after Charles II of England received Bombay as part of the dowry of Catherine of Braganza, the British began using Bombay for trade. They were not, however, unopposed. Regular raids by Shivaji, a Maratha leader, initially annoying, were eventually entirely quelled, and Shivaji suffered total defeat, his power and his holdings falling under British rule. Bombay prospered and grew.

The city was formally handed over to the British in 1665, and only three years later the East India Company assumed responsibility for it. In 1673, the fort of Bombay became the residence of the Council of Surat of the East India Company. Thirteen years after that, in 1686, the East India Company headquarters moved from Surat to Bombay. After that, the port was the main entry point of British colonialism in India, and was used for the lucrative trade of opium to China.

By 1818, the British were able to take full control, having routed the Marathas. The nineteenth century saw a great construction boom in the city which resulted in the Victorian Gothic structures best exemplified in buildings like Watson's Hotel.

On October 28, 1842, the ship *John Knox* docked at Bombay, and Burton disembarked at Apollo Bunder. At that time, the opium trade — a complex series of economic manoeuvres that included dealings in tea — was booming. This was the era of the "China Clippers." There were other kinds of cargo going through the port then, too. Lady Falkland, wife of the governor of

Late nineteenth-century photograph of Apollo Bunder.

Bombay, referred to the "fishing fleet." These were the husband-hunters who came by the shipload from England. They had been coming for almost 100 years, supported by the East India Company in an attempt to keep British men away from the *bubu* — the Indian "wife."

The Bombay to which Burton came was a thriving city with a population numbering more than a quarter of a million. Five years before Burton got there, regular steamboat service was established, and the Pacific and Orient steamship company had been calling at Bombay since 1840. There were already many stately examples of imperial architecture near the port and in the neighbourhoods beyond. The Bombay of Burton showed the influence of London, and in many ways it still does.

Today, Apollo Bunder is cluttered by a parking lot for the five-star Taj Hotel (1903); by hawkers and hookers; by a park with a wrought-iron railing that keeps the public away from the public facility most of the time; and, right on the sea front, by the Gateway to India — an imposing but useless monument to British grandeur — "something between the Arc de Triomphe in Paris and a segment of a Moorish palace," as Gillian Tindall describes it in *City of Gold*. Completed in 1927, the Gateway was begun in 1911 to mark the visit of King George V and his Queen.

The old Portuguese fort that Burton saw is now occupied by the Indian Navy (Western Command), which uses the harbour to control the Arabian Sea and the vast stretches of the Indian Ocean — a different kind of empire. The fort is closed to the public, and we had to obtain special permission to see and photograph the gate, the fort ramparts, and the old Portuguese sundial.

One thing that hasn't changed is the view of the sea from the upper floors of the Royal Bombay Yacht Club. Brilliant sunrises, different every day, are

Apollo Bunder today seen from Bombay Harbour.

greeted by Hindus with folded hands for *surya na-maskar* (sun greeting), the first of a series of morning yoga exercises. Pleasure boats anchor by the retaining wall. Ships line up to get into India's busiest port. In the distance can be seen the hills of Elephanta, a cave-riddled island to which Burton took Isabel in 1876.

Within walking distance along the waterfront is the Scottish Church, and just beyond that the Writers' Building, where the clerks of the East India Company toiled. Behind it is British Hotel Lane, named after the British Hotel, since demolished. Burton stayed there during the first week of his Indian sojourn, but abandoned it in disgust at the boorishness of its drunken British inhabitants. It was such excesses that prompted the construction of the

St. Thomas's Cathedral.

Anglican St. Thomas's Church (now Cathedral), named after the apostle who brought the gospel to India. "One of the reasons given for raising funds for the building of the church was that the British — Anglicans, that is — didn't have a religious presence," we were told by Bombay historian Foy Nissin, during one of our (later) interviews. "The British were not seen to worship. The East India Company managers were worried that the Catholics were seen to worship at the three Portuguese churches already here then; the Muslims were seen to worship, and the Hindus were seen to worship, but the British were seen to be whoring and drinking. They had mistresses. Many produced children. The Victorians were concerned about the souls of these illegitimate children. So they would ensure that the children were baptized. These children would stay with the Indian mother but would be sponsored and looked after by one or two British officers. They would be sent to orphan schools or church schools to ensure that they were reared in the Christian tradition." It was to counter the "whoring and drinking" image that the British built the church. And, in a true reflection of the social mores of the day, they allotted pews by rank and social standing, offering the worst seats to the Sahibs' brown mistresses, the *bubus*.

Burton found the church in bad shape — "splotched and corroded as if by gangrene." It has since been restored. The monuments, including gravestones on the church floor, were made by well-known nineteenth-century sculptors in London, whose works also grace St. Paul's Cathedral there: Hinchcliff, Weeks, Bacon, and Peart. "All of this was their way of being sanctimonious about death," according to Foy Nissin. "In fact, they were celebrating not so much the glory of God as those who died in the service of the Raj."

The cathedral is in the old fort area, an enclave of Victorian architecture around the Elphinstone Circle (1860), since renamed Horniman Circle after an Irish-born newspaper editor who became a staunch Indian nationalist. It is an elegant circle with a park in the middle whose railings came from a London foundry.

About two miles from here lived John Lockwood Kipling, the director of an art school. In the school's official residence, his famous son, Rudyard Kipling, was born in 1865. Rudyard was eventually to write a poem to the banyan tree in its front yard, which is still there, as are the frescos that his father designed and carved on the friezes of the Crawford Market across the street from the school.

That afternoon, Haroon Siddiqui and I began the interviews we had set up. We had agreed that we would learn everything we could before we got to India, and then write down everything that we discovered. Every detail, every observation, every sensation. We also agreed to state our opinions frankly, even if our views differed. We would ask questions even if the questions were embarrassing. We would keep to a strict schedule, however tiring — and it usually was — and we would plan each day and each itinerary well in advance. If an interview was to be conducted in anything other than English, Haroon would conduct it, translate it, discuss it with me and write it down before sleep that night. Explanations and translations were made to me during interviews, and my questions were translated and asked even if they disturbed the smooth flow of the interview.

Haroon is opinionated, sensitive, understanding, critical, curious, sometimes difficult to convince, but passionately enthusiastic. I could not have picked a better travelling companion. Nor could I have completed my mission without him. He was supportive every step of the way, and methodical in his inquisitive approach to interviews. Unselfishly, he regularly sacrificed his rest, writing far into the night to record details of our interviews while they were still fresh in his mind. I loved working with Haroon Siddiqui. He is a journalist and a professional far beyond my own qualifications. I simply had a theory. I gambled. He made my gamble work. I hope one day I can return the favour.

Our first interview was with Bal Samanth, author of *Richard Burton: The Fallen Agent*, written in Marathi. The book proved so popular that, Bal Samanth said, "I am now a household name here in Maharashtra" (Bombay is in Maharashtra State). Like any good interview subject, the seventy-year-old bibliographer and humorist turned out to be opinionated and amusing.

"I suppose at first some people bought my book because they thought it was about Richard Burton the actor!" As word spread, however, it became an instant bestseller. Everyone — kids, middle-aged people, seniors — loved it. One man, a well-known musician, Hudaynath Mangeshkar, told Bal Samanth that the story of Richard Burton changed his life. Before, on his innumer-

Bal Samanth, author, bibliographer and humorist.

able road trips, he had never paid any attention to the city or town he was in; he would perform, disappear into his hotel room, and then leave town as soon as possible. "But now, inspired by Burton's example, he talks to the local people, goes out and sees the cities he is in. This is what Richard Burton has taught him."

As Bal Samanth himself admitted, he did no original research. His book is mostly a rewrite of Fawn Brodie's and Isabel Burton's biographies, and Isabel Burton's travelogue, *Arabia, Egypt, India* (William Mullan and Son, London, 1879). Samanth's important contribution was in introducing Burton to non-English-speaking Marathas, people whom Burton had a lot to do with and whose language, Marathi, he learnt to speak.

It was Burton's fundamental empathy with Eastern societies and cultures that most appealed to Samanth's readers. As Samanth pointed out, "Burton loved Asia, particularly Muslims. He said, 'If the world is man, Europe is its head, but Asia is its heart.' When Burton read the *Kama Sutra*, he was so captivated that he said, 'We British never knew this kind of love and lovemaking. Had we known, we would not have ruined the lives of so many British virgins!'"

Asked if he felt Burton was a racist, Bal Samanth said: "No, Burton was not a racist at all. What he wrote was 150 years ago. It reflects some of the attitudes of those times. As an Asian, I am not at all offended by some of Burton's bigoted views of India, particularly Sindhis. I do not find his comments on India and Indians offensive. On the contrary, he condemned British colonialism; he said the British were plundering India's immense wealth, which they were. He also said harsh things about the Sindhis, and criticized certain Indian attitudes, but he never hated India or Indians.

"People like Burton are born rarely. You know, the British did not treat him fairly; they humiliated him. He was never a success in Britain, and Britain can take no credit for his popularity. Burton was not an Englishman; he didn't think like an Englishman.

"It is interesting that most Burton biographers — Rice, Brodie, and Farwell, for example — are not British. Only McLynn is British. Do you remember the Bible? 'A prophet is not without honour, save in his own country.'"

Bal Samanth readily agreed that India had indeed changed Burton's life forever, and the interview with him proved to be an early confirmation of so many of the ideas Haroon and I had formulated during our pre-trip discussions.

After the interview, we went out again into the crowds, past the Goan Catholic enclave of the Mahim neighbourhood, where we saw crosses on street corners and in front of houses. Many platforms seemed to have been erected specifically on which to plant these Christian symbols.

Soon after, we encountered an enormous crowd, a procession heading for the shrine of the Muslim saint Makhdoom Shah Baba for the *urs* (anniversary of the saint's death). It was an extraordinary sight — a frenzy of drummers, dancers and loud music. One bare-chested young man appeared to be in a trance. Crowds circled him. He held his head up, arms outstretched, and I watched in amazement as an older man pierced the skin on the young dancer's arms and chest, first with needles, then with skewers about a foot long. He also put the skewers through the skin of the young man's neck! I stood in shock, bewildered at what I was watching. I smelled fire, incense, smoke. More skewers were thrust through the man's forearms and the skin of his stomach. Drums continued to beat. Then, his eyes glazed, the young man raised his head higher still. He stuck his tongue out, and the older man, holding the tongue between his thumb and first finger, pierced it with a thick needle. The needle went right through the tongue. There was no blood, and the young man neither flinched nor cried out. All around me people murmured, "Bismilla hir Rahman ar Raheem," the first words of the Qur'an, which mean, "I begin in the name of Allah." The skewers remained in the man's body and still he didn't move. He was enveloped in smoke and incense from a small brazier at his feet. The drums beat faster and louder. "Ya Allah (Oh, Allah)!" "Alhamd-U-Lillah (Thank Allah)!" chanted the

Sunset over Bombay Harbour, from Chowpati Beach.

crowd, moving closer. With my camera, I made my way through the onlookers into the inner circle in front of the young man. No one seemed to mind. It was all part of the *urs*. All part of the celebration.

We were headed towards the shrine, which was about 200 yards away. The crowd inched forward, and we were carried along with it, part of a thick human river. It became harder and harder to move — either forward or backward. But we were part of whatever progress there was. We had to go with the crowd.

About 100 yards from the shrine, the street narrowed. It became almost impossible to go forward, and we gave up. We fought our way first to the side and then slowly away. But the crowd continued its slow, purposeful forward motion, pushing and shoving, not aggressively, but determined to reach the shrine and to lay *chadars* (cloths with inscriptions from the Qur'an) on the saint's grave and beg for favours.

I finished my first day in Bombay in a state of euphoria. The accidental coming upon the *urs* crowned the day's experiences. After only a day, I could see what Burton had been up against. He had somehow to capture all of this. Somehow he managed. Somehow — in India — he taught himself to be a writer.

Back in my own room, working on my own writing, I realized that I was starting to cough. Bombay is so polluted. Was that it? Just a reaction to fumes from the three-wheel taxis, the buses, the lorries? Or was the coughing something worse? There was a chemical smell in the air.

Night noises. Heat. The fan helped. I closed the window. That shut out the noise and, I hoped, some of the pollution. I was restless. I kept thinking about the *urs*. And about Burton and the countless small scars discovered on his body after he died. Had he scarred his body with skewers and knives like the young man in the *urs*? The experiences of the day left me full of questions and speculations. Was this how it was for Burton when he was first exposed to Indian culture and religion? I tossed and turned for hours before I finally slept.

At Bombay you admired the changes which the labours of the last quarter-century have effected .... a few tenements of stone and lime emerging from a mass of low hovels, mat and mud ... surrounded by tumble-down curtain-combastions.

Sɪʀ Rɪᴄʜᴀʀᴅ F. Bᴜʀᴛᴏɴ, 1876,
Sind Revisited

About 100,000 people live and sleep, and sometimes breed, on Bombay's sidewalks.

When the fit is induced, the rest of the company look with great respect at the patient till it is over.

Sɪʀ Rɪᴄʜᴀʀᴅ F. Bᴜʀᴛᴏɴ, 1851,
Sindh, and the Races That Inhabit the Valley of the Indus

Previous page: One bare-chested young man, arms outstretched, appeared to be in a trance. An older man pierced the skin on the young dancer's arms and chest, first with needles, then with skewers.

There were lots of British buildings here when Burton was here: St. Thomas's Cathedral, St. Andrew's Church, St. Columba's Church, the Scottish Church (opposite the dockyard), St. John's Church now called the Afghan Church; the Asiatic Society Library (1833), Castle Gateway; the Mint (1824); Gas Light (1833). The Methodist Church — behind the Taj Mahal Hotel by the Bombay Yacht Club; the British Hotel (now torn down). The Great Western Hotel (1797); the old Writers' Building (for the East India Company pen pushers by the docks); and two streetscapes that are still intact: Dock Yard Street and Perin Nariman Street (by Horniman Circle). If you walk down these streets you will get a sense of Burton's Bombay.

INTERVIEW WITH FOY NISSIN,
retired British consular affairs officer, Bombay, 1994

The crows woke me again. The second day. Not as good a sunrise as yesterday—but still a fantastic view out over the Bombay Harbour. Burton said the word "Bombay" came from "Mombadevi," a local tribal goddess. This couldn't be right. It is far more likely that it came from "Bom Bahia" — which loosely translated means "the good bay" in Portuguese.

Haroon and I met for breakfast in my room and exchanged notes and memos, then divided up our chores of writing, observation and opinion gathering and set off. Today, we had decided, we would try to visit as many as possible of the old British buildings that Burton had mentioned, or that he must have been in or seen while he was in India. I tucked a volume of Jan Morris's *Pax Britannica* into my pocket and we took to the crowded streets.

We began at St. Thomas's Cathedral in the old fort area in a relatively uncommercialized neighbourhood only a stone's throw away from the yacht club. This certainly seemed to be a very English area of town, with stately examples of Victorian architecture in Horniman (formerly Elphinstone) Circle. St. Thomas's struck us as quite beautiful. The oldest English building in Bombay, it was opened on Christmas Day in 1817, and is as imposing now, with its grand ceilings, as it must have been then. Its walls are completely adorned with marble memorials and tablets in memory of fallen British officers who died in the eighteenth and nineteenth centuries. Among these tablets we saw one to the memory of Lieutenant Gregory Grant, who died at Lucknow on July 28, 1857, from wounds received in the defence of the Residency. We also saw memorials to his wife, Eliza, and infant daughter, Ellen, who died there during the siege. He must have been one of the first casualties of

Marble tablet to the memory of Lieutenant Gregory Grant in St. Thomas's Cathedral.

the great Indian Mutiny of 1857. This revolt, which began as an uprising of sepoys (native soldiers serving with the East India Company), soon developed into the full-blown Anglo-Indian War. The resulting bloody conflict ended when the sepoys, who had been joined by Indian princes across northern India, were defeated through the efforts of Colin Campbell. As a result of the Mutiny, the East India Company relinquished its administrative powers in India directly to the Crown, ushering in the period called the Raj.

Next, our wanderings took us to the Asiatic Society Library, an imposing structure with neoclassical columns and steps. It houses 800,000 volumes, including six of Burton's works, 10,000 manuscripts and a rare first edition of Dante's *Divine Comedy*, said to be worth more than $3 million. We marvelled at the lifelike statues inside, including those of Elphinstone, governor of Bombay from 1819 to 1827, and Sir Bartle Frere, governor from 1862 to 1876, as well as of such "brown Sahibs" as Sir Jamsetjee Jejeebhoy, the most glamorous Parsee figure in the mid-1900s and the first Indian to be made a baronet, and the Honourable Juggonath Sunkersett (an anglicized version of the plain Indian name Jagan Nath Shankarseth), a distinguished citizen of Bombay. There was dust over everything. Rare books in disarray and disorder. Among them was a copy of *Sind Revisited*, which, I feared, wouldn't last long, despite the librarians' protective attitude. No copies. No photostats. No photographs. Nothing. An attitude we had also encountered among the librarians of New York and Toronto when we tried to get photos of pages of that particular Burton book, which is very rare.

After the Asiatic Society Library, we saw Biculla Station, the first railway station in India, serving the Bombay-Thana Line, starting in 1853.

Our discoveries were energizing us as we continued our survey. But not all we saw was imperially grand. I had seen the Bombay slums even before setting foot in the city. As your airplane approaches Bombay's Santa Cruz airport from the west, you see, first, a breathtaking view of the western *ghats*, then suddenly one of the world's biggest and worst slums. Row upon row of tiny hovels of beaten-out tin and corrugated iron, an apparently endless panorama of dirt and misery, the sight of which gets seared on your mind and sinks into your consciousness for life. As the aircraft loses altitude, you are almost skimming the rooftops, and the settlements stretch right up to the runway, separated from it only by the airport fence. But jet noise is the least of the slum dwellers' worries. Theirs is a ceaseless struggle against the rigours of urban existence — far worse than the most Dickensian nightmare.

Half of Bombay's approximately 12.5 million residents live in such slums, without proper hygiene or sanitation. Many have no running water and rely on nearby ponds. Still, they are not the worst off. About 100,000 people live and sleep, and sometimes breed, on Bombay's sidewalks. Keeping their possessions to a minimum, usually a bundle that can be tucked away, these sidewalk dwellers, most of them bachelors, come here only at night to sleep, vacating their places early in the morning, before the daily commerce and hustle and bustle resume. Their plight is made worse by the fact that the sidewalks are controlled by the local mafia, who charge a rent, passing on part of it to the police.

From scenes like these, we retreated to lunch at the Bombay Yacht Club, which, however run down I found it, was luxurious by comparison. Then we explored the Bhindi Bazaar. One woman, a prostitute, allowed me to take pictures of her tattooed hands and feet. I couldn't help noticing other needle marks — not from tattooing — on the inside of her left arm.

From the bazaar we took a jaunt to Chowpati Beach on Marine Drive. The poor come here for relaxation and entertainment, and it is a beehive of activity. We saw horseback riding, monkey shows, levitation, card sharks, hustlers — and crowds. Everybody willing to try everything. In less than forty-eight hours, the complex, kaleidoscopic culture that grabbed Burton was beginning to pull me in.

Burton's chameleon-like nature was nowhere more evident than in matters of religion and sex. In religion, for example, he distanced himself from Protestantism and Catholicism. And he became fascinated with Islam, and its mystical current, Sufism. He had some involvement with Sikhism and Hinduism, too. Burton is one of the very few people who have experienced a variety of religions. It strikes me as odd that he did not write about or discuss Buddhism — but I suppose he was not exposed to it, even in its place of birth. Buddhism apart, he knew many religions, their contradictions and their appeal, and also their position in each social culture.

Because of his wide-ranging interests and his ready sympathy with many different forms of religion, it is difficult to know where his real sympathies lay. I pondered this problem as we set out for a meeting with Yogi Battunathji.

This was an odd interview, but interesting. After driving for about two hours to a little town north of Bombay, we found ourselves approaching a small, one-roomed building off a narrow pathway adjoining a row of houses. There was a carpet on the floor. Four or five attendants stood around. In the centre, against one wall, sat Yogi Battunathji, dressed in saffron robes. He had a long, impressive, well-groomed beard, black and grey, divided in the middle and veering off to the left and to the right. Above this was an

Our ignorance of aphrodisiacs is considered the most remarkable phenomenon: there being scarcely a single oriental work on physic that does not devote the greater part of its pages to the consideration of a question which the medical man in the East will hear a dozen times a day.

SIR RICHARD F. BURTON, 1851
Sindh, and the Races That Inhabit the Valley of the Indus
Prostitute openly selling her wares in the Bhindi Bazaar.

equally impressive handlebar mustache. The hair on his head, long and unruly, fell down over his shoulders.

The interview was mostly conducted by Haroon Siddiqui, and mostly in Hindi. I interjected with several questions, which the yogi answered in English.

Yogi Battunathji explained that he had spent a number of years in the foothills of the Himalayas — fourteen years, in fact, starting in 1967 — with a guru Ardooth Maisnathji, who has been in meditation in the Himalayas for more than forty years.

The yogi's philosophy is summed up in the following five M's: *madham* (drink/alcohol); *masham* (meat); *maishyam* (fish); *mundra* (wealth/possessions); and *maithoon* (sex). All these, the yogi informed us, must be avoided to achieve yogic status. Too much of any of these and you will not be reborn.

Instead of *madham* (alcohol), a yogi is taught by his guru to drink "the sweet juice" that drops from the brain into the mouth when a yogi has the connecting tissue of the lower part of the tongue slit by a sharp knife, thus enabling the loose tongue to be moved up from the gullet toward the head. "I drank the sweet juice called *shastrael dal* because my guru taught me how to do it." *Masham* (meat) creates fat in the body (as does *maishyam* — fish — if you have too much of it), and makes it less supple and suitable for the eighty-four positions of yoga. Very few yogis practise all the positions now; most concentrate on fewer than twelve. "I myself use six to eight positions," the yogi informed us. One of these is *siddharsan* (the legs are crossed and the right foot is pulled over the left leg): "This is a position I can sit in for seven hours." Another is *padmasana* — the famous lotus position, used in tantric sex. "I can also stand on my head for up to thirty minutes using *sirsashan*."

Mundra does not just mean wealth. It means all worldly affairs — which must be renounced. Yogis block out the humdrum ebb and flow of worldly life by a yogic posture — a finger in each ear, another two shutting each eye, two more blocking off the nose, and another two to shut the mouth tight.

"You try and close all doors on worldly affairs to get *shanti* (peace)."

While *Maithoon* (sex) is one of five desires to be shunned, the yogi embarked on a long justification of why tantric yogis have frequent sex with women. "Some yogis reach the state of *brijnoli*, the power to have women

... the production of a Sufi, a tribe of mystic devotees who hold tenets somewhat similar to the Platonists and the Gnostics of your faith in the early days, and it teems with the commonplaces of their poetry: the negative entity of the world of matter, the positive existence of the human Soul as a particle of the Eternal Spirit; enjoyment of what the Hindus call Máyá, or the illusions of mundane existence, and devotion to earthly, the imperfect type of heavenly, Beauty and Love.
SIR RICHARD F. BURTON, 1851

The yogi's philosophy is summed up in five M's: madham *(drink/alcohol);* masham *(meat);* maishyam *(fish);* mundra *(wealth); and* maithoon *(sex).*

have sex with them, as a way of cleansing a woman of her sexual drive. After such a session with a tantric yogi, she would not need sex for three to six months."

"In other words," Haroon pointed out to me, "you can cure her of sexual desires through sexual excess — an orgy, if you will — the chief beneficiaries of which are the yogis themselves!"

I remembered reading in the Rice biography about how tantric yogis would make love to a woman or many of them, or indulge in group sex — a group of yogis sitting in a circle in a lotus position and passing a woman or women around from lap to lap.

Haroon then asked the yogi whether the women ever get pregnant. "No. Because there is no ejaculation. The yogis have trained themselves not to have ejaculation."

"Yogis can also cure people of illnesses, calm people's nerves and wash away hardships and worries. Also cast out the devil." Haroon here noted that *bhoot utaarna* is a common Indian phenomenon. Those "possessed" by the devil often go to holy men, Hindu or Muslim, yogis or Sufi saints, whose religious incantations, *shloks* (sayings) in the case of the Hindus and Qur'anic injunctions in the case of Muslims, calm them down and supposedly drive out the devil.

For physical ailments our yogi said he uses *jadi-booti*. This literally means roots and branches, some metals (such as silver wafers, mercury, iron) and his own tantric incantations, or *mantras*. However, the yogi stated that nothing works unless he can invoke *shakti* (inner power) in your heart and mind. The three elements must work together: *mantras*, tantra, and *shakti*.

On the way back to Bombay, Haroon explained to me that the yogi, like most mystics and Eastern philosophers, uses a sort of circuitous logic, not the point-by-point linear Western style of reasoning. The yogi starts off in a small circle and keeps going into bigger circles — like ripples in water. It's all part of the tradition. Most yogis, indeed most Sufis, are taught orally by their master. The guru-student relationship, as indeed the *pir-murid* (master-student) relationship among the Sufis, has been the foundation of most learning in the East. The student would spend years with the master, listening, observing, learning by osmosis. "This kind of learning makes it virtually impossible for them to summarize a hypothesis, say, in a hundred words," Haroon explained. "You ask a simple question, and what you get is this outpouring of knowledge, most of which you cannot grasp. 'Never mind,' they say. 'Listen. Pay attention. Eventually, you will understand.' And you do."

Our discussion of religion had led to the topic of sex. But our next interview, which started on the topic of sex, led to a discussion of art. On our first Sunday in Bombay, I met Lance Dane, co-author with Dr. Mulk Raj Anand of a new edition of the *Kama Sutra*. Dane is an eccentric, single, seventy-three-year-old Englishman — ex-army — who stayed in India after the war and after Independence in 1947. Dane's *Kama Sutra* is illustrated with photos of art works from private collections, as well as of rare objects found in Indian temples and shrines.

In Dane's view, Burton's translations in his *Kama Sutra* were not very good. Published privately by the Kama Sutra Society in London, they provided the first real money Burton made from writing.

The *Kama Sutra*, Dane pointed out, outlined a formal approach to life. The social niceties of life for the man about town were beautifully portrayed: how to fix himself up; how to behave; how to conduct relationships — with money lenders, at the market, with go-betweens; how to arrange picnics, and so on. It was not a quick guide to sex. It was

Lance Dane, co-author of a new edition of the Kama Sutra.

meticulously worked out, with a long build-up: gambling, hunting, playing cards, how not to be seen in bad company.

Dane's fascination with the *Kama Sutra* dates from the time in his British Army days when he came across a pirated Indian edition published in Allahabad. In Delhi, the Indira Gandhi Centre now houses Dane's collection of more than twenty editions of the *Kama Sutra*. The first Indian English edition of the *Kama Sutra* came out in 1921, published in Lahore.

After he first saw the *Kama Sutra*, Dane visited the Calcutta Museum in Chowringhee and was astonished at the Indian sculptures he saw there. He purchased a camera in order to photograph them and, by trial and error, perfected his technique. In this way he began what was to be a lifelong career of photographing Hindu sculptures and Indian art. "It's amazing what infects a person's mind and starts a lifelong love affair," he said. "Overnight, from a soldier, I became a scholar. This also happened to Burton. I went through the tunnel. It was a new life. I turned my back on the past. After that, I could only concentrate on what I loved. I learnt to photograph art in the natural light the artists originally used."

Of course, the camera had barely been invented in 1842 when Burton was in India. "All the topographical records of the time were made by commissioned officers in the British Army," Dane pointed out. "Topography as an art has made a considerable contribution to illustrating history…. Burton must have been very frustrated in trying to record what he saw. That is why he sketched … and he became quite good at it."

My mind was full. Full of Burton and opinions about Burton. Clearly, Burton was no ordinary soldier. He was an individualist, a talented linguist who was quite possibly used as a spy to keep Britain informed about the

Maharaja Raj Singh of Dungarpur in Rajasthan.

region. It was already clear that language was the *key*. A man who knows the languages of India and Pakistan can enter and unlock the secrets of those places. This was Burton's task. It was ours, too. Once again, I was grateful for Haroon Siddiqui's presence. He was beginning to be my passport.

On another day, we met with the Maharaja Raj Singh of Dungarpur, a small principality north of Baroda, in Rajasthan. Dungarpur was carved as a state out of the great Rajput House of Mewar in the thirteenth century. Unlike most of the maharajas, who could not make the transition to democratic India well, Raj Singh's father won five elections to the State Assembly in post-Independence India, and was speaker of the assembly in the province of Rajasthan.

The Maharaja was impressive, outspoken and opinionated. He is the head of India Cricket, quite a powerful man, who seems not to have forgotten the past, but who understands it and has moved into the present using his knowledge and political power. He has lived in Bombay for thirty-two years, and is a businessman, dealing in tube wells, granite and marble.

We met him at Khyber, a new restaurant decorated in the traditional style, with Urdu sayings cast into clay plaques on the walls. It seemed to be a haunt of the rich, the emerging capitalist class of India.

It was Raj Singh's opinion that the British did a lot of good for India. He felt that the British used the Raj to exploit people, but did good as well. They were not just traders, like the Dutch or the Portuguese. He admitted that he did not know a lot about Burton, since he himself was not very army-minded. However, he was very outspoken about the current Indian situation and India after Nehru.

Indira Gandhi, in his view, was a clever, scheming woman, who understood power and used it. Twenty years after 1947 and Independence, despite all the agreements, she moved quickly, once she was in power, to take away the princes' privy purses (large sums of money initially pledged by the government of India to the princes in return for peacefully merging their states with India). By this move she eliminated their financial power, made their very survival extremely difficult and thus attained some popularity with the masses, who did not identify with the old nobility. "The British used the Raj, but the nobles gained from British rule. Indira Gandhi used the nobles as fall-guys, scapegoats."

To Raj Singh, the "old days" had their advantages. Before Independence, he noted, not a single one of the 586 states had Hindu-Muslim communal riots, and not a single prince was ever assassinated. "This is very unlike modern India, which is characterized by repeated communal killings, which the politicians often feed and governments seem incapable of stopping. Three prominent leaders have been assassinated: Mahatma Gandhi, Indira Gandhi, and her son Rajiv Gandhi.

"Indira Gandhi destroyed democracy in India and perpetuated family rule. She groomed her first son, Sanjay, to succeed her, and when he died in an air crash, she brought in Rajiv, her younger son. It was her dictatorial style. She imposed a draconian emergency rule for eighteen months in the 1970s, and started the process of Balkanization in the country, starting with the Punjab. There, she dismissed the duly elected government in an effort to control the state from Delhi. This process ended in 1984 with her ordering troops into the Golden Temple, something the British would never have dreamt of doing. She alienated the Sikhs, who were a more patriotic people than the majority of Hindus.

"How had the Mughals ruled India so successfully? By not interfering in the states. They left that to the governors, giving them local autonomy. Under Indira Gandhi, and later Rajiv, our state chief ministers (premiers) were like *chaprassis* (errand boys) in the Prime Minister's court. They spent sixty per cent of their time in Delhi and the rest in their state capitals.

"I think the British and the maharajas did more good than bad. They opened a window to the rest of the world for us. They gave us language; even today, an Indian from Jammu and another from Madras can converse. This is only in English. It's a disgrace, but it's a fact. I can't really say that the English exploited us."

"Did the British introduce corruption? Compared to the level of corruption now, corruption under the British was not very bad. It is true that they cleverly alienated the princes from their own people. First they educated us in Western ways. The rulers' children were brought up by British nannies and educated by British tutors. That was how I was brought up and educated, for example. Then the English set up five colleges for the children of the royal families — Aitchison College in Lahore, Mayo College in Ajmer, Daly College in Indore, and two campuses of Raj Kumar College in Rajkot and Raipur. They asked us to cast off our own clothes and wear suits. They taught us cricket and polo and pig-sticking. The princes built houses in Bombay, Delhi, Simla, Calcutta and Ootacamund to socialize in clubs and play polo. More than half the royal families lived outside their own states. This took them farther away from their own people. The British created a big gap between the rulers and the ruled. They introduced us to a foreign culture. They made us look like aliens in our own land.

"And so, by 1947, when Independence came, the princes stood naked. They no longer had the roots to resist the winds of change. Sardar Patel, India's first Home Minister, who negotiated deals with the princes on behalf of the federal government, knew the weaknesses of the rulers: 'Give them their privileges, their palaces, their hunting lodges, their diplomatic immunities to go abroad with no border customs checks, and they will give up their states.' And they did. The sad part of that, and Indira Gandhi's decision to take away the royal privy purses, was that it annihilated the cultures of the

586 states. Each had had a distinct culture: music, food, paintings, architecture, literature, rituals. All that disappeared. That is the tragedy."

The next day, I spent some time in the morning with A.K. Essajee, an antiques dealer near the Royal Bombay Yacht Club. There I discovered a very old and intricately carved Tamil Nadu gold necklace. He also showed me some knives and betel cutters from southern India. I decided I'd have to visit him again when we next got back to India and I asked him to try to keep them for me. There was no way I could carry rare knives and antique jewellery around with me in the Sindh!

We had lunch at the Cricket Club with Major General (Retired) A.H.E. Michigan, MVC, who provided a good background on regimental life in the Burton era: "The British East India Company needed guards for its factories or trading posts, whom they armed. As the business expanded, this need expanded. The three armies of the company — the Presidency Army, the Bengal Army, and the Bombay Army — reflected the three presidencies. But the officers of the army would definitely rank second compared to the company's civilian staff. They received lower pay, got few or no perks, were afforded no good family privileges. For this reason, the company army attracted a different calibre of Englishman from the regular army. The officers became indolent, undisciplined and slovenly. And they mistreated their Indian soldiers. This fed the unrest that eventually led to the 1857 Mutiny, after which the Crown took over the army and took three immediate steps: They made a career job of it. They selected more educated and dedicated people. They paid better and hiked the perks. They also built "hill stations" for the wives, such as those at Ooty, Simla, Darjeeling, Naital — where the women were kept entertained by the chaps on leave.

"Of course Burton was a spy. That used to be part of the terms of reference of some officers. Spying was part of their job. It was common practice during those days. Burton must have been detailed to do these things. So Burton may have undertaken all his activities partly on assignment, and partly out of personal interest."

As for the British legacy: "it was good, as far as the army is concerned. But it was horrible as far as the bureaucracy was concerned. For the army, they created good discipline, and left it very well organized. But more than discipline and organization, they left us traditions. Each regiment had its own set of traditions, which are being followed even today.

"The British also believed in roads and railways and telegraphs, which opened up the country. There was a reason for it. They had to move large numbers of troops from presidency to presidency. They also left us a good education system. They were actually trying to train only clerks, but the Indians had a much higher IQ than they thought! Finally, they left us cricket!"

It was this interview, and one with Foy Nissin, that really whetted my appetite for the next stage of the journey.

Foy Nissin is an impressive individual. A retired consular affairs officer, he is a self-described lover of Bombay. He is still active in the city's British Council. An Englishman born in Bombay, Foy Nissin is one of a handful of British people who opted to live in India after Independence. His great-grandfather was Captain George Nissin, a cavalry officer in the Baroda Army.

"Burton covered his tracks very well, didn't he? None of the biographies tend to explain Burton's experience at all! I find him a mystery. He is surrounded by legends — some of them with no basis in fact. I can understand Burton the man and his reactions: A man who makes up his own mind, who is not easily swayed, who is curious, who wants to do his own thing, an original not at all involved in the Victorian rat race in which officers charted their careers by the Red Book, which laid down rules for your career in the same way that multinationals do today. There was no great career for Burton in the army. He realized this. He was far more interested in scholarship and in doing interesting things.

"We don't know for sure that he was a spy. Official reports on Burton—from his superiors in the field—are not available from the India Office in London. There is only Napier's book, with references on Burton. But the India Office say they cannot find Burton's records. Or they say they don't exist.

"Lots of these British characters did some spying, although that may not have been their primary role. Why not Burton, too? What was John Seeley, the topographer, doing in Nagpore and Madhya Pradesh, deep in the heart of central India? What were Burton and Scott surveying in the Sindh? Let's face it, surveying work was a cover. They were advance men for the Empire — its eyes and ears in the field.

"But they don't say that. They would never say that. Whether he was hired specifically as a spy or used as one later by virtue of his capacity in the field, we will never know. But it is pretty obvious that he was used. He was a good man to have around — full of intense curiosity, with good reporting skills and a desire to record the truth, not fabrications. In fact, a damn good diarist.

"Spying was Burton's way of getting an opportunity. I mean, how else would life have been interesting for this obviously talented young man? As an ordinary officer there was no career for him in the army. As a surveyor? Come on. Burton does not fit the map-making mould.

"If Burton was being used as a spy, he was definitely also filing secret reports to his bosses. But where are those reports? And even if you could find some secret reports in official British records, they might not be in his name. They might have been written anonymously and forwarded by his superiors."

The theory that Burton was a spy is, he said, borne out by the fact that he went to Goa. He could have been in Goa because the British had twin fears at that time that the French might cut off the route to India or that they would take over Goa or India or intrigue with the Tipu Sultan in Mysore.

As the interview drew to an end, Nissin's parting comments fuelled my impatience to step beyond the threshold of Bombay and plunge deeper into our Burton adventure. "Stranger's Lane on Back Bay is where Burton pitched a tent for a week on a trip to Bombay from Baroda," he told us. "That's the Oval Maidan [parade ground] — which is where Bombay ended then. It was a sort of encampment. Government bungalows for officers at the edge, and a tent city for junior officers travelling through. It was just the sort of place Burton would have loved to stay — a place where he would not have had to mix with officialdom. And it would have been cheap accommodation, which would have appealed to Burton. You know, it was also the area where people living in the stuffy fort area would move out to during the hot summer months. They would just pitch tents there."

The thought of Burton pitching his army tent filled me with a sense of excitement — the excitement of knowing that it was time to move on. Our next stop would be Baroda and the army encampment — the first real posting of Burton's long career.

Besides receiving an enormous rate of interest, the creditor, who can read, write, and compute, turns the ignorance of his debtor to profit by keeping his accounts in a state of confusion most advantageous to the only one that understands them, himself.

SIR RICHARD F. BURTON, 1851
Scinde; or, the Unhappy Valley

Baroda

*Before him was Baroda, a true Indian city, his first —
feudal, primitive, old as history, a sharp contrast to
Bombay, with its dense Portuguese and English
imprint. Baroda was India, with all the exotic finery,
pomp, tawdriness, dirt, smells, decadence, and danger.*

EDWARD RICE
***Captain Sir Richard Francis Burton,
1990***

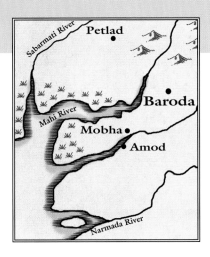

3

Baroda

Baroda is an important city in the Republic of India and has considerable historical significance. It lies in Gujarat State, on the Viswamitri River, about 230 miles north of Bombay. Originally called Vadodara, the busy congested city still has boulevards lined with flaming gulmohar trees. The word "vadodara" actually means "in the heart of the banyan trees," a reference to the profusion of banyan trees in and around the city. In the mid-nineteenth century it was an important military town and is where Burton was sent immediately upon his arrival in India to start his army career.

Burton arrived at the cantonment of the 18th Bombay Native Infantry—stationed a half-hour out of Baroda — after six weeks in Bombay. The area provided Burton's first real introduction to the life of the officer in the mid-nineteenth century. Fawn Brodie quotes from *Falconry in the Valley of the Indus* to give a hint of what that life was like:

> [H]e could see that the average officer lived rather handsomely. He had "a horse or two, part of a house, a pleasant mess, plenty of pale ale, as much shooting as he can manage, and an occasional invitation to dance, where there are thirty-two cavaliers to three dames, or to a dinner party when a chair unexpectedly falls vacant." The subalterns had at least five servants; one stood behind his master at meals, turbaned and gorgeously dressed, ready to place silver lids on the tumblers to keep out the insects. "But some are vain enough to want more," Burton wrote, "and of these fools was I."

The "more" that Burton wanted was a richness of life that could not be supplied by the rather banal amusements of the average officer in Baroda,

It was in Baroda that Burton first came to care for the charms of non-white women, women who, in India, were trained in the art of man-pleasing.

The usual Moslem prejudice against female education is strong in the Sindh.

Sir Richard F. Burton, 1851
Sindh, and the Races That Inhabit the Valley of the Indus

Previous page: A Muslim girl stands beside the world's largest Qur'an.

men who began their day with a cup of tea brought to their quarters by one of the ever-present servants, then set out for morning horseback exercises. After breakfast, the men spent their day at billiards, pig-sticking, shooting — it was indeed a world of knives and guns. That was one of the things Burton liked about it. But he came to abhor hunting, and in Baroda, as everywhere else, he began to seek diversion in the areas that always provided it to him: sex, religion and exploration of other cultures.

It was in Baroda that Burton first came to care for the charms of non-white women, women who, in India, were not only beautiful and trained in the arts of man-pleasing, but who were also educated in poetry, language, conversation and other arts of the mind. Like many others, Burton set up housekeeping with a *bubu*, or temporary Indian wife.

In Baroda, Burton also moved inexorably towards the magnet of religious adventure. He became intensely involved in Hinduism, delving into the cult of the *nag* — the snake-god that we had seen guarding the lingam in Bombay. And, under the tutelage of a Goan priest, he also practised Catholicism.

In Baroda Burton immersed himself further in the study of languages — Hindustani, Gujarati, Sanskrit — and began his regular forays back to Bombay to take the government language examinations, at which he always triumphed.

The life that Burton made for himself in Baroda was bound to set him apart from the other officers, and it did so in a way that marked him for the rest of his career. He became known as the "White Nigger." Partly this was because he found life among the natives of Baroda far more interesting than life among the British. But he was also a "White Nigger" because he was an outsider. That would never change, for the rest of his life.

When Burton first arrived at the cantonment outside Baroda he encountered only a few men and eight officers. Almost everybody else was 160 miles away guarding the East India Company's opium fields—the opium trade being one of the things that sustained Britain's commercial triumph in India. Nigel Leask, in his *British Romantic Writers and the East*, explains:

> [O]pium was produced by the British East India Company in India for export to China, as an exchange commodity for Chinese tea. This formed a delicately balanced trade triangle: the Chinese had to pay for Indian opium, Britain's Indian subjects had to pay for the privilege of British rule, and the British consumer had to pay for China tea. These outstanding claims were cancelled one against the other, to the benefit of Britain's worldwide trade. When in 1839, the Chinese, worried by the economics of the international situation and growing indigenous addiction to the illegally imported drug, confiscated a quantity of British opium at Canton, the British government maintained that Chinese courts had no jurisdiction over British subjects and could not authorize the seizure of their property. As was the case in India seventeen

*years later, the cry was for vengeance upon the inhabitants of the
subterranean world. War was declared: the British navy seized
Hong Kong and bombarded Canton, forcibly opening China to
western markets at the Treaty of Nanking in 1842.*

*British reactions to what would become the biggest narcotics
traffic in history were at best ambivalent, at worst hypocritical.*

Obviously, England's involvement in India was a complex and shifting thing.

The British presence in India was above all for commerce and material gain. The yardstick by which administrators were judged by the Crown was the amount of the yearly revenues they sent back to the Crown's coffers. War, treason, treaties, proper administration — all were equal tools employed opportunistically to extract as large a share of revenues as possible from the more than 550 principalities, at the expense of the local peasantry. Indeed, when the costly wars embarked on by the viceroys Clive, Hastings and Cornwallis prevented them from meeting their revenue targets, they were disgraced upon their return to Britain. Although all three men greatly enhanced the British presence and power in India, and historians regard them as very successful, in their own time they were generally considered failures.

Colonization in the true sense of the word was never really possible in nineteenth-century India, nor was it the principal objective of the British presence. What the British did was use long-standing local rivalries, factions and historical mistrust among India's local nobility — the nawabs and maharajas — to enter into a bewildering set of arrangements and treaties with them. These arrangements allowed the British to administer the provinces and collect tax revenue, in return for providing the princes with armed protection and a share of the revenues. The system worked well until the 1850s. Then the British began a series of blatant moves to strip the princes of all their power, such as the 1856 dethronement of the Nawab of Oudh in north-central India. This bold violation of an existing treaty created huge mistrust, and a national movement of resentment and resistance began with the first war of independence in 1857. It was not until nearly a century later, however, that India finally succeeded in ousting the British.

The difficulty of uniting the former princely states into a democratic country has persisted. Following Indian independence in 1947, an Indian Union was established, and over a period of several years, but principally between 1948 and 1951, the princely states joined the Indian Union in return for "privy purses" for the princes (eventually abolished, in 1967). The architect of the creation of this modern Indian state was Home Minister Sardar Vallabhai Patel, who annexed many reluctant princely states under the thinly veiled threat of force. In the case of Hyderabad, the largest state, this was done by marching in troops, and in Kashmir, the most contentious of all, by ignoring a U.N. Security Council call for an internationally supervised plebiscite.

Before independence, Baroda was a vast and strategically located area in northwestern India, not far from Surat. It was the second most powerful state after Hyderabad. It was ruled by the family of Gaekwar (or Gaikwar or Gaikwad), a dissident offshoot of the rulers of the Maratha Confederacy based in Poona, near Bombay. When the inter-Maratha feud came to a boil in 1803, Anand Rao Gaekwar signed a treaty with the British. In exchange for receiving British help, he ceded military powers to the East India Company. It was typical of the way the British annexed rather than colonized India. In all, about 70 per cent of the enormously diverse country was annexed by the British by clever intrigue and negotiation with the various rulers. The Company protected the rulers and helped manage the territories in exchange for a large share of the taxes — usually 50 per cent. The army of the British East India Company was indispensable to this plan and allowed the Company to pursue its enormously profitable commercial enterprises. It was an army of commerce and a tool of imperialism.

Even with all the changes, the domain of the Gaekwars, which means "protector of cows," was one of the richest princely states in the subcontinent. In Burton's time, the family was still powerful, as Rice has noted: "By Burton's time the Gaekwars' humble origins had been forgotten. Now they were rulers possessing great power and wealth of a type and shown in a manner that offended English sensibilities, although Burton was most appreciative of certain ways in which it was expressed. The current Gaekwar had two great guns to which *pūjā* or adoration was regularly offered: 'They were of massive gold, built around steel tubes, and each was worth about £100,000,' said Burton."

When I arrived in Baroda, I found the Gaekwar family of today still influential but, like the British Empire with which they had made so many deals, scarcely at the peak of their fortunes.

Our minds full of history and recently reread research, we flew via Indian Airlines from Bombay into Baroda very early in the morning. My first impression was of a busy and aggressive town. It looked far more congested and crowded than Bombay. Half an hour at Hotel Vadodara and we were out into the streets, contending with the crowds and the traffic and the pollution. My cough was getting worse and worse. Lorries and three-wheeled taxi cars belched black smoke. The pollution seemed to hang over the hot, crowded Indian metropolis, shielding us a little from the sun's direct rays. I remember Burton once saying of one part of India, "Everything in this place seems to hate us. Even the pet tiger, as he catches sight of our white faces, shakes off the purring little cats who amuse themselves with walking over his broad flanks, springs up, glaring at us with blood-thirsty eyes, and ears viciously flattened...."

Almost our first visit was to Jami Masjid — the main mosque of Baroda.

The front was rebuilt in 1912, and one wouldn't know there was an old mosque behind this "new" facade. The mosque's enormous courtyard was a peaceful haven after the bustle and congestion of the narrow street leading to it. This mosque is only a few yards away from the old palace of Maharaja Sayajirao (sometimes spelled Saijirao) II, who ruled during Burton's time, and also from the Grand Palace of Sayajirao III. Nearly 25 per cent of the population of Baroda has always been Muslim, so it was not surprising to find a 400-year-old mosque right in the middle of the Muslim sector. It couldn't have changed much since Burton's time.

In the crowded bazaar near the mosque, merchants displayed their wares in tiny boutiques at the edge of the narrow pavement. The variety was bewildering. Trinkets, clothes, food, wooden spoons, earthenware, henna, *kohl*, *surma* (a black powder that is a precursor of modern eye drops) and *itr* — perfumes from natural sources such as musk. The perfumes were interesting. There were all kinds of them — and all decanted from glass bottles into small, skin containers. These skin containers must have been very old — they seemed almost as rare as the perfumes. There were various scents: flowers, *khas* (sweet-smelling grass) for men and other potions from light floral to sickly sweet. Other cosmetics were *missi* (a paste used as lipstick); and *ud* and *lobaan* — cones from trees that when sprinkled over hot coals produce a dense aromatic smoke that women use to aerate and perfume their hair. We saw saris for women. Also *shalwars* and *kameezes*; these are the long shirt and baggy trousers featuring popular tribal Maratha prints. Our eyes were captivated by a dazzling array of multicoloured glass bangles, by silver anklets, silver- and gold-thread designs on brocade ribbons for borders on saris or shirts.... Everywhere we looked, something different.

Attached to the main mosque was an Islamic school, and we were invited in by the man charged with delivering the *azaan* or five daily calls to prayer. The school is a sort of theological seminary for the teaching and memorization of the Qur'an, a practice Burton wrote about with great admiration. On the second floor of the mosque was a rare treasure: a fifteen-volume 208-year-old hand-written copy of the 88,000-word Qur'an. It was a labour of one man's love — that of a calligrapher named Muhammad Gauth, of the famous Indian Sufi family of Bandagi Muhammad Gauth. He worked at it from the age of eighteen until he was sixty-five — for forty-seven years — using the famous *dahka malmal* (a wafer-thin cotton from Bengal which, it was said, was so fine that you could stuff a yard of it into a matchbox). He had artisans from Ahmadabad (a town northwest of Baroda) make him sheets of paper measuring 6¼ by 3¼ feet — about 1,200 of them — on which he penned the thirty chapters of the holy book, writing two to a volume. His was not simple calligraphy. He also wrote the Persian translations under each Arabic line. And, along an elaborately flowered border, he wrote his own commentary on the holy book. This was an exacting, stupendous undertaking, even by Muslim standards. The Prophet Muhammad enjoined his followers to read the Qur'an often, to memorize all of it if they could, or at least parts of it (as Burton did) and to write it often. This tradition gave rise to the art of calligraphy and its various writing styles: Kufi, Naskhi, Taliq, and so on. Such work was not left to professional calligraphers alone. Noblemen strove to learn the art of writing and penned the Qur'an in their spare time as an act of devotion as well as a tool for spreading God's word at a time when there were no printing presses.

According to Haroon Siddiqui, the practice of writing the Qur'an continued on even to the generation of his own grandfather, who used to write the Qur'an every day for an hour or so. Whenever he was travelling, he took along his little writing desk, ink pot and reed pen. His staff would spread the *qaleen* (rug) on the floor, set up his desk and pens and paper, and he would sit down *ukdu*-fashion (with both legs tucked under his buttocks) and write a few lines or pages every day. As soon as he finished one Qur'an, he would give it away as a gift to a young groom or student graduating from a seminary.

The enormous Qur'an of Baroda is mentioned in the *Guiness Book of Records*. Fourteen of the bound volumes are kept in a glass enclosure, while one of them is opened and spread out in a display case. The pages are turned at least twice a year to mark special religious occasions. This ensures that the book gets some airing, but it is still in bad shape — fraying at the edges. Unless some further protection is given to this wonderful treasure, it will just rot away — a victim of age and the elements.

We were to interview several of the successors of the old potentates of the region. The first was Maharaja Ranjit Singh Gaekwad (the anglicized version of Gaekwar), at the Laxmi Vilas Palace, built by His Highness Sayajirao III. The palace was begun on January 12, 1881. It took twelve years to complete and cost £180,000. The architect, a Major Mant, also designed palaces at Kolhapur and Darbhanga, but he had a tragic career. Arriving in India in 1859, he became fascinated by local architecture and sought to unite the functional qualities of European designs with the native styles. He became one of the greatest exponents of the Indo-Saracenic style — a synthesis of Muslim and Indian features favoured by European architects. He produced designs for the

Maharaja Ranjit Singh Gaekwad of Baroda.

maharajas of Darbhanga, Baroda and Kolhapur, but the foundations of all three palaces had scarcely been laid when he lost control of his senses and became convinced that he had done his sums wrong and that the buildings would fall down. He died while still in his forties.

The palaces stood up perfectly well, of course, and Laxmi Vilas Palace is a

The Laxmi Vilas Palace, built by His Highness Sayajirao III. It was begun in 1881 and completed twelve years later at a cost of £180,000.

tribute to the young architect's genius. Mant's designs were eventually carried out by Robert Fellowes Chisholm. The result is a palace with stately dining rooms, billiard rooms, great apartments for distinguished European visitors, and many, many rooms to suit the Baroda family's increasingly Western lifestyle. The best elements of several periods of Indian architecture were incorporated, together with some of the functional touches and decorative flourishes of different European schools. The sheer size of the palace — the facade is more than 500 feet long — made it possible to include all these elements while avoiding stylistic chaos. It is a wonderful creation.

The exterior of the Maharaja's apartments was in the tradition of Hindu martial architecture, with most of the detail borrowed from the fortress of Bharatpur. The public apartments, however, were more in the Mughal style, while the women's quarters ended in a forest of domes and canopies copied from the Jain temples of Gujarat. We saw Venice in some of the arches, and a decided feeling of Gothic in others. Towards the south end of the building, however, there appeared to be a distinct leaning to an earlier and somewhat purer type of classical European architecture. The palace, with its eclectic Indian exterior and lush European interior serves as a characteristic monument to the memory of Sayajirao III, and to the curious bridging role that the princes were obliged to play in the era of British rule.

The palace is featured on the cover of the illustrated book *Palaces of India* by Fatesingh Rao Gaekwad, the previous Maharaja. He was a Ranji Trophy first-class cricketer and president of the Cricket Control Board of India who won election to Parliament and then to the provincial Gujarat legislature, where he was named State Minister of Health. He died in 1989 without a son. He was the current Maharaja's elder brother. Another brother runs the family's big business empire, Baroda Rayon, in Bombay.

After the hustle and bustle and traffic and chaos of Baroda, the Laxmi Vilas Palace might have been in a different world, an idyllic haven of peace, where you could hear the quiet and see the birds, including peacocks. We followed a long driveway through a park with wonderful views, until, quite suddenly, there was the palace. It simply took my breath away — a stone Mughal mansion with domes, parapets, porticos, pillars, columns, frescos, carvings and inlaid work. In the palace foyer were bronze statues and marble floors. Farther inside were endless corridors and rooms. On the walls, the stuffed heads of tigers, leopards and bisons. But the paint on the walls and ceilings was peeling. The carpets were fraying, and the floors were dusty — a great family's grand surroundings disintegrating because of a severe lack of funds.

The Maharaja, a greying man in his early fifties, had been a first-class cricketer. He was now rather slow of step, but very polite and courteous. We chatted informally in a grand old library-cum-reception room lined with books in built-in wooden shelves. He, too, was coughing. I wondered if he was having the same allergic reaction to the pollution that I was! We were served tea, and he spoke of the old ways of royalty, and the more prosaic contemporary problems of urbanization, deforestation and environmental degradation. I got the impression of a man living in the past. It was almost with relief that he turned to the subject of Burton and the time of his own great-great-great-grandfather.

It was not surprising that Burton was seduced by India, he said. "India does suck you in. It is so old, so rich, so wonderful. Something you cannot find in any other part of the universe." And he also understood how Burton became, or pretended to become, a Hindu, a Sikh, and a Muslim. "I can do that too. We in India live so close to each other and each other's faiths and religions. I can move from one religion to the next easily. Just as Burton did. As a Sikh, or a Hindu, or a Muslim. You know, religion plays an important part in our lives. Your religion, on the other hand, doesn't really count for much in your daily dealings with others."

Unfortunately, he told us, he could not show us any artefacts or documents proving a Burton connection with the nineteenth-century Gaekwars. "There was a period when the British ruled Baroda directly for ten years because the Maharaja was issueless. My great-grandfather was actually brought from a village and adopted by Mullarao's wife. And so the records, not only for those ten years of British rule, but prior to that, are lost to the family. They must have been sent either to the India Office or to the local government archives. But the local governments have not been very good at looking after the records, or anything with history. This is probably why we don't seem to have any Burton memorabilia in the family."

I asked him about the two great guns that Burton had said the Gaekwars

Jami Masjid — the main mosque of Baroda. The front was rebuilt in 1912.

owned, and he not only confirmed the story but provided the most authentic account so far of their whereabouts: "The two cannons that Burton mentions were here. One was of gold and the other of silver. Not solid gold but covered with gold and silver. They were taken out for parades in the city. However, the silver one has now been melted. The gold one, on the other hand, is still here in our collection, but we don't let anyone see it anymore. It is locked up."

The Maharaja then took us on a tour of the palace, which has a Spanish Moorish courtyard, entered from a corridor running around all four sides. He complained at some length that there was not enough staff to look after the palace or even to clean away the dust gathering everywhere.

"Baroda has become very dusty. This is because of all the deforestation going on. We are going to close off segments of the palace and not allow the public in. We simply don't have the staff to provide proper security. People can just walk off with art objects. Nothing is under lock and key."

The audience hall, called the Durbar Hall, is a grand room, at least thirty feet by sixty feet, with high ceilings and beautiful chandeliers. Portraits and busts line the walls. The Maharaja now rents out the hall for lectures and concerts, and when we were at the palace there was a gathering of sixty-five architects and students from several Asian cities on a nine-day tour of India. They sat on cushions on a rug on the floor listening to — of all people — Indian-born author (now living in the U.S.A.) Bharati Mukherjee, with the Maharani of Baroda in attendance, sitting in front.

Following our interview with the Maharaja, we visited the Central Library, which he said his family had donated. Though the library appeared to be very organized, the books themselves were dusty, fraying and neglected. The chief librarian, S. Chantranand, read my palm while I was waiting for Haroon Siddiqui and Mahnoor Yar Khan to finish looking at some of the previous Maharaja's photographs, on the second floor. The librarian surprised me by accurately relating some of my past history. Then he gave me a strange warning about our journey: "You must go with some military help. Otherwise your planned trip will not be a success."

Before dinner we made a brief stop at Thamilvadi Hall, a very old building with murals on its interior walls that date back several centuries. The murals depict scenes of Indian mythology — and of British red-coats fighting natives. This hall was certainly visited by Burton. It was the mansion of a Maratha Mughal who was prime minister to the Maharaja of Baroda.

We also stopped at the Indian Arts Emporium in the basement of the Hotel Vadodara where I looked at Gujarat knives and an elephant knife. There were some betel cutters, too. These were the very first weapons from the ancient state of Gujarat that I bought — an important addition to my collection.

During dinner we were introduced to wonderful vegetarian cuisine of Gujarat. It features unusual and delicious combinations of aromatic spices, crisp, fried delicacies, lots of thick milk and butter and seemingly endless variations on lentils and vegetables.

We discussed the complicated genealogy of the present Gaekwads: Sayajirao II, who ruled from 1819 to 1846, was the maharaja Burton might have met. There were also Khander Rao Gaekwad, 1856-70; Mul, his brother, 1870-75; and Sayajirao III, 1875-1939. Of the three brothers of the current generation, Fatesingh Rao, mentioned earlier, had died. His next younger brother is the present maharajah, Ranjit Singh, whom I had already visited; and the youngest brother, Sanga Ran, is the head of the Baroda Rayon business in Bombay. Sanga Ran is rumoured now to be suing Ranjit Singh over the division of the property and other assets, marking an unhappy chapter in the history of one of India's greatest dynasties.

The next day began with thunder, then a downpour, followed by the earthy smell of rain on dry, dusty ground. I drove in darkness to pick up the guide to go to the Maharaja's *shikhar ghar* (hunting lodge). It was soon clear, however, that the roads were a mess of churned-up mud after the rain, so we postponed the hunt.

The rain changed the whole character of the town. There were fewer people about. Some crouched in doorways or sheltered under umbrellas, covering their heads with newspapers and plastic sheeting. Lame beggars somehow moved quickly to cover. Vendors kept hawking their wares. After the rain, the streets glistened and steamed in the hot sun. The hustle and bustle continued, but the dust and pollution had vanished. The much-needed soaking cleared it all away and gave our lungs a brief respite. I was able to breathe deeply again, enjoying the clear air and the wonderful earthy smell — unique in the tropics.

I spent the time after breakfast writing instead of touring. Then at 11:00, we left to visit the Laxmi Vilas Palace again. This time we concentrated on the armoury, which had an incredible collection of old knives, swords, cannons and spears, all beautifully displayed.

We also visited the Laxmi Vilas Palace Museum nearby. The personal museum of the previous maharaja, Fatesingh Rao, it is filled with paintings and *objets d'art* collected by his ancestor, Sayajirao Gaekwad III. It is a small, intimate art museum holding portraits and bronzes by the versatile Italian sculptor Felici — who also advised his patron on the purchase of Western objects for the museum.

At noon we found ourselves at the Museum and Picture Gallery of Baroda in Sayaji Park, a larger gallery founded in 1887 by Maharaja Sayajirao Gaekwad III. He was a visionary. Here, too, we saw many wonderful paintings and *objets d'art* — including one portrait of Maharaja Sayajirao II.

After lunch and a visit to St. James's Church (Anglican), which Burton certainly visited, we made our pilgrimage to Burton's camp at the Outram Lines, where nothing remarkable remained to be seen. We also saw Sir James Outram's residence, a reminder of his days as a colonial administrator.

Maharaj Kumar Ashok, a retired Indian army officer from the Sindh Horse Regiment.

Finally, we finished this busy day with a meeting with Maharaj* Kumar Ashok Rajai Gaekwar. (His name is Gaekwar, while the other branch of the family uses the anglicized Gaekwad.) He is the uncle of the present maharaja, Ranjit Singh. A retired Indian army officer from the Province Horse and later the Sindh Horse Regiment (until 1972), the Maharaj was one of the first three Indians named to Lord Mountbatten's staff when Mountbatten became independent India's first governor general. Now in his late seventies, the Maharaj is writing a book on the early Gaekwars.

Maharaj Kumar Ashok lives in a relatively small palace — a manageable mansion, unlike the overpowering palace of his nephew. He has a clipped British accent and a correspondingly dry sense of humour. "I am the last of the fogeys," he said.

For our interview, he wore a jacket and tie, and offered us British hospitality. A white-jacketed bearer served us open-faced chicken sandwiches after handing out cotton napkins hand-embroidered with the Gaekwar family crest. Maharaj Kumar Ashok was very interesting and knowledgeable about Burton. He was confident that Burton was "used" by the British for his knowledge and his ideas about keeping the balance of power among the

---

* "Maharaja" is used to refer to the king. Uncles and others are "maharaj."

various contenders for local sovereignty. During Burton's seven years in India, the Maharaj reminded me, he spent a lot of time away from the military bases. His excursions into the countryside, often for surveying, took him all over the Madras Presidency south and the Bombay Presidency. He held the view that surveying was very probably a cover for spying.

He believed that Burton would certainly have met Maharaja Sayajirao II. He would have wanted to know what kind of man Sayajirao was. Also, Burton was too young for anyone to suspect. He was the perfect person to send to check on the Maharaja, who was at loggerheads with the British.

"Sayajirao II had an ongoing fight with the British," recalled the Maharaj. "According to Baroda's 1803 treaty with the British, we used to give a contingent to the British, and part of the agreement was that we would share the spoils of victory. However, they never did give anything to us after the third Maratha war of 1818. So this argument between the Maharaja and the British went on and on. He was doing black-magic mumbo jumbo on them. He even had a special tantric temple of the goddess Bhavani Devi built here, hoping to be able to put a curse on the British.

"If there is any record that Burton and Sayajirao met, it could be in one of two places: the British political records, or what they thought was all right for us to keep here. The rest they took back to England. Because Burton was a spy, his records should be at the India Office. There won't be much in the archives here because Burton was not on the local payroll.

"Although we cannot say for sure, I believe that Burton and Sayajirao must have met. Burton delved deeply into Indian culture. At first I thought that since he wanted to translate the *Arabian Nights*, he felt he had to go through the whole gamut of Eastern cultures and religions — Hindu, Sikh and especially Muslim — to understand their concept of life and their way of thinking.

"However, I now think he may have been specially sent off to spy. Was he actually in the army? Or was he just given army rank and then used? You can never really understand the English. You never know what they're thinking and what they're going to do."

Kumar Ashok Rajai had strong opinions on everything, including Napier's famous telegraphic message, "Peccavi" or "I have sinned [Sindh]": "He never said that. There is no actual record of him saying that. I am from the Sindh Horse Regiment, and there is no record of this. However, it's a good story."

Village settlement on the outskirts of Baroda.

Surat

*And now, having happily escaped the gaieties of a
Bombay "season," you propose a trip to Sind, or the
Unhappy Valley; chiefly, I believe, because all the
Presidency world declares that the sun is fatal; that
small pox and cholera rage there; that plague is
coming down, full gallop, from "the Gulf" — briefly,
that it will be the death of you.*

RICHARD F. BURTON
Sind Revisited,
1877

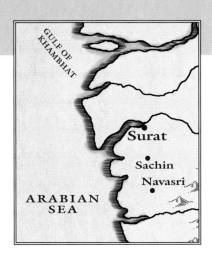

4

SURAT

Burton called Surat "a kind of nursery of the Anglo-Indian Empire." Surat was the most important of the many ancient ports along the coast of western India, which is broken by numerous rivers that run through groves of banyan trees before emptying into the Gulf of Cambay. The port lies at the mouth of the Tapti River. Founded by a Hindu Brahman, Surat became an enormously important international trade centre whose prosperity was coveted by the Mughals, Portuguese, Dutch, French and English. Surat was conquered many times, and its Portuguese fortress, built in 1546, had many masters. The Mughal emperor Akbar the Great captured it from the Portuguese in 1573, after which it became a gateway to Mecca, the Muslim holy city in Saudi Arabia across the Arabian Sea. A century later, the Maratha ruler Shivaji raided the city.

Surat also provided a toe-hold for the British in India, starting in 1608 with an agreement between the East India Company and the Delhi-based Mughal emperor Jehangir, son of Akbar the Great. It was a "must see" on our journey. We left very early on the long, bumpy car ride from Baroda to the coastal town where the Nawab of Surat had first allowed the British to trade. It took almost four hours and was absolutely exhausting. It was hot, dusty and chaotic, the roads crowded with cars, buses and lorries. But we got there, and it gave us a look at the countryside of Gujarat — Gujarati farmers dressed all in white, women in flared red skirts working in fertile-looking fields, men in coloured turbans, women carrying sticks. The people and the countryside seemed to be constantly changing. Eventually ... Surat. It was bigger than I expected, and busier.

Below the walls of the Portuguese fort and above the water level of the Tapti River estuary were some of the worst slums I have ever seen. Far worse than in Bombay. Or Delhi. Or Kathmandu. Hundreds and hundreds of people, living in cardboard and tarpaper shacks, existing in congested, desperate

The entrance to the old fort in Surat.

Previous page: Below the walls of the Portuguese fort and above the water level of the Tapti River estuary were some of the worst slums I have ever seen. Far worse than in Bombay. Or Delhi. Or Kathmandu. Hundreds and hundreds of people, living in cardboard and tarpaper shacks, existing in congested, desperate near-futility.

near-futility. There was filth and putrid waste everywhere. Mud, excrement, refuse, vermin. It was appalling, and I felt incredibly guilty, as if I were a voyeur gazing on some terrible scene — a witness to the very depths of hell. People in the utter hopelessness of their base existence didn't even *try* to beg. Their eyes alone spoke their desperation. As I made my way through the street, I was noticed but almost ignored. Only the children, in their naivety, begged. The air was foul. Mud and excrement covered my feet. I needed to photograph the fort — for the book, for the story. But this was something else. My camera recorded a terrible plight.

In September 1994, eight months after my visit, the world was shocked and horrified to hear of the outbreak of plague in Surat and the huge western state of Maharashtra. The world's press reported that it was the worst since 1926, when the disease had ravaged Hyderabad and Deccan. The Indian government took immediate steps to prevent panic. Plague was also reported in other states, but there was no town worse affected than Surat, where it was believed to have begun and where many, many confirmed cases of both bubonic and pneumonic plague were recorded.

The rat population had grown immensely in rural Maharashtra, spurred on by the earthquake that wiped out 10,000 people just before we arrived in Surat in January 1994. Also, contact between rats and humans increased dramatically when the monsoon rains flooded the city's many slums. Both bubonic and pneumonic plague are transmitted by fleas from infected rats, although the pneumonic form, which affects the lungs, can also be spread from person to person through coughing. It is incredibly contagious, far more so than bubonic plague. A single sneeze can infect a whole roomful of people. Disease spreads quickly, especially in areas where narrow streets and small buildings lead to close contact between people in bazaars and shops.

Epidemics of plague have occurred throughout history. The bacillus *Yersinia pestis* may lie dormant for many years, before a flood or man-made change in the environment drives rats into closer contact with human beings. The Romans interpreted plague as punishment for an insult to one of the gods. The Christian church came to view the fourteenth-century outbreak of the Black Death in a similar way.

Most people in the West have learned about the Black Death in grade school, but often do not know that it was neither the first nor the last plague epidemic in Europe. There had been a similar outbreak about 800 years earlier, and London was also struck by the disease in 1665. Only the great fire of 1666 halted the contagion.

Practically everybody infected with pneumonic plague will die if not

Men, women, and children besieged my door, by which means I could see the people face-to-face, especially that portion of which Europeans, as a rule, know only the worst.

SIR RICHARD F. BURTON, 1851

Early sketch showing the Castle of Surat, which Burton called "a kind of nursery of the Anglo-Indian Empire."

treated, and up to 50 per cent of those infected with bubonic will die. Although plague is now curable, it must be treated immediately, and the drugs must be available.

The real fear is for Bombay. The authorities are frightened that the plague will reach the heterogeneous mass of tin-roofed huts in the heart of Bombay — which may be the biggest slum in Asia. Bombay has a population of about 12.5 million people — many of them living on the sidewalk — and, it is thought, five times as many rats. In such a place, the plague could go off like a bomb — a time bomb. The world is terrified by the possibility that plague will be transported to other places — particularly the West.

Although I am now sure that I couldn't possibly have contracted the plague, my coughing was really becoming a problem, and it was very bad in Surat. In Baroda, I got some antibiotics from a pharmacist. Later, in another city, I went to a doctor who gave me a huge dose of antibiotics that kept me reeling for over a week. God knows what it stopped. But eventually I did get better.

After the first agreement between Britain and the Mughal emperor Jehangir in 1608, Sir Thomas Roe, Britain's first ambassador to the Mughal court, travelled through Surat in 1615 on his way to Delhi and Agra. Surat was already a bustling port, especially for Mecca-bound Muslim hajis (pilgrims). It was one of the richest cities in the world in the sixteenth century, with state revenues of 500,000 rupees a year. The British East India Company established a "factory" (office agency) on the banks of the Tapti River, and continued doing business while the city was sacked twice, in 1664 and 1670, by Shivaji, the Maratha warrior from Poona, principally with the intent of looting the hajis. With the death of the last great Mughal emperor, Aurangzeb, in 1707, the hold of Delhi began to weaken all over India, and in Surat, the local nawab,* Tegbeg Khan, declared himself the city's autonomous ruler. His position was weak, however, and the British conquered Surat in 1759 and occupied the port, placing a garrison there, but allowing the nawab to remain as a figurehead.

The British further eroded the position of the local royalty when they pensioned off the nawab in 1800 with an outright payment of 100,000 rupees and another 50,000 in annuities, and placed his pliant son, Nasiruddin, on the throne. By this time, Surat was a city of 600,000, according to the *Gujarat Gazette* of 1877, and its economy was booming, with shipbuilding augmenting the traditional industries of silk and cotton weaving.

In 1843, Burton came to Surat from Bombay by boat on his way to Baroda, 150 kilometres inland. Surat was also the transit point for his various trips back to Bombay. Even then, the East India Company was still feuding with the local royalty. When the nawab at the time, Afzaluddin, died on August 8, 1842, and left no heir, the British cut off the pension to the royal family and froze their properties under the Doctrine of Lapse. The dead ruler's son-in-law, Jafar Ali Khan, went to England in 1843 to lobby the Company's directors, but without success. He went back again in 1855 and convinced an M.P. to move a private member's bill in the House of Commons to restore the royal title and pension. The latter was partially reinstated in 1857.

For all intents and purposes, therefore, Jafar Ali Khan was the local nawab when Burton was in Surat.

We visited the crumbling old palace of Nawab Jafar Ali, now occupied by his descendant, Nawab Mir Usman Alam. Built as a *shikhar ghar* (hunting lodge), it is a well-preserved seventeenth-century building with a private game sanctuary extending for a furlong around it in all directions. It was originally provided to spare the nawab the trouble of going to a real jungle to shoot.

We met Mir Usman Alam, the present holder of the title "Nawab of Surat and Belha" (Belha is a small principality near Poona). He responded to my question, "What do you do?" with the poignant remark, "Well, you know, we have lots of properties. We are trying to survive...."

His struggle is easy to see in the crumbling of the grand old palace. Plaster is peeling off the walls, picture frames are covered in dust. The grand Durbar Hall on the second floor is almost empty of furniture. "This hall was known

* "Nawab" is a derivative of the Urdu/Arabic word *naeb*, meaning deputy (to the king). It is the Muslim equivalent of "maharaja," a Hindu term for king. "Nawab" is the source of the English word "nabob," or potentate. Also heard are the expressions "Nawab Saheb" (Nawab Sir) or "Nawab Sahebzada" (Nawab Exalted Sir). The greatest nawab of them all, the king of Hyderabad in India, preferred "Nizam" (Grand Governor) because "nawab" was not good enough for him.

as the biggest *cheeni khana* (house of china) in Gujarat, but most of it is now gone," he lamented, "taken — pilfered — by other members of the family."

He was referring to the soap-operatic quarrels between the feuding wings of the family. The last nawab had four wives. The third one was an *ayah* (nanny), according to Mickie, the present nawab's journalist son. "The fourth was his servant woman." The children by the first wife are feuding with those of the other three. One wing of the old palace in Surat is occupied by cousins who are rude to the present nawab's visitors; one of the surviving wives, who lives in Bombay, does not speak to the rest of the family.

In our travels around Surat, we located another old fort that is now a government office with nothing more than a small tablet at the gate to mark its history. The Moorish-style structure has a huge gate, with metal spikes to repel attacks by elephant-led forces, and three semi-circular fifty-foot-high ramparts on the river. Another slum — a relatively small one — has sprung up in the fort's shadow, and the grounds are a sloshy mess, with no one realizing the significance of the spot.

The first headquarters of the East India Company was located in this old part of the city, but in which building no one is really sure. On one side of the street, is an squat old three-storey building, now occupied by a Parsee family. Parsees in Surat go a long way back. They sought refuge in the city, fleeing persecution in Iran (then Persia). From Surat, they went to Bombay in the mid-seventeenth century, and became "honorary Europeans" — partners of the British. The building may once have been a Parsee travellers' lodge. A building on the other side of the street was built in 1840 and is now an Irish Presbyterian mission school. Originally, it was either the headquarters of

The palace of Nawab Jafar Ali, now occupied by his descendant, Nawab Mir Usman Alam. It was originally built as a hunting lodge in the seventeenth century.

the East India Company or one of its warehouses.

As we went down a gully, a narrow path to the river, we saw a dilapidated building on the right with a really old gate, again with anti-elephant spikes. The entrance to the East India Company office complexes, perhaps? This led into a cluster of homes, most of which had either collapsed or were about to collapse. A local resident told us that one of the biggest houses had already disintegrated, leaving behind an empty space where, he claimed, the residence of the governor of the East India Company used to be. On the edge of the property was what looked like servants' quarters, with the nameplate "Cooper Villa." Farther along the cobbled street was a crumbling two-storey villa with another plaque reading "Cooper Hall" and, on its veranda wall, a framed picture of a Parsee priest. According to Mickie, this was the East India Company's waterfront building. The East India Company's office requirements were reduced once it moved its headquarters to Bombay in 1686, while the "factory" continued in Surat.

Two kilometres away is the cemetery where Burton looked unsuccessfully for the grave of Thomas Coryate, an early English traveller to Persia and India, a scholar and a brave and unstoppable man, who died in India in 1617. No doubt the young Burton — just beginning his adventure in India — identified with this rogue adventurer of another age. Coryate ended his life a beggar and a religious mystic. His grave was, in fact, upriver from where Burton sought him in Surat.

The once-impeccable British graveyard is in a shambles, its gravestones vandalized. People have defecated on the graves. No one cares — not the government, not the British High Commission in Delhi, nor the consulate in Bombay. Though Coryate is not here, the graves of several seventeenth-century Englishmen are, among them that of Gerald Angier, a governor of Bombay.

About Burton, Mickie said, "In all my readings on Surat, I have not come across any mention of Burton. In his travels through Surat, he might have stayed at the Governor's residence, but more likely he put up in the barracks nearby."

After our search for the remnants of the East India Company, we had another interminable drive back to Baroda. To avoid the thick traffic jams and the endless stream of trucks, we bumped along the side of the road, got off the beaten track and took short cuts over fields and through villages. It had been a long, tiring day.

Karachi

Karachi, thou shalt be the glory of the east! Would that I could come again to see you in your grandeur!

**SIR CHARLES NAPIER,
1843**

5

KARACHI

On arriving at Karachi airport, we were met by Abdul Hamid Akhund, secretary, Department of Culture and Tourism, in Sindh. We found this powerful man to be charming, knowledgeable and keenly interested in our project. He had just republished Burton's 1877 work, *Sind Revisited*, for the Sindhi government, and had been given the task of looking after us.

I arrived at the Sind Club at about 1:30 a.m. Despite my tiredness, I couldn't quell a feeling of deep excitement. We were moving farther into our journey, stepping from the realm of research and speculation into the realm of action and discovery. We were also moving towards a more unsettled region than the one we had just left, and also towards more unsettling questions about Burton than we had dealt with so far.

Burton's description of the Karachi of the early 1840s was sometimes humorous but, I imagined, also critically to the point. He found it to be "a mass of low mud hovels and tall mud houses with flat mud roofs, windowless mud walls, and numerous mud ventilators, surrounded by a tumble-down parapet of mud, built upon a low platform of mud-covered rock."

Kolachi-jo-Kun (Whirlpool of Kolachi) was little more than a fishing village before the British took it over in 1839. It was formed of the three islands of Manora, Bhit and Baba in the harbour of what came to be known as Karachi. It had a population of about 6,000 when Burton arrived early in

The shrine is visited every morning and evening; if the devotee be a stranger and his business very urgent, he takes up his abode on the spot. Perseverance is of course the only means of success, and when the Pir has been so slow in his movements as to allow his visitor to die before the prayer has been granted, all believe that there will be a greater proportion of reward in heaven. Some votaries are so grateful as to continue their visits to the tomb, and presents to its guardians, even after success.

SIR RICHARD F. BURTON, 1851
Sindh, and the Races That Inhabit the Valley of the Indus

Previous page: Veiled women enter a mosque at Mangho Pir outside Karachi.

A sketch of the harbour and fort of Karachi—about one year after the British took it over in 1839.

1844 to carry out his military, surveying and other investigative responsibilities for the British East India Company.

He made note of the town's apparent lack of ambition, but he found that changed on his return visit with Isabel. As he noted in *Sind Revisited*: "In those days the port of Karáchi had no pretensions to be called a port.... Presently Karáchi developed pretensions of her own; and she detected in her position, the point nearest to Europe, a pride of place, a virtue, a natural value, which, improved by Art, would soon raise her high above obsolete and rococo Calcutta, Madras, and Bombay...."

Nevertheless, it took time for Karachi to reach its potential. As late as 1947, before Partition and Independence, the city still had a population of less than half a million. But after Partition, with the influx of millions of Muslim refugees from India, rapid growth changed the city considerably, and it became the new Pakistan's first capital. Later, in 1963, the capital was moved to Islamabad by President Ayub Khan. Karachi is now the capital only of the Sindh, and perhaps it is better that way. Sindhis seem to be much prouder of being Sindhi than Pakistani. And Karachi certainly has the depth of culture necessary for the capital of Sindh province.

Looking down on the city from the east end of M.A. Jinnah Road, the tomb of Muhammad Ali Jinnah is a modern monument that cannot fail to impress. Because of his determination in demanding that Pakistan become a separate Muslim state, Jinnah is considered to be the father of the country, and was its first governor general. It was he who engineered the rift that led to Partition during the 1947 negotiations for Indian independence. The creation of Pakistan was Jinnah's dying political achievement — and his greatest. The enormous marble dome of his huge white tomb is softened with high pointed arches and copper grilles. This is not only Pakistan's most impressive monument, but also its proudest.

Karachi is still the largest city in Pakistan. It is the hub of the country's commercial activity and a considerable international port. It now has a population of perhaps 7 million. The long, slow growth in the nineteenth century followed by the rapid growth in the twentieth has given Karachi a very different look from Bombay. Together with Victorian Gothic buildings, there are now modern skyscrapers. The city throbs with activity and is full of startling contrasts. Ancient, narrow, market alleys open up into tree-lined boulevards and thoroughfares. The old and new do not seem to mix easily. I felt I was constantly having to shift from the old world to the new and back again. History was never far away.

Karachi now has an international airport, two railway stations, and a sheltered natural harbour serving as the port. The city is the easternmost point on the Indus delta, and other ports now seem to have fallen into disuse. Roads and highways connect the city to the rest of the country, and communication is easy. You can instantly feel the energy of this sprawling city.

It is by far the most important centre in the Sindh, the southernmost province of Pakistan. At the core of this region is the Indus River, which cuts it in two and gives it its name. For millennia the area has depended on the river as its chief source of moisture; there is little rain. Winter in the valley of the Indus is the temperate season, with temperatures ranging from 10 to 30 degrees Celsius. For the uninitiated, summer is a fair imitation of hell, with the thermometer often reading 50 degrees Celsius (125 degrees Fahrenheit).

The inhabitants of the valley are some of the world's most efficient managers of water, and where the valley is irrigated, it provides lush harvests of grain, fruit and other valuable crops. Where there is no irrigation, however,

The tomb of Muhammad Ali Jinnah (1878-1948), rightly considered to be the father of modern Pakistan.

The children of Sindh live the same lives as their great-great grandparents, who Burton said survived by "cultivating patches of ground to provide them and their families with bread."

there is desert. And where there is desert, there is dust.

In the irrigated regions, where descendants of the ancient Balochs work their tenant farms, and in the deserts, where both settled and nomadic tribes abound, many things have not changed for 5,000 years.

In ancient times, in Burton's time and in our own time, this region — the valley of the Indus and its surrounding desert — has been a land of courage and cunning, daring and perseverance, mystery and romance. This was the land that Burton gave his soul for. Its inhabitants were the people that Burton sought out, identified with, understood and wrote about — the people who changed his life forever.

The civilization of the Indus existed at the same time as those of Mesopotamia and Egypt. Alexander the Great conquered the main towns along the Indus, arriving in 326 B.C. Then in the third and second centuries B.C., the Sindh was part of the great Mauryan Empire of India. The dominant Buddhism of this era was eventually eclipsed by Hinduism between the sixth and eight centuries A.D., the period when the caste system was introduced.

When the Sindh was conquered by Muhammad bin Qasim in A.D. 712, the Arabs introduced Islam into the subcontinent. Until 874, the Abbassid Caliphate, the leaders of the Sunni Muslims, ruled the Sindh from Baghdad. It is their court that is so exuberantly described in the *Arabian Nights*, which

was eventually translated by Burton and published in 1885.

After 874, various peoples wrested control of Sindh, beginning with the Sumras, a local tribe who ruled for nearly 500 years. They were overthrown by the Sammah Rajputs in 1337, and Thatta was made the capital. The conquerors were themselves conquered in 1524, when the Sindh was captured by Shah Beg Arghun from Afghanistan. He then met defeat in 1545 at the hands of the Tarkhans, who first ruled independently, but then became governors under the Mughal Empire (1526-1858) based in Delhi. The Kalhoras controlled the Upper Sindh starting in 1736; and then they were overthrown by the Talpurs in 1789, who moved the capital to Hyderabad. The Talpurs originally came from the Indus: from Marri and Derajat, north of Sindh — a barren land on the banks of the river near the mountains, in more or less desertous country. In 1843, just after Burton arrived, the British defeated the Talpurs at the infamous battle of Miani under General Napier. British rule of the province continued until Partition and Independence in 1947. It was the British who really created the city of Karachi and set in motion its transformation from a tiny fishing village to an enormous industrial metropolis.

In describing the Sindh of Burton's day, Edward Rice comments that it was, "a vast, broiling, often hateful province with a great marshy delta into which the Indus River emptied."

Burton, when he arrived, exclaimed, "A regular desert! — mere line of low coast, sandy as a Scotchman's whiskers — a glaring waste, with visible as well as palpable heat playing over its dirty yellow surface!"

My own first hours in the Sindh, though not without their challenges, were far more pleasant — largely because of the amenities of the wonderful Sind Club.

On that first morning, I was woken by Mohammed Younus — my tall, elderly bearer at the Club. He was very apologetic at waking me up at 6:15, which I really didn't need. Not only was the time half an hour behind India, but the *muezzin* had just called the Faithful to prayer. I had forgotten that would be the case in this very Muslim state. Also, a multitude of crows, kites and even a few falcons were soaring overhead and making quite a noise outside my bedroom window. Looking out, I saw an empty lot where a considerable amount of garbage had been dumped. I supposed that was what the birds were after. The scene made me think of one of Burton's descriptions of "Kurrachee," in *Scinde; or, the Unhappy Valley*, where he mentions, "the mountains of old rubbish which surround and are scattered through the native town...."

Younus was totally in white. He had on long white *pajamas* and a "Sind Club" white jacket. On his head he wore a white, fez-like hat on which the words "Sind Club" were embroidered in red.

"What do you wish for breakfast, Sir?" he enquired or I thought he enquired. I asked for something simple. "*Acha*" (yes), he replied. I was still extremely tired, and all I really wanted was some strong coffee. The morning was quite cool. Younus was very attentive, sorting out my dirty clothes, hanging up my shirts, turning on my bath, attending to my breakfast tray. And he couldn't speak a word of English! The Sind Club,

Mohammed Younus, my attentive bearer at the Sind Club.

though, is very British and still treats its members in the traditional manner.

The Club was founded in 1871 and at its inauguration had 76 members, all British civil servants. Indian and Pakistani members began to be accepted in the early 1950s. Today the membership is nearly 2,000, of whom 10 per cent are residents. In the beginning, the Club was in a bungalow rented at ninety rupees a month. Now, however, it occupies a large piece of land. The grounds are magnificently landscaped, and the Club is smoothly run. It has retained a unique position throughout a period that witnessed profound changes in Indian and Pakistani society, elegantly bridging the gap between imperialism and Independence.

The Sind Club was formed after Burton first left India, but it was very much in existence on his second visit in 1876. In 1871, at the time the Club was founded, the Indian Mutiny (1857) was fourteen years in the past, and Sindh had been under British control since the battle of Miani in 1843. Among the original members of the Club were men who had participated in that battle. One of these was a Colonel Marston, who was credited with saving Sir Charles Napier's life at Miani. Sindh's only railway — Karachi to Kotri — had started running in 1861, and the Suez Canal had been open for only two years. At the time of the Club's founding, the population of Karachi had reached 56,000.

The original clubhouse was in the staff lines, but I don't think it still stands. The current clubhouse was completed in 1883. It is a grand building. Long, low porches stretch away on either side of a main entrance portico, and a balconied second storey runs the entire width of the building. There are elegant gardens, tennis and squash courts, attentive servants in white uniforms and a general air of tranquillity and ease. Everything is protected behind high walls and a large, black, wrought-iron gate.

The furnishings throughout are in the colonial style: tasteful fabrics and carpets; old Sindhi prints and other pictures; silver cups, trophies and presentation mementos.

The veranda, attached to the dining-room, overlooks the garden. There are also a drawing-room, a bridge room, a reading room, a cocktail bar and several other comfortable meeting rooms. There are residential quarters on the first floor, and also in some newer buildings behind the main clubhouse. It was a comfortable haven. It was wonderful to be here after the rigours of Bombay and Baroda, and, as I was to learn, would be a welcoming headquarters to return to from the various excursions into the world of the past and Richard Burton.

No liquor was served anywhere in the Club, as prohibition was strictly observed; and I was not allowed to take any photographs. This last rule I did not observe quite so strictly.

My first briefing by Abdul Hamid Akhund took place in the Governor's Mansion. We discussed our busy schedule, and then it was out onto the porch and into a station wagon that had been provided for us for the duration of our stay in the Sindh. Luckily for us, it came with a driver, Gul Hassan, who, I was to find out, was very curious, very humorous and almost always late!

We proceeded through the gardens, past the armed guards at the enormous gate of the Governor's Mansion and into the streets of Karachi. The city seemed different in daylight — newer than Bombay and the buildings cleaner. Where were the slums? I knew they were there because I'd read about them — but they are far less extensive here than in Bombay and less immediately visible. The traffic was just as hectic, however, and the crowds were just as thick.

My early experiences in Karachi included interviews with two authors, Suhail Lari, who had recently written a history of the Sindh, and Mrs. Yasmeen Lari, a renowned architect and author of a well-known book, *Traditional Architecture of Thatta* (I was soon to visit Thatta), and another on Karachi, *The Dual City: Karachi during the Raj*. Suhail took a positive view of the British conquest of the Sindh, while Yasmeen was more critical. Her book on Karachi focuses on the effect of the Raj on one particular area. Both writers were highly knowledgeable and offered valuable observations. They told me that there was a time when Karachi was little more than cactus and sand! Karachi did not have a municipal water system until 1883. Before that it was a very dusty town with constant dust storms. Even twenty years ago there were dust storms in Karachi. The addition of buildings as the city expanded changed the wind patterns and ended the storms.

We talked about where Burton might have stayed in Karachi. Probably in the barracks, but not necessarily so. At the Napier Barracks in the European Infantry Lines, the officers lived in front. In 1876 Burton may have stayed with some dignitary, though we know the Burtons preferred good hotels. The Napier Barracks were first built in 1843-44. The second storey was added before Burton arrived in 1876.

In the old days, they told me, one could see the sea from the cantonment. There was nothing in front of the area then. The camp was in what is now the Sadar Bazaar. The army camp followers who brought supplies settled in the area, beginning in 1839. They were encouraged to open stores, and these eventually evolved into the bazaar of today. An old Parsee fire temple, which was destroyed, has been succeeded by a new one, also in the bazaar area. There is a Roman Catholic convent near the old cemetery which Burton commented on in *Sind Revisited*. The old Free Mason's Lodge was on the present site of the Sind Club.

We also discussed the whereabouts of the famous "Karachi Papers." As Fawn Brodie has said, "Burton was first stationed under Sir Charles Napier in 1844, when the 18th Native Infantry was sent to the Sind.... It was some months before the old soldier learned of Burton's special linguistic accomplishments and began to use him in intelligence work."

Burton later described how this led to his being asked to provide Napier with information on the boy brothels of Karachi, which Napier had good reason to suspect his soldiers of frequenting. Because he was the only British officer who could speak Sindhi, Burton was the inevitable choice for the job, but he took it on condition that the report he wrote should not be sent to Napier's superiors in Bombay.

Using his ever-increasing powers of disguise, Burton says he "passed many an evening in the townlet, visited all the porneia and obtained the fullest details, which were duly despatched to Government House."

Yasmeen Lari mentioned that Zulfiqar Ali Bhutto, the former (and eventually executed) prime minister, had used his considerable influence to try to locate these notorious reports, but — like everyone else who has tried — could not discover their whereabouts. The interview was followed by lunch, after which we toured some of historic Karachi.

A drive through the crowded older part of Karachi brought us to the busy boat basin. A government launch was put at our disposal, and we motored out to Manora Island (locally called Manhorro). The channel out there is about thirty-five feet deep, and runs between the naval section on the left and the container docks on the right. Strict security was demanded and I was warned about this constantly. I could see why. In Keamari Bay, we threaded our way through destroyers, their large grey shapes looming over us, until we finally arrived at the Manora Observatory Tower, built in the British period. The lighthouse, built in 1887, is a "new" one, replacing an older version.

We saw the site of Fort Manora, built by the Talpurs — the kings of Sindh. We also explored Keamari Bay, which is seven and a half miles long and one and a half miles wide. The area is home to ethnic communities that have survived from ancient times to the present day, among them the Kutchi Memon.

The Bazdar came softly out of the tent, carrying on his fist Khairu, the Laghar, who was sitting erect, as if mentally prepared for anything, with head pressed forward, and pounces firmly grasping the Dasti. Her hood was then removed, her leash was slowly slipped, and ... cast off with a whoop, [she] dashed unhesitatingly at the enemy.

RICHARD F. BURTON,
Falconry in the Valley of the Indus, 1852

Haroon and I drove to an interview with Hamidullah Paracha, a wealthy industrialist who lives in the suburbs of Karachi and is a member of the Sindh Wildlife Management Board. His house is in the Defence Colony — an affluent suburb with a gate controlled by a Kalashnikov-toting guard! Paracha is a coal-mine owner whose passion is falconry — as it is for his fourteen-year-old son, Yusaf.

After being shown around his spacious, rambling house, we were offered tea and cakes. I immediately asked about the gun-toting guard. Mr. Paracha then gave us our first hair-raising tale of dacoit (bandit) activities in the Sindh. These brigands are ruthless and violent. The risk of being kidnapped is a very real one everywhere in the Sindh — particularly for anybody who seems to have money. Guns are a necessary evil for protection and for retaliation against banditry. The Paracha family had recently been held up and robbed while on a hunting trip.

Hamidullah Paracha is a *bazdar* (falconer). He told us that both falconry and hawking had just about died out in Pakistan until they were revived by wealthy Arabs from Bahrain and the United Arab Emirates, Qatar, Oman and Saudi Arabia.

We saw some of Mr Paracha's hawks and falcons, perched on low wooden stoops in his garden. There are a number of differences between hawks and falcons. Falcons are black-eyed. The hawk is easier to train, and can be used to hunt practically anything — even deer and gazelle. There is no doubt that the peregrine is the fastest and most versatile of the falcons. It too can be trained to hunt almost anything — including ducks. According to Burton:

*There is a great difference, here as elsewhere, between the proper-
ties of the long-winged falcons and the short-winged hawks. The
former have ever been the general favourites in Europe, on account of their docility, ardour, and perseverance. These "denizens
of the cloud and crag," swoop from the air upon the quarry with
the rapidity of lightning, and fell it to earth with a single stroke of
their powerful avillons, or hind-talons, slantingly delivered from
behind, so as to lay open the shoulders and loins, the back of the
neck, or the skull. Of this order is the peregrine, the "Saccer ales,"
who "deserveth no meaner a title than Jove's servant," and to her,
as the type of the race, falconry profusely gives every attribute of
nobility.*

RICHARD F. BURTON,
Falconry in the Valley of the Indus

The Saker falcon — one of the largest falcons, and second only to the gyr-falcon in size and strength — is very popular among the Arabs, and obvious-ly also a great favourite of Hamidullah Paracha. It is a powerful, bold and aggressive bird, and may be priced at anywhere from 20,000 to 500,000 rupees.

"An expensive falcon," Mr. Paracha told us, "is a status symbol for the Arabs. However, a 20,000-rupee Saker will hunt just as well if trained properly!"

The birds are used in the Sindh mainly for bustard hunting. The season is usually in February. "Bustard hunting is banned to Pakistanis — but not to foreigners. Visiting Arabs kill an incredible number of birds every year: almost 10,000. Despite the ban, Pakistanis seem to kill 2,000 or 3,000 every year. That's a lot of birds. Although there is an enormous outcry from environmentalists calling for a ban on bustard hunting, the government will not disallow the sport. Arabs bring a great amount of economic benefit to the country. They pay the government for the land they hunt in, and they spend a lot of money locally.

"Besides bustards, the Arabs also hunt for sand grouse, rabbits and partridges. But I'm afraid they have really spoiled falconry and distorted the market. Some Arabs combine falconry with guns. They use the falcons, and they also shoot from their Jeeps. This is not at all sporting. But they pay exorbitant prices, and they get away with anything. They have not only distorted the market but created an environmental hazard. Small falcons are being used to catch larger falcons, and these fetch huge sums of money that the

Hawks, in Scinde as elsewhere, are of two kinds, the "eyess" (or Nyess), and the "passage-bird." Young hawks grow quickly; as soon as they begin to fly strongly they must be taken from the hack. Then their education commences in earnest; eyesses are not seeled like haggards and birds of passage; their reclaiming commences with being broken to the hood.

SIR RICHARD F. BURTON, 1852
Falconry in the Valley of the Indus

Arabs seem willing to pay. If a poor man can capture a large falcon for an Arab, he can sometimes make enough money in a single transaction to support himself for the rest of his life. Locals are now tying weights onto smaller falcons and stitching their eyes up, so that when they are released they cannot fly. The bigger falcons are captured when they swoop down to steal these lures. Thousands and thousands of smaller falcons are dying like this. It really is quite cruel.

"A good falconer will hunt with his falcon for only two years and then release the bird into the wild. But this is seldom done these days."

That evening, we had dinner with Abdul Hamid Akhund at his house, and it was a real feast! There was chicken *qorma* (in gravy), spinach cooked in ghee (clarified butter), a grain dish called *roti* (regular wheat *roti* and also a *roti* made with millet — a Sindhi speciality), goat-meat curry, fried onions with spices, aromatic basmati rice, and a fantastic dessert called *qulfi*, which is condensed milk with pistachio nuts, frozen and served in a cone. All very tasty!

But where were the women? In *purdah*, seclusion. And, of course, no alcohol. Yet it was a very pleasant dinner, very friendly, with the conversation dominated mostly by a single, rather remarkable guest, Ali Ahmed Brohi, a seventy-four-year-old former journalist who is the only surviving member of the 1946 naval mutiny against the British. He was court-martialled and condemned to die, but was released on a technicality. Despite the court-martial, Mr. Brohi remains an Anglophile. He is well read and very opinionated. He is also a diehard Sindhi, but is nevertheless very critical of his own people and his own country.

"Ah! Burton. He was a great man. You must concede that. Whether you like him or not. He didn't beat about the bush. He wrote exactly what he thought."

He agreed that much of what Burton accomplished was the direct result of his unusual gift for languages. This was something that Burton's contemporaries had noted as well. Walter Abraham said of Burton, "When I knew him, he was master of half a dozen languages, which he wrote and spoke so fluently that a stranger who did not see him and heard him speaking would fancy that he heard a native. His domestic servants were — a Portuguese, with whom he spoke Portuguese and Goan ... an African, Persian, and a Sindi or Belochee. They spoke their mother tongue to Sir Richard ... and it was a treat to hear Sir Richard talk; one would scarcely be able to distinguish the Englishman from a Persian, Arabian or a Scindian."

Even so, Brohi noted, it was not only his knowledge of many languages that set Burton apart, but also his rare gift of sitting down with absolutely anybody anywhere and being able to make them open up and speak to him. "He had some milk of humanity in him that somehow made others confide in him, tell him things, and tell him, sometimes, their innermost secrets."

Colonel James Outram, who clashed with Napier over military strategy for the British conquest of Sindh.

Burton possessed to an amazing degree the ability to find common ground with anyone — a remarkable gift, especially for a person coming from his background. He could deal with the people of the East, who, Brohi maintained, "are totally inscrutable. You must understand that here everyone is a puzzle. You don't know whether he is going to love you or kill you." Unlike other people I had spoken to, Brohi didn't think Burton was a spy. "He was just doing his job. Mostly surveying." In any case, Brohi was more interested in the man and what he was thinking than in what he was doing.

"Perhaps Burton *was* 'used' by the British," he conceded. "He was a difficult man to handle and harness. He didn't really belong in the army. He was not disciplined enough. So he was given isolated jobs and excursions to utilize his talents."

"We don't know for sure if he was a homosexual. But surely a lot of men have either done it or thought about it. I feel that Burton either practised it, or else he had definite homosexual tendencies. But why did he probe homosexuality in Karachi? Let's face it, prostitution is the one industry which is the same the whole world over. What was there to probe? How can an army exist without homosexuality?

"Some people are crazy," he continued. "But they are also geniuses. Certain people have vistas open to them which are denied to the rest of us.... Burton had syphilis, you know. This also causes a kind of genius or madness. He must have contracted it somewhere in India or here. Sickness sometimes drives people to greatness."

I enjoyed Brohi's outspokenness and his lack of inhibition in expressing controversial views. He was scathing about General Napier, whom he blamed for slaughtering Sindhis to advance his career. "General Napier had been one of the greatest English failures before he came here. He had hardly done anything throughout his entire military career. He was driven by an inferiority complex. He was already old when he came to the Sindh. I feel he wanted to prove himself and win some glory. And it was he, not General Outram, who started the war against the Sindhis at Miani and Dubba. In fact, Outram accused Napier of provoking and starting the war. There is no doubt in my mind that Napier instigated the war to gain glory and fame."

Brohi's views of the British legacy were quite positive, though he made it clear they were not widely shared. "Every politician in Pakistan abuses the British and blames them for all our problems. Yet our language, law, justice, roads, canals and railways were all established by the British. They ruled us as colonizers all right, but they ruled us wonderfully. Compared to our present-day politicians, they were absolute angels. I have seen their justice, and I've seen our justice. And I can tell you their justice was infinitely better, and much fairer. British rule was the greatest blessing that we could ever have received."

I couldn't tell if it was just courtesy to a visitor that led him to praise the British — and to enjoy relating some anecdotes that showed his own countrymen in a humorous light. "There is a story," he said, "of a Sindhi general who was showing off his medals, one of which he said was for 'saving the honour of a woman.' 'What did you do?' he was asked. 'Oh,' he said, 'I changed my mind.' Another general, also sporting his medals, was asked, 'What did you get that medal for?' He answered, 'I was honoured for chopping off the legs of a rival general.' 'Why didn't you chop off his head, instead?' he was asked. 'Because,' replied the general, 'it had already been chopped off by somebody else!'"

Everywhere he goes (as he recounts in "Sind Revisited," which he wrote from our journal on return) he visits the old scenes of his former life, saluting them, letting the changes sink into his mind, and taking an everlasting farewell of them. He was very apt to do this in places where he had lived. He notices the ruin of the Indian army — the great difference between his time and now. He said, "Were I a woman, I would have sat down and had a good cry." There was only one of his joyous crew still breathing ... the old hospitality was gone; there was no more jollity, no more larking boys; everything so painfully respectable, and so degenerated.

ISABEL BURTON,
The Life of Captain Sir Richd F. Burton, K.C.M.G., F.R.G.S., 1893

Though the Burtons found the army of the East India Company much diminished on their return to Karachi in 1876, they did not feel the same about the buildings. On his first visit, Burton noted, it had been little more than "a mass of low hovels."

"And now Karáchi," he continued, "after growing from 6000 to 45,000 souls, has become, externally at least, mighty respectable and dull. The straggling suburbs have been removed, and the general shape is a broad arrow-head pointing northwards, and striking the Fiumara, or Sukhi Naddi (dry river).... The material is still the old, dull-grey ... foundations of stone; but it is lighted up and picked out with more chunam and whitewash. The dark, narrow alleys have been improved off, except in the bázárs; the streets are wide, open, and glaring; each has its name and its pair of *trottoirs*, whilst the quasi-civilized *reverbère* contrasts with the whitewashed and beflagged tombs of various Pírs, or holy men, still encumbering the thoroughfares. There is a general Bombay look about the place, the result of deep eaves supported by corbelled posts...."

The intense military aspect and sound of Karachi had also vanished by the time Burton returned. Gone were "the days when she contained, besides artillery and cavalry, three white and as many black regiments.... The steamer and the railway, the telegraph and the counting-house, the church and the college, have gained the day against artillery, cavalry, and infantry. The 'mercantile' element has become a power...." Burton commented: "Time, which found Karáchi camp built of unbaked brick, has now turned it into stone." By the late 1870s, the administrative powers of the army were gone, and the imperialism of which the army was such a proponent was waning; but the imperial buildings of Karachi remained — and many of them still do.

No doubt echoing the comments of her husband, Isabel Burton said of the Karachi of 1876, "The buildings had grown magnificent, but everything else had changed for the worse...." One of those magnificent buildings is Frere Hall, set in the lovely Jinnah Gardens, next door to the Sind Club. This building, constructed after Burton's first journey to India, was built by Sir Bartle Frere, governor of the Bombay Presidency from 1862 to 1876. It is not exactly charming, but it is unique — a real Victorian Gothic conglomerate. Governor Frere intended it as a functional centre in 1865, but it is now a public library. It is certainly a landmark — impossible to miss. It stands now as an epitaph to the British and Victorian presence in Sindh in the mid-nineteenth century.Quite near to the Sind Club and Frere Hall is Holy Trinity Cathedral, the largest Protestant church in the Sindh, built as a garrison church in 1855. This building is typical of the colonial church architecture of the era, but I found the inside more interesting than the outside. Brass and marble memorials all around the interior walls recall details of the history of British life in the Sindh. I could have spent a long time poring over

these details. They are memorials to the glory of
Britain; but it is part of church architecture to
glorify the builders as well as the Lord!

Leaving the neighbourhood of the Club, I took
a long drive around Karachi with my driver, Gul
Hassan, and my camera. We drove past Gimcona,
the place where Hindus meet. Along McLeod
Road we wound, through the bazaars and behind
Boulton Market. Past camels, donkeys, carts, into
narrower and narrower streets. Some men wore
coloured turbans — they were probably Balochs.
Market stalls lined the narrow lanes.

It seemed as though anything one might want
must be available. Not only was there a huge diversity of products, but there were special markets for many of them. The Sarafa Bazaar for

*Frere Hall, built in 1865 by
Sir Bartle Frere, governor of
the Bombay Presidency.*

silver. The Bartan Gali for pots and pans. The Cloth Bazaar, where I saw marvellous Sindhi fabrics in a wide array of colourful materials and designs. The
Khajoor Bazaar — for dates! And then the Sadar Bazaar, the very centre of
shopping in Karachi — possibly all of Sindh — with every conceivable variety
of shop. Stretching between the two main thoroughfares of Abdullah
Haroon Road and Zaibun Nisa Street (previously known as Victoria Road
and Elphinstone Street, respectively), it is a busy, noisy, rabbit's warren of
narrow alleyways in which a bewildering array of goods is offered for sale:
copper and brass, cloth, jewellery, food, handicrafts.

Farther up the Abdullah Haroon Road, we reached the Zainab Market,
which proved to be more of the same: crowds and commerce, busy vendors,
carpets and rugs. And the Bohri Bazaar, another cloth bazaar. We also saw
the Empress Market, an enormous Victorian Gothic building opened in
1889. This market is enclosed, housing a great many stalls mostly selling
food: meat, fish, vegetables....

Though I have seen some of the world's most elegant shops—and some of
the most spare — I will always think of the markets of India and Pakistan as
the most vibrant example of how commerce captures the richness of a country's daily life and its continuing culture.

For me, Burton was nowhere more present than at Napier Barracks, the
long, stone-built stretch of row housing that was the centre of British army
life in the Sindh. Napier railed against the squalid conditions of barracks
like these, knowing that the death rate of his Indian soldiers was more than
three times as high as that of soldiers at home — a difference not accounted
for by combat alone.

The barracks are different now. This huge structure, with its second floor
that was added later, is now surrounded by the growing, bustling metropolis.

That evening, Hamid Akhund joined us briefly at the Sind Club and introduced us to Mohammed Hussein Panhwar, a sixty-eight-year-old engi-

neer, collector and author, with whom we had dinner. Mr. Panhwar was very learned and obviously well read — particularly about the Sindh. He gave us a bibliography of Burton's writings, and he recommended that I look again at volume ten of Burton's *Arabian Nights*, the "Terminal Essay." Mohammed Panhwar thought that the Terminal Essay was perhaps a summary of the Karachi Papers without the details.

"When Burton wrote his notes in the *Arabian Nights*," he said, "his writing really came to life. In the notes he was, of course, master of his subject.

"Burton was a very clever man who even got access to our women. That, no outsider could do. The women, not just Muslims, but many Hindu women, too, observed the *purdah* (seclusion) in

Abdul Hamid Akhund, secretary, Department of Culture and Tourism, in Sindh.

those days. They could be seen only by males of their immediate families and the pirs (saints) and the shopkeepers. So he became a shopkeeper and a travelling salesman. That was very clever of him."

Panhwar was referring to the fact that when Burton chose a disguise for the purposes of intelligence gathering, he set up business as "Mirza Abdullah," a merchant. As Frank McLynn, paraphrasing Burton himself, explained in *Snow upon the Desert*: "He would take a house near the bazaar, so as to be handy for the evening conversations. For the purposes of credibility he occasionally rented a shop and furnished it with clammy dates, viscous molasses, tobacco, ginger, rancid oil and strong-smelling sweetmeats. His shops were always crowded but did poor financial business, hardly surprisingly since Burton gave the heaviest possible weight to all the women, especially the pretty ones, to gain their favour and avert all suspicion."

Although McLynn implies that Burton's motives in doing so were those of a spy, Fawn Brodie, in *The Devil Drives* (1967), seems to prefer the explanation that Burton simply had a weakness for women: "Burton ... recorded his pleasure in Arab women whenever he glimpsed a pretty face or figure. 'I have often lain awake for hours listening to the conversation of the Bedouin girls,' he wrote, 'whose accents sounded in my ears rather like music.'"

The *purdah* code emanates from the Islamic injunction that women ought not to expose themselves or become sex objects for males they are eligible to marry. In other words, women could be seen by male members of the family (uncles, etc.) but not outsiders. How much of their face or body they could expose, and to whom, has been hotly debated within Muslim societies for 1,400 years. Customs differ according to culture and region. In some countries, custom simply holds that women ought to dress modestly — from a Qur'anic injunction that urges both women and men to do so. In other cultures, men have used the injunction to put their women in veils, with varying degrees of concealment. In some families, women are expected to wear over their clothes a tent-like *burqa*, all white or all black, covering them from head to toe, with eye-slits for them to peer through. Others have a veil that covers the body but exposes the face, or covers the mouth and nose but not the eyes. This adds an aura of mystery and sexual tension to the scene. You see a woman from a distance, all covered up. As she gets close you are pleasantly surprised that her face is exposed, and that she is beautiful or has gorgeous eyes. That is why so much Persian and Urdu poetry is on the subject of eyes. That is all the poets could see. And that is precisely why women in the East say so much with their eyes — a furrowed brow of irritation, a squint of disapproval, a stare of interest, a quick wink of flirting. In his note to the "Persian Girl," for example, Burton praised her eyes; "The rose-bud of my heart hath opened and bloomed under the rays of those sunny eyes...." In fact, Burton wrote eloquently about the eyes of Eastern women:

> *Her eyes are large and full of fire, black and white as an onyx stone, of almond shape, with long drooping lashes, undeniably beautiful. I do not know exactly whether to approve of that setting of Kajal which encircles the gems; it heightens the colour and defines the form, but also it exaggerates the eyes into becoming the feature of the face — which is not advisable. However, I dare not condemn it....*
>
> RICHARD F. BURTON,
> *Scinde; or, the Unhappy Valley,* 1851

In Mohammed Panhwar's opinion, "Burton was preoccupied with sex. He was obsessed with it. He was either writing about it or indulging in it. His *Arabian Nights*, for example, was a book that contained much pornography. And then *Ananga Ranga* and *Kama Sutra*. He also used women as a learning tool. Wherever he went he would engage two or three women as servants, to learn the local language and customs. I suppose some of them were his mistresses, too...."

Outside the protection of the Sind Club, Karachi had a sometimes grim face.

I took photographs of drug addicts inhaling through some sort of long, thin, metal pipe. They wore blankets covering their heads. Dazed addicts

> *Among females of the Syyid race, especially in the northern parts of Sindh, the Burka of Arabia and Persia is much used. It is intended to present an appearance of peculiar modesty, but fails to do so, if we may believe the native proverb, which declares that the wearer of the Burka is a little worse than her neighbours.*
>
> SIR RICHARD F. BURTON, 1851
> *Sindh, and the Races That Inhabit the Valley of the Indus*

Drug addicts inhaling heroin in the streets of Karachi.

stared into space, resting against the city's walls. Squalor. Stench. Hostility. They were willing to pose for money. People passed unnoticed by the posers; cars and trucks honked incessantly. A small crowd gathered as soon as I started taking the pictures. Bloodshot, glistening eyes looked up pleadingly. No conversation. Begging without words.

On one of our evenings in Karachi, we had dinner with Hamid Akhund at the Kubla Khan Restaurant. At last — something different: a Chinese and Pakistani buffet. Fantastic food. Then after dinner, at about 10:00 p.m., we were taken to the preliminaries of a Pakistani wedding.

It was a rich family. The son was marrying an English girl. She was tall, slim, actually quite Iranian looking, but her accent was British. We were ushered into an enormous, patterned tent, decorated for the occasion and with a throne-like seat at one end. There was a bar at the other end, where all the men seemed to congregate. There is prohibition in Pakistan, but the guests all seemed to be enjoying themselves drinking. Admittedly, it was quite an international gathering.

The women were already seated around a huge, cloth-covered dance floor. Dressed in their finery, they were talking, gossiping, happy to see and to be seen. Most of the women had had their hair done professionally, a rare practice in a nation where 99.9 per cent of women merely tie their hair into a sim-

The Jelali Fakirs in Sindh are, generally speaking, poor, and live from hand to mouth. Their Pirs are said to receive about one-third of their gains

SIR RICHARD F. BURTON, 1851

ple *choti* (braid). I noticed some very expensive designer saris and gowns, set off by fabulous jewels, all conspicuously displayed. The groom's mother was dressed in black embroidered with gold, and sported a twenty-four-karat gold necklace and earrings set with rubies.

Eventually, the bride demurely tripped towards her throne. A lady close by was heard to whisper in Urdu, "They might at least have taught her how to walk!"

A short while later, the groom and his cohorts joined the bride with a lot of giggling and whispering. Many inside jokes.

There was music, followed by gift-giving, then by the sound of drums. After a while, the wedding pair left, and the guests moved in to leave only a small enclosure for the *mujra* dancers (sometimes referred to by Burton as Nautch girls). The drums sounded again, and the overweight dancing girls went through their routine.

A flurry of tossed rupee notes from onlookers greeted this effort. I found the whole affair to be a glittering display of new wealth. Upbeat but traditional. The evening's festivities would be followed the next night by *qawwali*, a genre of group singing devoted to praises of Allah and his prophet, Muhammad. The day after that the actual wedding would take place.

I learned more later from Haroon about the history and traditions of the *mujra* dance we had

Mujra *dancer. This sexy, evocative dance, originally done in brothels for an all-male audience, has been a tradition for centuries.*

seen that evening. *Mujra* is a sexy, evocative dance done in brothels — *kotha*, in Urdu — for an all-male audience. It has been a tradition for centuries in the Indian subcontinent. The dancer must also be a good singer, reciting romantic Urdu poetry — usually stories of heartbroken lovers pining for their beloved or paeans to the beauty of a woman you were in love with or had just developed a crush on, as Burton had for the Persian Girl. Burton praised her "features carved in marble like a Greek's...."

A brothel would come alive late at night, as customers, usually nawabs and other well-to-do Muslim gentry, arrived bearing the small, white, highly fragrant jasmine and mogra flowers, sewn into strings four to six inches long. These they tossed at the dancer, or if they managed to entice her close enough, tied onto her wrists or pinned in her hair.

The customers sat on the floor along three walls, supported by *gao takiya* (round cushions). The musicians — playing *dholak* and *tabla* (two types of drums), a harmonium (an accordion-like Indian instrument central to most singing), and a violin, or perhaps even a *bansri* (flute) — sat against the fourth wall, leaving the central space for the dancer.

She wore *churidar* (tight trousers) and a long *kurta* (dress or shirt), with elaborate bead or mirror handwork that shimmered in the lights, plus a *dupatta* (a long, thin, muslin scarf). She had *kohl* around her eyes, henna painted in fine geometric patterns on her hands, and wore a jasmine flower in her hair, a diamond stud in her nose, silver or gold earrings and *ghungroo* (dancing bells) tied to her ankles.

The customers waited patiently, as the etiquette required, while she bowed to her musicians, especially the *ustad* (teacher) and then to the brothel madam, who nodded her permission for the performance to begin.

The harmonium sounded, and the *mujra* dancer whirled towards the audience, her long, gathered *kurta* rising up in a circle. She moved her dance steps to the beat of the drums, leaving a trail of the fragrance of musk or other natural perfumes. She sang of love, romance, beauty, the joys of mating and the agony and pathos of parting from her lover. The men in the audience — most of them discerning patrons of Urdu poetry who would themselves know the verses she was singing — showered praises on her: "Wah wah" (Well done); "Shabbash" (Bravo!); "La jawab" (Without parallel); "Kya kahna" (No words of praise can do justice to you). Many threw money at her feet and urged her to sing a verse again: "Mukarrar irshad" (Repeat that, please).

As the evening progressed, attendants replenished the drinks; the songs — and her dancing — became naughtier, with poems on the pleasures of a stolen kiss, an encounter in the fields, and finally, of the conjugal bed. But unlike at a striptease in a Western bar, both the poetry and the bodily movements were kept just this side of vulgarity, the phrasing suggestive but never crude, the dance poses evocative rather than explicit. The more evasive the words and the dancer, the more heightened the sexual tension. "Hi, tadpa diya" (You've made me quiver), a customer might say, dangling more currency, which she would pluck out with a flick of her index and middle finger.

The rules of Indian society laid down strict boundaries for how far one might go in flirting with the Nautch girl. Nobody dared attack her sexually. Those too inebriated to keep the prescribed etiquette were shown the door — the worst insult a man could suffer. "Nautch wali ke kothay se nikal wa diye gaye" (He got thrown out of a Nautch girl's house) used to be the ultimate insult for a social outcast in the red light district.

A preferred customer could, some day, take the Nautch girl to bed, but she would never be an ordinary prostitute. The man would have to win her over, and bid for her favours. She might take weeks or months to consent. The Nautch girl would remain in demand — and keep her price steep — by not being readily available. She made her living primarily by singing, dancing, teasing and flirting. But she might give herself to a nawab if she liked him. She was the queen of her street, and she, not the nawab or the nobleman, called the shots.

In the old days, even small towns had a Nautch girl in the red light district. Burton found one — "Moonbeam" — in Larkhana in the northern Sindh. But only the capital cities of princely states boasted the classy brothels, and provided the patronage for the *mujras*.

"It is a dying art these days," Haroon Siddiqui noted. "Social mores have changed. Customers have neither the luxury, the time, nor the patience to sit through an all-night *mujra* session. Nor, thank God, are there the indulgent wives who will allow it. It is also a mark of our times that the customers want immediate, full sexual gratification, not just sexual titillation and arousal! Now, as we can see from the wedding, the *mujra* girls come to the customers to sing and dance before a mixed audience."

Many women in the audience here were smoking and drinking, and some had the *bindi*, the dot of Hindu women, on their forehead. This was surprising in an Islamic nation. In the confines of their private party among friends they trust, people seemed to revel in making a defiant statement. A supposedly progressive female audience was attending a late-night session of *mujra* given by two heavyset, out-of-shape dancers who could neither dance nor sing, but merely lip-synched their way through popular Indian movie songs. I was disappointed. The dancers were as phoney as their audience!

Burton might have had to go to rundown seedy brothels in Larkhana or near Hyderabad to watch a *mujra* in all-male company, but he would at least have had the pleasure of seeing and enjoying the real thing.

In attending events like the wedding, I began to understand the pleasure Burton found in anthropology. And in my own, albeit amateur, observations of the lie of the land, I began to see how he took such pleasure in studying the topography of the regions he explored.

One morning I went alone with Gul Hassan towards Hawkes Bay, about fifteen miles southwest of Karachi. The communities grew progressively poorer farther from the city. Eventually we headed for the sea, to what Gul Hassan said was "Griks village." I'm not sure of the spelling of this name, nor could I get it from anyone else. The village was right on the ocean and was clearly a fishing community — very desolate and poor — and entirely made up of thatched huts. The people seemed different from the inhabitants of Karachi. Later, Hamid Akhund told me that the area is still much the same as when Burton first visited it 150 years ago. There are Baloch and Kutchi people here. It is a very old community.

Farther along we came to Maripur, another thatched-hut community also mainly populated by Balochi tribal people. I was staggered at the poor maritime existence, but I felt quite at ease — with myself and with the people — as I wandered through the humble village. There was a hot sun, a clear, cool, unpolluted breeze from the sea, and the Balochi tribespeople smiled easily. The women were shy, but didn't seem to mind posing for photographs. At one point I found my path blocked by a group of people sitting on the road outside the door of a clay-built house. I wondered about this unusual sight until it was later explained to me that these were mourning residents who were seated outside their deceased friend's dwelling.

Fifteen miles southwest of Karachi the people seemed different. I was staggered at the poor maritime existence.

Then Hawkes Bay. This was one of the areas where residents and tourists came to swim. Certainly the stretches of sand around the bay seemed clean, although I was warned that the strong undertow makes the place quite dangerous to swimmers. Gul Hassan explained that only Sindhi people came here. There were no Balochi tribespeople, despite the fact that Baluchistan was very visible on the other side of the bay. This was desolate, brown, windswept country; and the people had bleak, weather-beaten faces. There was very little vegetation. I saw two camels unattended in the distance.

In order to get back, we had to drive through Lyari, on the outskirts of Karachi, where there are three communities: Punjabi, Kutchi, and Balochi and Sindhi mixed. Here the traffic was mostly transport buses and trucks. We made our way very slowly down Lyari Road. It was terribly congested. The unpaved dirt road was little better than a country lane; I was told that it floods during the monsoon season. For long periods the traffic barely moved, the congestion made worse by carts pulled by donkeys, camels blocking everyone's way, vendors out in the open selling barbecued chickens and other items, including textiles, pots, fans and trinkets. The road got even narrower, and to the foul pollution in the air was added the pervasive stench of urine. Camel urine. Was this the real Karachi? Finally, we bulldozed our way through the traffic and people and, with a tremendous sense of relief, got off Lyari Road onto the open, paved thoroughfare.

That afternoon, Haroon and I had an anthropological adventure of a different sort: a visit to a sex specialist!

Sex shops are common in India and Pakistan, especially in the older part of Karachi. One can see them from quite far off because of their brightly coloured Urdu messages advertising cures for impotence and other problems:

Every wish fulfilled.
Guaranteed to have children.
Cure for unmanliness.
Cure for impotency.
Enjoy life to the full!

I wasn't, of course, unaware of the danger of exposing myself to God knew what, but the temptation to investigate was overwhelming. When we were discussing Burton's potion for the Persian Girl, Haroon had told me that the "prescriptions" doled out by such specialists were usually from the homeopathic or Unani schools of medicine — natural and harmless.

So when I saw a large circular sign advertising "Sex Problem — Help" at the corner of Arambagh and Bans roads in the very heart of Karachi, I stopped Gul Hassan, navigated my way through perilously busy traffic and approached the physician's shop.

Pushing my way through saloon-type swinging doors with a great deal of Urdu writing on them, I came upon the expert, whose name I later found out was Hakim Minhas. He was fast asleep on a dirty platform next to an empty desk.

Awakening him, Haroon explained in Urdu that I was sixty years old, recently married to a much younger woman, and was anxious both to have more potent sex and to beget an heir. It was a story we'd cooked up just seconds before we stepped in the door, and it seemed plausible enough.

Apparently happy at the prospect of serving a customer — and a foreign one at that — Hakim became fully awake and began his diagnostic investigation: "How often do you go to your wife?"

I replied uneasily, "Three or four — maybe five times a month."

He showed great surprise. "Oh!" he said, "That's sometimes less than once a week. Not good with a young wife." He paused for the sake of reflection — or politeness. Then he said, "Do you get regular erections?"

"Yes," I replied, "I get erections." Now it was I who hesitated. "But what I would like is — you understand — to sustain them."

More reflection on the part of the specialist. Finally, he explained that he could prescribe a full course of medication that would cure my ailment for 5,500 rupees (about $170). But he had to examine me first. It was mandatory.

Hawkes Bay was desolate, brown, wind-swept country. The inhabitants had bleak, weather-beaten faces.

Previous page: Goat herders still barter livestock in the central Karachi market.

I had to respect him for that. After all, it might be a matter of honour to him not to give medicines for ailments without examining the "patient."

Telling myself I was crazy, but consumed by curiosity, I accepted his proposal and allowed myself to be led into a dimly lit chamber at the back of his rudimentary dispensary. He instructed me to lie on a sort of dingy platform, and I complied.

Alone in the gloom, I stared around me. I saw a series of bottles, pipes, wires and an enormous plastic tube measuring two and a half inches in diameter and at least eight inches long. I could make out a syringe beside me on a shelf. What was it for?

I looked again at the fat, ugly tube. At the end, a curled black wire attached itself to a cylindrical metal hand pump. Suddenly, I was terrified and my heart started to race.

But before I could do anything, the doctor came back. He ordered me to lower my trousers and lie prostrate on the none-too-clean, brown plastic platform. Then he put the giant test tube over my penis.

I tried hard not to move, as if that would prevent my skin from touching

The sex shops in Karachi are visible from quite a distance because of their brightly coloured advertisements.

the plastic. How many other men had been there before me? Had the tube ever been washed? My terror grew. But there was nothing I could do. I was in another man's domain and my safety lay in respecting its rules.

The doctor began violently pumping the device. He held it hard against my groin with one hand and went at it as hard as he could with the other. It didn't take much to figure out that he was trying to excite an erection, though I didn't know whether he was attempting to pump something into me or suck air out of the tube to create a vacuum.

Either way, not surprisingly, nothing happened.

As abruptly as he had begun, he stopped his pumping. "Master problem," he concluded. Shaking his head and shrugging his shoulders, he motioned for me to sit in a chair in the same dark chamber. It was a familiar gesture — the one a doctor uses when he is about to give you his diagnosis and his prescription.

"You have problems with the nerves in your penis," he said, "from old age and overuse. Your past is catching up with you!" He waited for my response, and when I nodded, he went on, "However, I can definitely cure you for the 5,500-rupee fee, if you take what I give you and follow my instructions exactly."

I nodded again, and he explained his prescription.

"This is Eastern medicine. Good for the Western man, too. It will take fourteen days. You need four oral medicines — two bottles of *Ijwaan*, of which you must take one teaspoon each day. You also need one gold pill and one red pill." He took the pills from a small vial and showed them to me. In the faint light, they looked like little stones.

"Also, you require two ointments for your penis." From his stores, he selected a bottle of yellow ointment with heavy flakes of what looked like silver suspended in it, and another bottle that held a tamarind-coloured mixture with traces of silver leaf. Both ointments had an indefinable but pungent odour.

Without thinking about what I was doing, I reached out and took a drop of the yellow potion on my finger. I lifted it to my mouth. It tasted both sweet and tart. The doctor nodded approvingly.

Talk turned to the 5,500 rupees. Sensing my unwillingness to pay that much, the specialist suggested a seven-day trial course for 2,750 rupees, half the price.

I told him I was very tempted to accept his offer and subscribe to the full, fourteen-day treatment. However, Haroon, supposedly my "interpreter" who had come in to help me understand the diagnosis, recommended that I think it over. He said we could always return the next morning if I wanted to.

With those words, we politely escaped after paying fifty rupees for the examination. We walked out into the bustling street, which boasted three other sex shops in the immediate vicinity, all plastered with Urdu lettering advertising cures for "impotency, childlessness, sexual weakness," and promising "youth, sexual drive, prolonged enjoyment, and happiness for you and your *begum* (wife)."

Actually, this was my second attempt at finding a sex "doctor." A day earlier we had gone to the Banari Circle in another old part of Karachi and entered three separate sex clinics, only to be told that they had nothing to say to "foreigners." Our visit to the last of these so-called clinics was, in fact, a hair-raising experience. We had walked up the steep, narrow steps to the second floor, but an attendant shoved us away. Suddenly our way out was blocked. Standing in the doorway was an angry young man with fire in his eyes: "What are you foreigners doing here?"

Told we were merely paying a visit, he shot back, "You are here to write bad things about our people, aren't you?"

It took some cool — and reassurance in Urdu — to calm him down. He let us out reluctantly. It turned out he had seen us getting out of our car across the street, and had watched us enter the clinic. He was clearly irritated that "foreigners" were snooping around in the underside of his society. An underside that everyone knows about but rarely discusses.

At 9:00 p.m. that evening, we were picked up at the Sind Club by our driver and an assistant from the Department of Culture, and driven to police headquarters. Then with an armed escort, and previously arranged radio contact with three other officers on Jeep patrol, we sauntered deep into the red light district on Napier Road. This is a dangerous area. Pimps flaunt power over their women, who can legally entice clients to their evening *mujra*, and not-so-legally invite further amorous advances for steeper and steeper payment. Extortion is rife. Kidnapping has been reported, and an argument or encounter could easily lead to a stab wound or cost one an eye — or even a life. I was glad I was not alone. I had been warned against such a visit, but this was where Burton, almost 150 years before, had spent so much time — and researched his doomed "Karachi Papers."

The exclusive Sind Club in Karachi.

Mujra *dancer in the red light district of Karachi.*

I do not know when and where the red light district in Karachi first start-ed, but it has been located on Napier Road since 1842 — a year before Burton arrived there. It was named after the governor of Sindh at that time. The red light district here is far smaller than Bombay's infamous Kamatipura, and far less seedy. Here, six-storey buildings lined the narrow street. Most activi-ty appeared to be centred in two buildings on the main road and another three located in a dead-end street off Napier Road. With their narrow, dimly lit corridors, they seemed well suited to the business in question.

The small shops were only just opening. Vendors sold *paan* (red betel nut), cigarettes and other non-alcoholic stimulants. There were money-changers to provide small bills for potential customers, merchants discreet-ly selling condoms, *cha khanas* (tea houses), *mochis* (cobblers), tailors and a whole host of others. Men and a few children (but no women) congregated on the streets, deep in conversation or busy with their evening program. Two heroin addicts covered their heads and crouched against a wall of refuse, intent on inhaling their deadly potion, unconcerned with us or the world around them. Slowly we groped along dark corridors and up narrow stairways whose steps had been worn down by the feet of many generations. Rows of six to eight rooms on each floor housed the so-called *mujra* dancers, preparing themselves for the evening guests. The rooms were small and quite neat and clean. A sharp contrast, Haroon reminded me, to the tiny, grimy hovels and "Cages" of Kamatipura in Bombay.

Unlike in India, prostitution is illegal in Pakistan. Entertaining with

mujra song and dance is not illegal, however, even though it is obvious that the entertainment is a cover for the not-so-legitimate activity that takes place behind the hanging curtain or blanket suspended at the rear of the room or small dance floor. The flimsy barriers preserve the dignity of the women. In Bombay's Kamatipura, on the other hand, the women stand in doorways advertising and selling their wares openly to the public. There was no open solicitation here, neither on the streets nor in the corridors.

The street doesn't really come alive until well after 10:00 p.m. Then, gradually, the *tablas* begin to be heard, and the music of the harmonium and the jingle of dancing bells waft down to the street, heralding the start of business at such appropriately named buildings as Sangeet Mahal (Singing Palace), Moosiqee Mahal (Music Palace), Noor Mansion (Light Mansion), and the grandly titled Bulbul Hazar Dastaan (Mynah and a Thousand Tales), named after the famous Arab folk tale.

This is the area where Burton came to gather information for his famous report on pederasty. But now there are no homosexual brothels. Today gay life has gone underground in Pakistan and India, and it is difficult to find any openly gay brothels anywhere. However, the colour, the sexual tension, the sleaziness and the raciness of the oldest profession in the world are still very much alive.

One by one we visited each chamber, asking permission to take photographs — first from the dancers and then from their pimps or masters. Most refused — perhaps understandably. Besides the dancers, there were residents, too, who appeared to live alongside the dance rooms. An easy camaraderie existed between the dancers and the residents, although people were reluctant to talk to strangers. Finally, on the fourth floor, one "master" agreed to allow his dancer to pose. Her name was Kanwal, and she was only fifteen. Drums and an accordion lay on the floor. She put on her make-up and clothes, I photographed her and we paid her "master."

We returned to the street and visited two other buildings looking for the photo opportunity that would best illustrate the Karachi activities. Nothing satisfied us. Then, nearly an hour later, I returned to the first building and convinced Kanwal and her master to allow us a further series of poses. They were now far more cooperative and I had a busy half hour. Iron-patterned doors, red dress, sultry look, good night atmosphere. It was almost midnight, and the music was starting. Fifteen or twenty people had gathered

Prostitutes in Sindh are of two kinds. The Rangeli, or Khobli, is a courtezan of the Jatki Race.... They inhabit villages close to the main roads, and support themselves and the males by the contributions of travellers. Another and more respectable class is the Kanyari who, like the Nautch girl of India, generally unites the occupation of dancing with the more immoral part of her trade.

SIR RICHARD F. BURTON, 1851
Sindh, and the Races That Inhabit the Valley of the Indus

147

around our fourth-floor landing. The area was coming to life.

We photographed other dancers, outside and inside their chambers. One sultry young temptress lured us to her door and posed hiding behind a collapsible screen. She could have been no more than eighteen years old. As we made our way slowly down the stairs we revisited a few more dance chambers. Girls heavily made up waited patiently for clients, sitting on carpets or richly patterned tiles. Some, for money, now permitted us to photograph them. A wrinkled old woman with untidy hennaed hair grasped a banister rail and stood proudly for a photograph. A complete portrait of a madam — or someone who has seen better days. Very pleased with her fifty-rupee windfall she tucked her prize into her sagging bosoms. I kept clicking away, photographing the scene and the people, but was soon out again in the street, glad of the cool night air. We smelled of incense from the dance chambers. My adrenaline was running high as we made our way out of the district.

We had a morning interview with Dr. G.A. Allana, the vice-chancellor of the University of Sindh, Hyderabad, the second-largest university in Pakistan. Dr. Allana is a very refined and highly respected Sindhologist who thought long and carefully before answering each question.

Dr. Allana made two very important points about Burton's contribution. The first was that Burton's *Sindh, and the Races That Inhabit the Valley of the Indus* is still used in schools and is the main reference work on the tribes and customs of the Sindh. Dr. Allana agreed with us that this was an extraordinary book for so young a man. Dr. Allana also emphasized that Burton's role in the Sindh was clearly two-sided. Burton must have realized early in his career that he had to live two lives: that of a young army officer serving his country, and that of a writer observing the customs of an exotic civilization. He kept the second activity to and for himself. It launched his literary career.

"Burton studied Sindh and its people — and its falcons — very carefully, very minutely. He studied our educational institutions, the *madarsah*s (Islamic schools) and their curricula, which were not restricted to just theology but included philosophy, logic, lexicography and the study of Persian and Arabic. He studied the history of all the towns and villages that he wrote about. He studied the races that inhabited the valley of the Indus."

Burton's second, profoundly important contribution was that he recommended the Arabic script for uniform use in the Sindh. As Dr. Allana noted: "When the British came, there were about twenty different scripts in use. Every Hindu caste had its own script, and sometimes more than one script. For example, the Bhatias of Hyderabad had one and the Bhatias of Sukkur had another. The Muslims, too, had more than one, such as that of the Kutchi Memon." To try to resolve the problem, the British established a committee of two British officers, four Hindus and four Muslims.

Burton's case for using the Arabic script for Sindhi was laid out in a detailed memo to the commissioner, dated May 2, 1848. He gave, in effect, a summary of his arguments in *Sindh, and the Races That Inhabit the Valley of the Indus*.

Burton had left the Sindh by May of 1849. But the language controversy continued. Governor Frere used Burton's memo to convince the East India Company in Bombay to agree to the Arabic script, which it did in the early 1850s.

The Muslims had opted for *Naskh* (Arabic) script, the Hindus for Devanagari, used for Sanskrit, Hindi, and other Indian languages. Captain George Stack, who was the author of two Sindhi-English dictionaries (1849 and 1851) using the Devanagari script, sided with the Hindus, but Burton had opted for the Muslims' choice, *Naskh*. His chief reason was that there was already an abundance of Sindhi literature in that script which would all be lost if everyone switched to Devanagari. He also argued that certain Sindhi names and phrases could not be written in Devanagari (for example, "Quazi Qutbuddin Sala Mahu Rabbahu" — "May the jurist Qutbuddin be showered with God's blessings"); this would come out distorted in Devanagari as "Kaji kuttu (dog) buddin sal (hole) amahu rumbo (pickax)," totally changing the meaning. The committee's report went to a B. Ellis, inspector of education, who sent it to Governor Frere, who sent it to the East India Company, which opted for the *Naskh* script.

"So Burton's greatest legacy to Sindh and Sindhis is our Sindhi language script. For that alone we owe great gratitude to him. That is why he is so well known in Sindh. Ask any primary school teacher in Sindh, and he or she will acknowledge that. Every time there is some discussion about the script his name crops up, even today."

Haroon and I were surprised and pleased to hear about this. It is a new point that none of Burton's biographers seem to have written about.

Dr. Allana told us that Sindhis remember Burton and Frere fondly, Frere for a variety of good works, including promoting literacy and education and the use of Sindhi as the language of instruction in schools and the courts. He also set up a legal system, constructed buildings and roads and improved the canals. "The one who is not loved much here is Napier, the conqueror of Sindh, who initiated the battles of Miani and Dubba. He was out to win himself glory in the Sindh. This was his last hurrah. But he did get his glory and his rewards — at our expense. He got his statue in Trafalgar Square.

"When I was in London," Dr. Allana added, "my British hosts took me to see Napier's statue. But I said, 'Why have you brought me here? Do you think I will salute him?'"

He told us that a translation of Burton's *Sindh, and the Races That Inhabit the Valley of the Indus* into the Sindhi language was undertaken by the Sindhi Adabi (literary) Board about ten years ago. A committee was formed for the purpose, and among the first arguments was whether or not the translation should leave out the highly critical comments Burton made about the Sindhis, and also the things he wrote about the use of *bhang* (a local intoxicant) and other vices. "We are a very conservative society, and we don't like a

Muslim devotees at prayer.

public discussion of some of these vices of ours, especially by foreigners. I suppose we don't tolerate criticism of our bad habits. We tend to say 'Let's not publicize them.' Eventually, however, the Board decided to translate the book as is, and it was an instant bestseller. There was some criticism of it and much discussion in the newspapers about whether it should have been published. But the majority of the people, especially the young, appreciated it. The majority of Sindhis, who do not speak English and who had heard Burton's name but had no access to his works, read the book with great interest. Now it is part of the curriculum for undergraduate and graduate students of history."

We asked whether this book is seen as being bigoted and racist, and were told that this is no longer discussed. "I certainly don't personally find his caricature of Sindhis offensive. As a writer myself, I appreciated what he had to say. I appreciate the total picture as presented, something that only a foreigner can write, something that I cannot write, and even if I could, I would be criticized." Overall, he concluded, Burton had done a great service to Sindh.

"Even today, I use his books as references. His body of work is a lexicon for educational and official purposes. That is, after all, an amazing legacy."

One of Dr. Allana's final comments to us was: "It's ironic that most books on Richard Burton, the traveller and adventurer, have been written from bookish knowledge, by authors cloistered in libraries rewriting old material. I have not read much from anyone writing from personal, original knowledge, or from travelling the route that Burton did, seeing all that he saw, meeting the people of the various races he met and wrote about."

Gharo, Thatta and Mangho Pir

*Burton quickly learned the rudiments of surveying....
The great Indus, the vagaries of which brought life and
death to the area like the Nile to Egypt, was the third
river in Burton's life. As a child he had watched the
Loire in flood with admiration and fear. At Oxford he
had trained in sculls on the Thames, competing
among the crew before his expulsion. But the 900-
mile-long Indus — extending three-quarters to a mile
in width — was the first great river of his life.*

FAWN BRODIE
The Devil Drives, **1967**

6

GHARO, THATTA AND MANGHO PIR

It was as surveyors of the Indus valley and its irrigation canals that the British made one of their greatest contributions to nineteenth-century India. Mohammed Panhwar, the engineer, collector and author whom I had met earlier, and who had spent most of his life engineering in the Sindh, had compiled a list of more than 700 canals of the Indus system, 529 of them inherited by the British from the Talpur rulers, and which would have been subject to the type of surveying that Burton engaged in after 1843. In his book about the nearly 500 maps of Sindh made between 1600 and 1843, Panhwar wrote: "it is now confirmed that [the] British were surveying Sindh [from] 1808 A.D. ... After the treaty with [the] Talpurs in 1832 A.D., large scale surveys were undertaken in which Carless, Campbell Margary, John Jacob and Messuir did most remarkable work. These officials used most[ly] indigenous methods and instruments for the purpose and one cannot but credit them for untiring work in the oppressive climate of Sindh" (M.H. Panhwar, *Historical Maps of Sind, 1600-1843 A.D.*).

The science of measurement in the Sindh dates back to the ancient Indus civilization. One of the exciting discoveries of our trip was learning of the work of Dr. N.A. Baloch, pre-eminent Sindhologist, who, in 1983 when he was the director of the Institute of Historical and Cultural Research at the Islamic University in Islamabad, revealed his findings concerning the measurement systems of ancient Sindh. According to Dr. Baloch, techniques for measuring size and distance based on various parts of the human body, such as the hand and the foot, are still employed today. The ancient Sindhis used the simple phenomena around them to measure not only large and small distances, but also days, weeks, and the seasons. In his surveying work in the valley of the Indus, Burton also used some of these time-honoured techniques.

Before joining the Sindh Survey, however, Richard Burton spent nearly a year working as a translator in court-martial trials at the cantonment at "Gharra" — now called Gharo — which was located in a barren desert forty miles southeast of Karachi. His succinct description of it reads: "Look at

The unique houses of Thatta are made of mud and wood, with walls up to two feet thick.

Previous page: The arid landscape of Sindh supports only the hardiest of animals: camels, goats....
Burton called the area near Gharo a "hideous landscape."

that unhappy hole — it is Gharra."

Thirty years later, time would alter his opinion somewhat, but not much, as Isabel Burton explained: "Then we went back to ... Gharra, where he had to live so miserably. He traces the foundation of the lines of his old regiment, where he says, 'None of us died, because we were young and strong; but we led the life of salamanders.' He says, 'There lies the old village, which saw so many of our "little games"; a cluster of clay hovels, with its garnishing of dry thorns, as artlessly disposed as the home of the nest-building ape. How little it has changed; how much have we!'" (Isabel Burton, *The Life of Captain Sir Richd F. Burton, K.C.M.G., F.R.G.S.*, 1893).

Yet, despite its discomforts, the cantonment at Gharo was to provide Burton with some of the central adventures of his Indian sojourn. It was here that he encountered the legendary Aga Khan, the leader of the Ismaili Muslims. It was here that he may have made his first commitment (however tentative) to Islam, at least to Sufism. And it was here that he came to know the Persians, among whom he would find the "Persian Girl," a woman who may have been the love of his life—or merely the object of a fine but fleeting flirtation.

We set out for Gharo and nearby Thatta along the old Hyderabad road, following the Indus River north-eastward. It was to be a day of fascinating experiences.

About seventeen miles east of Karachi, we noticed masses of stone tombs stretched along the crest of a low ridge. These were the historic Chaukundi Tombs, built between the fifteenth and nineteenth centuries by Balochs and Burbats. Hundreds of stone tombs, between five and fifteen feet high, crowned the hills. Some had roofs supported by pillars, but most had a rectangular base with a pyramid-shaped roof, and were covered with amazingly intricate designs.

I had never seen anything quite like it. The air was hot and dry, and the countryside arid and brown. Swirls of dust billowed up with the wind under a cloudless sky. I could taste the dust. The long, low, brown ridge of tombs looked down over a green valley. The quality of the light was great for photographs, and I saw a wonderful opportunity to get depth of vision illustrating the grandeur of the tombs against the vast horizon.

Rosettes were frequent in the geometric designs on the tombs, as were squares, diamonds and zigzags. I had learned that the small rosette might have had some connection to ancient sun worship. Sometimes images of horses and riders decorated the tombs. These were usually on the graves of men, sometimes of warriors. Men's graves also sometimes had a stylized stone turban on top. The Rajput custom of burying a fallen warrior with an upright sword capped by his turban may have been the origin of these tomb designs. Muslim culture frowns on the representation of animals and people, so these tombs suggested a pre-Muslim influence. Wherever jewellery and other objects of personal adornment were illustrated on the tombs, we assumed those to be the graves of women.

There was no sign of water anywhere, but there must have been some to make the valley below us green. Strangely, also, there were armed guards everywhere, making us feel a little unwelcome. It was fascinating, but we didn't linger among the Chaukundi Tombs.

It was on our way from the tombs to Banbhore that we were rudely waved down and stopped, fifteen kilometres from the Makli Hill, at a military check-post. Armed guards approached our Jeep, waving a piece of paper. Not a good omen.

"Are you Mr. Christopher?"

"Yes."

"We have been told by headquarters in Hyderabad to provide you with an escort."

"Why?"

"It's just safer that way."

Relieved, we nodded our heads in assent, and a soldier with a semi-automatic rifle climbed into the rear of our Jeep as we drove off. A friendly force he may have been, but we couldn't quite shake off the queasy feeling created by the pres-

An armed guard keeps watch over ancient desert ruins.

ence of a semi-automatic rifle twelve inches from the backs of our necks. This weapon was in the hands of a complete stranger, a man whom we'd never set eyes on until a few minutes before.

Later we learned that Hamid Akhund had ordered the armed escort for us because he had learned of stepped-up dacoit activities in the area. As it turned out, the guard, Mohammed Munawwar, was a middle-aged man of a level of calm forbearance not usually seen in the Sindh constabulary. An ex-army man, he had joined the Sindh police five years before, and his platoon had been seconded to the army to man the check-posts.

At every historic site we visited, there were at least two armed sentries posted at the farthest reaches of the ruins so as to deter dacoits.

We drove through semi-desert countryside and tiny villages. It was poor scrub land for twenty miles before we reached Banbhore on the northern bank of Gharo Creek near the mouth of the Indus.

Burton hated Gharo immediately and said it was a "hideous landscape." It must have been the middle of summer when the regiment was moved there, because the heat was an outrageous 125 degrees Fahrenheit in the canvas army tents. Despite the fact that Gharo was on the banks of the Indus, it was absolutely arid when Burton arrived and would stay that way until the monsoon rains. A vast wasteland, flat, parched and barren. There would have been no shelter for the army except their regulation Bombay Native Infantry canvas tents. It was hot enough when we were there in January, so the summer heat that Burton had to endure must have been

appalling. There was no escape.

Even such desolate surroundings could not quell Burton's curiosity, however. His almost obsessive desire to learn new languages now focused on Persian. And his anthropological observations, later captured in *Sindh, and the Races That Inhabit the Valley of the Indus*, continued apace.

There is not much to see in Gharo now, and there was no way of knowing where Burton's cantonment had been. But Gharo was once an important port, which may have been founded by Alexander the Great in 325 B.C. In the Gharo museum there were remnants of Greek pottery dating back to the first century B.C. Nearby Banbhore also may have been the site of Debal, the port taken in A.D. 712 by the first of the Arab invaders, Muhammad bin Qasim. There is excavation at Banbhore, and the walls of the city still remain.

From Banbhore, we went on to Makli Hill, which, with its millions of graves, is probably the largest necropolis in the world. Though it is a Muslim resting place, Burton here noted the presence of Hindu practices: "certain upright stones stained with vermillion, and decked with huge garlands of withered flowers, upon the margin of a small deep tank...." The sacredness of Makli — and its strangeness — persists. It fills the visitor with a sense of haunting eeriness.

It served as the graveyard of the nearby city of Thatta, which was the capital of the lower Sindh from the fourteenth to the seventeenth century, and many of the graves testify to the incredible prosperity of that city. The larger tombs obviously belonged to royalty and military commanders, and the smaller ones were for more humble occupants. There were tombs here of the Tarkhan kings who ruled Sindh from 1545 to 1614, and also even older tombs of the Sammah kings. These were the magnificent mausoleums of Thatta's élite: kings, queens, generals. The long low hills and the graves stretched for at least five miles.

In her biography of Burton, Isabel mentions that when in the Thatta area Burton exercised one of the gifts most dear to himself but not appreciated by many — his talent as a poet.

"He next goes to Nagar (everywhere pronounced Nangar), and to Thathá, and Kalyan Kot, and the Mekli Hills (holy places), where he composed the following poem:-

> *LEGEND OF THE LAKKÍ HILLS.*
> *In awful majesty they stand,*
> *Yon ancient of an earlier earth ...."*

ISABEL BURTON,
The Life of Captain Sir Richd F. Burton, K.C.M.G., F.R.G.S., 1893

Thatta, a short distance away, and about sixty miles from Karachi, may be the site of the ancient city of Pattala where Alexander the Great rested his

Makli Hill, with its millions of graves, is probably the largest necropolis in the world.

troops before his near-fatal march across the Makran Desert in Baluchistan. Thatta's history is known to go back at least 600 years. From the fourteenth to the sixteenth century it was the seat of the Sammahs; in the mid-sixteenth century, the Portuguese destroyed the town. In 1592 it became part of the Mughal Empire. It then prospered for 150 years as a port famous for cotton weaving and woodcarving. Its glorious days were over when, in the eighteenth century, the Indus again shifted its course. As well, Britain began exporting to India cotton that was better and cheaper than the once-famous Thatta product. By the mid-nineteenth century and Burton's day, Thatta's population had fallen from a peak of 300,000 to a mere 7,000. Now only a few of its old and beautifully carved houses remain standing.

Many of these unique dwellings are featured in Yasmeen Lari's book. They are made of mud and wood, with walls up to two feet thick. A number of the houses are two and three storeys high and listing precariously. Some of them sway with the wind. Some are as much as 250 years old. Burton would certainly have had to stay in one or more of these buildings. There was nowhere else to stay.

After a brief visit to Kalankot Fort — referred to by the Burtons as Kalyan Kot — a little way southwest of Thatta on the Makli ridge, where we saw the twelfth-century fort now in ruins, we made our way to the village of Pir Patho, where we interviewed Seema, a handsome *hijra* (transvestite). I first noticed him in a roadside tea shop in the village. The twenty-five-year-old told us his story in Urdu, referring to his sexuality as that of a *fakir* (literally "beggar"), a word that is usually applied to Hindu yogis and Muslim Sufis who renounce the world and live off what they make by begging. It is also an elliptical appellation for homosexuals, especially cross-dressers.

"I was born in this village," Seema told us. "When I was twelve I knew I was going to be a *fakir*. I knew. I told my parents, and they let me do what I wanted. They didn't resist. I started begging and living off whatever people gave me. Five years ago my parents died. Now I live alone in my hut a little way from here.

"I am the only *fakir* in this village. People here accept me for what I am. They don't really bother me much. I have met very few other *fakirs* — maybe four or five in Thatta. I met my friend there."

Seema was vivacious, svelte, clean-shaven, well kept and well groomed. He had applied a light lipstick and a light rouge to his face. He had *kohl* around

The Afghans are commercial travellers on a large scale and each caravan is accompanied by a number of boys and lads almost in woman's attire and Kohl'd eyes and rouged cheeks, long tresses and henna'd fingers and toes, riding luxuriously in Kajawas or camel-panniers: They are called Kuch-i-safari or travelling wives, and the husbands trudge patiently by their sides.

SIR RICHARD F. BURTON, 1885
The Book of the Thousand Nights and a Night

his eyes and a reddish eyeliner. He walked with a gentle swaying motion of his hips. Seema's openness about his sexuality and readiness to speak to strangers was very unusual for a transvestite, since they face daily taunts and ridicule and tend to live in their own ghettos. Perhaps, as the only transvestite in the village, Seema had learned to live with the rest of the society. This may also have explained his refusal to acknowledge any problems with the villagers — who had gathered around us by this time and were openly snickering at him and at us as we interviewed him.

We asked if there was a national organization of transvestites in Pakistan, like the one that had been established in India, but the answer was no. The Indian organization had recently held a conference to discuss the obligatory chopping off of the penises of *hijras*, the paying of obeisance and the sharing of their beggings with their guru or master, who is a male version of the brothel madam. The conference also discussed rape and the increasing AIDS problem.

Seema was keen to know more about this conference, but as we talked, we heard the *muezzin* call the Faithful to prayer over the mosque loudspeaker. As would any woman, Seema then picked up his *dupatta* (Muslim scarf) and draped it over his head, as a mark of respect whenever God's words are announced. Asked if he was allowed in the local mosque, where only men pray, he said, "Yes, they allow me," but not as a cross-dresser. He would have to wear male attire in order to enter the mosque.

After this we headed back to Karachi. It was getting late, and I was coughing badly. Haroon was getting quite worried about me, and he insisted on taking me to a doctor that evening.

The doctor thought that what I had was a fine-dust allergy. He wasn't sure. Anyway, he prescribed some cough medicine, which I drank by the bottle. It made me quite drowsy but seemed to suppress the cough. I was ready to take drastic measures. The constant hacking really was getting me down. I was beginning to tire easily.

Of one thing I was certain: Burton was right about life in the Sindh. It *is* a different world. The farther north we went, the more different it became. I could see how a willingness to give oneself up to this culture was necessary for understanding. Without doing so, one remains an outsider. But how was I to bridge that gap — to solve the mystery of Burton? The answer certainly didn't lie in the luxurious confines of the Sind Club of Karachi....

Although it was a Friday, a weekly holiday in Pakistan, Gul Hassan was back again with the Jeep early the next morning. Hassan looked awful. Since Friday was usually a day off, perhaps it was his habit to spend Thursday night on the town! He didn't look too happy to be there. But he was willing enough to drive us to Mangho Pir, which is eleven miles north of Karachi. It was an interesting adventure for us, as I had read a lot about Burton's visit to this shrine in his and other people's books.

Isobel Shaw, in her excellent *Pakistan Handbook*, relates an amusing legend: "when the saint Pir Mangho came from Arabia in the 13th century, he inadvertently brought crocodiles with him in the form of head lice. Soon after his arrival two oases sprang up from the desert, with hot springs gushing out from a clump of date palms; the crocodiles jumped in and have lived there ever since."

The drive out of Karachi ran northward through some poor slum areas. However, just outside the city, there were no slums, although there were definitely poor villages in quite arid countryside. We seemed to be moving into hill country, and

Gul Hassan, our tardy but always loyal driver in Sindh.

eventually we reached the village of Mangho Pir. Of course, it was no longer quite the way Burton had described it. Like other shrines, this too had become quite commercial, and as we climbed up the small hill away from the road, we passed many boutiques and concession stands, all with multi-coloured triangular flags flying above them.

There were quite a few people about, moving to and from the shrine. As on a weekend in North America, people used their day off to come here to seek blessings and cures. People were hoping for relief from all sorts of ailments, but particularly rheumatism, skin diseases and leprosy.

The shrine itself is simple enough. What make it unusual are the two hot sulphur springs beside it. In one of these, people were bathing. In the other, which was surrounded by a low wall, were several crocodiles of the snub-nosed variety, lying around the outside of a relatively small, murky, spring-fed pool. There appeared to be no way for them to get out and nowhere for them to go, so they must have been trapped there. Perhaps the Hub River had changed its course, stranding the beasts in this isolated pool. Zoologists claim that the snub-nosed crocodiles are not related to the long-snouted gharial of the Indus, so these must have come from somewhere else. They are reputed to be much more dangerous than other varieties.

The crocodiles seemed to have been well fed. I took innumerable photographs, trying for something dramatic, but without much luck. Eventually a man, presumably their keeper, arrived and invited me to jump the wall to stand with him among the crocodiles. I did this — but only to take closer and more dramatic photographs of the beasts. I hoped to get one with a lump of raw meat in its jaws, but couldn't see one with its jaws open. At first, I kept to the edge of the pool, but eventually I got braver and stood among the crocodiles. I saw the guide lift the upper jaw of one of the animals to put some meat into its mouth. It didn't seem too active or too interested. Finally, full of confidence, I gave my camera to Haroon, and he took a few photographs of me standing among the crocodiles.

Mangho Pir, 1878. The "Rajah" crocodile.

Burton said of this place, "The poor devils of alligators, once jolly as monks or rectors, with nothing in the world to do but to devour, drink, and doze; wallow, waddle, and be worshipped; came to be shot at, pelted, fished for, bullied, and besieged by the Passamonts, Alabasters and Morgantests of Karachi."

Burton talks a bit about the fun the young English army officers had with these crocodiles (or alligators as he calls them). He describes how a Lieutenant Beresford hopped across the tank on the backs of these beasts, and also that he himself stood on the back of one of these crocodiles after tightly tying its jaws together, then took a "ski" ride across the pond.

Before I went to Mangho Pir I thought the stories about the crocodiles were absolute fantasy. But I can now believe that a nimble-footed person could well have some fun tripping over, walking on, and perhaps even riding one of the beasts without too much damage or danger. When the crocodiles are a little hungrier, however, I think the story might be different.

As we drove back to Karachi, we saw more dry and barren terrain, but found the topography interesting. There were numerous tribal settlements. And cricket everywhere. I photographed a cricket match of some children playing in the desert — a strange contrast to the green cricket fields of England.

Even in Burton's own family, only his sister knew of his passionate and ill-fated attachment in Sind, a love which occupied an unique place in his life. During one of the many romantic rambles ... he met a beautiful Persian girl of high descent, with whom he had been able to converse by means of his disguise. Her personal

Mangho Pir, 1994. Crocodiles sometimes live for more than a hundred years.

charms, her lovely language, the single-hearted devotion of one of those noble natures which may be found even amongst Orientals, inspired him with a feeling little short of idolatry. The affectionate young soldier-student, separated by thousands of miles from kith and kin, expended the full force of his warm heart and fervid imagination upon his lustrous-eyed, ebon-haired darling; never had he so loved before, never did he so love again. She worshipped him in return....

GEORGIANA M. STISTED,
The True Life of Capt. Sir Richard F. Burton, 1896

In our travels throughout this area, Haroon and I found ourselves debating the true role of the "Persian Girl" in Burton's life. The story is that he saw the young beauty near a desert camp of Persians and that the girl may have been a niece — or even a daughter — of the Aga Khan. Burton's own version of the story was told first in *Scinde; or, the Unhappy Valley*, then repeated without modification in *Sind Revisited*.

In Burton's version, he catches sight of "one of the prettiest girls ever seen," summons one of her minions by means of whom he dispatches a love letter on bright yellow paper, to which, in reply, he receives a request for "European remedies." Undaunted by the fact that he is neither doctor nor pharmacist, he cooks her up a prescription and sends it by means of the same messenger. There is no further word from the girl, and Burton now glimpses only her "latticed face," as she leaves with her caravan. He never sees her again.

The Stisted version is unsubstantiated unless one accepts as autobiographical a poem, believed to have been written by Burton during the India years, in which he mentions a young woman who is poisoned for having violated the code of her family, and the avenging of that murder by the lover with whom she compromised herself.

I said to Haroon, "A lot of this about the Persian Girl is imagination and speculation. The English were always romantics, particularly Burton. I find it hard to swallow. How do we know she was a princess? It's tempting to rely on Georgiana Stisted, who seems to write knowledgeably about it and to have strong opinions about the girl being Burton's true love. But she may be dramatizing the whole thing. Burton himself dramatizes the incident— brief as it is. His description strikes me as having been written by Burton the storyteller rather than Burton the lover. But we also know that the Victorians were notoriously reluctant to engage in true self-revelation in autobiography."

Like me, Haroon had given the matter a great deal of thought. "Burton does not say how he knew that the group was Persian. Maybe they looked Persian or spoke Farsi. He also gives no hint as to how he knew that the girl was being ferried to her father's house in Karachi, except to say that she was a Bee Bee (princess) in the house of the Great Sardar A___ Khan.

"Burton beckons her slave boy in the caravan, 'who scarcely numbered twelve summers,' and gives him a note of courtly love to the girl, praising her beauty. The boy, who does not even tell Burton the girl's name, disappears with the note (written perhaps in Persian). The boy later reports back, saying that he did deliver the letter, but that she said 'nothing' beyond wondering if he had any European remedies. Burton, who is disguised as a Muslim merchant, concocts a questionable potion of sugar, simmered over a slow fire and mixed with a cheap cologne he was carrying with him...."

"It makes a good story," I replied. "The boy as go-between. The woman perhaps weak or ill, looking for some sort of help — or even salvation—from a man she may suspect is a foreigner, despite his disguise. Burton does say that the girl emerged from the tent muffled and wrapped up...."

"But," Haroon said, "there is no indication in the story that he even saw her up close, let alone exchanged a word with her directly. I think this is nothing more than a simple story told by a congenital liar writing for a faraway home audience. Over the years it's been further exaggerated — first by his niece, Georgiana Stisted, and later by his many biographers."

"I admit," I answered, "that the Stisteds were a little awe-struck. And they

They are Persians, escorting one of the prettiest girls ever seen to her father's house near Karachi. Is she not a charming girl, with features carved in marble like a Greek's; the noble, thoughtful Italian brow; eyes deep and lustrous as an Andalusian's, and the airy, graceful kind of figure with which Mohammed, according to our poets, peopled his man's paradise!

SIR RICHARD F. BURTON, 1851
Scinde; or, the Unhappy Valley

Children playing cricket in the desert — a strange contrast to the green playing fields of England.

had a bone to pick with Burton's wife."

"Yes," Haroon agreed. "Stisted *was* an awestruck author, writing about an uncle she adored. She was also a woman of limited knowledge about India. And you're right in saying that her story was coloured by her dislike of Isabel Burton. Georgiana was out to prove that her uncle's real love was someone other than Isabel. Georgiana claimed that he was smitten by the Persian Girl's 'lovely language.' But we know from Burton's own accounts that the girl in the desert never uttered a word to him. Georgiana also claimed that the Persian Girl 'worshipped him in return.' This is clearly rubbish. Georgiana further claimed that he would have married her and brought her home to his family. Burton himself never told us so in *Scinde; or, the Unhappy Valley*, nor when he reproduced the story thirty years later in *Sind Revisited*."

I pointed out that I thought Georgiana reduced her credibility by dramatizing the Persian Girl's departure, by writing about how she was "snatched from him," and later suffered an "untimely end." "There are problems with such contrived melodrama. There is no proof that she was snatched away from him. The caravan might simply have stopped for a brief while; the timing when it moved on may have had nothing to do with Burton. There is also no proof that the girl met any sort of untimely end. That's just an inference drawn by Georgiana from Burton's poem. Georgiana offers no evidence that the victim in Burton's poem was the Persian Girl."

"It's true," Haroon pointed out, "that Edward Rice cites the same poem as a basis for speculating that the Persian Girl was killed for having communicated indirectly with Burton. McLynn mentions the poem, but he doesn't offer theories about what really did happen to the Persian Girl beyond saying, 'Later came word that she had died suddenly of a mystery illness.' So, was it murder or was it an illness that wiped her out? Most likely, neither. McLynn is on the right track in asserting that 'the "death" looks like rationalization on Burton's part, an inference strengthened by a poetic fragment found among Burton's papers.'"

I responded, "It's also unclear what Rice's evidence is for asserting that

the princess had attempted to defy custom and was flouting a very rigid social code. In the first place, the princess had not indulged in any great act of
social defiance. Even if she had, we don't know that her misdemeanour was
noted by anyone in her entourage beyond her slave boy...."

"Yes," replied Haroon. "And if we accept, as Rice does, that the girl had
broken custom and that Sindhis were given to murdering women who violated taboos, why didn't they also go after *Burton* for revenge?

"Here is what I think of the whole 'Persian Girl' incident," Haroon concluded. "Burton was what in Urdu is called a *dil phayk* — literally, one who
drops his heart readily, a romantic, always smitten by this or that pretty girl.
In the India of the nineteenth century, male-female flirtations were brief and
often carried on surreptitiously, through stolen glances, a flicker of a smile,
or messages conveyed through third parties, usually little boys. The lack of
direct contact, the absence of any conversation, enhanced the nuances of the
encounters and made them seem more important than they really were. If
the girl was from a family that observed the *purdah*, the passing glimpse of a
beautiful girl's face and her features lent an enhanced aura of romance to
the occasion.

"The scene as described by Burton is one that happened all the time. It is
Indian to its core: an incurable romantic, a foreign one at that, posing as a
local Muslim, is pleasantly surprised in the middle of the desert at the sight
of a good-looking girl; he catches her eye; he's brazen enough to dash off a
note to her; even gets a response of sorts; sends her a potion; and waits. Only
to have reality intrude rudely. The girl is gone. He is left with a sweet memory, the tale of a smitten man, which gets exaggerated in the telling and
retelling."

Into the heart of Sindh

The East provided Burton with material to indulge his urge to live robustly, his love for adventure, his penchant for the curious and "anthropological"…. Burton found everything he needed in the East.

THOMAS J. ASSAD
Three Victorian Travellers, 1964

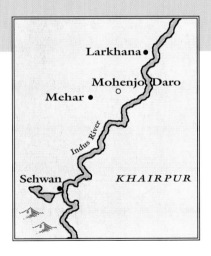

7

INTO THE HEART OF SINDH

I started the day with a scorching onion and green-chili omelette. Thank God for the strong coffee to neutralize some of the spicy heat!

After breakfast, we piled into a Jeep and set out for the airport with Hamid Akhund and Dr. Mohammed Rafique Mughal, the director general of the Department of Archaeology and Museums. We were on our way to Mohenjo Daro, the site of an ancient city in the northern Sindh.

Mohenjo Daro was one of the great settlements of the early Indus civilization. The name means "Mound of the Dead." On this site are the ruins of a 4,000-year-old Indus city — one of the most advanced of its time. For thousands of years, the site lay undisturbed until it was rediscovered in 1922 by the British archaeologist Sir John Marshall.

At the airport, a private Cessna 46 "Caravan" awaited us. On board: Abdul Hamid Akhund; Dr. Rafique Mughal; Sherazam Muzari (Vice-president, Citibank, Pakistan); Rana Talwar (Executive Director, Citibank, South East Asia Division, Singapore); Hamid Haroon (Deputy Executive Chairman, Dawn Group of Publications, including *Dawn* daily of Karachi, Pakistan's largest English newspaper; M.A. in economics from Harvard, classmate of Benazir Bhutto). Hamid Haroon is from a very influential Sindhi family. His uncle, Mahmoud Haroon, organized enough Independent members in the National Assembly to form a coalition with the People's Party after the 1993 election and ensure Benazir Bhutto's majority government.

The flight from Karachi to Mohenjo Daro took an hour and twenty minutes, and gave me a panoramic view of the arid countryside just outside Karachi. Pakistan really is a desert! Only where there is water is there any green. The Indus is the lifeblood of the country. It used to be much wider, until India's diversion of four rivers out of the Punjab. Although still very mighty, it is now a much smaller river. The banks are cultivated, and canals leading off from the river provide — as they did in Burton's time—the much-needed moisture to sustain intensive cultivation. But the rest is dry, brown, sandy—scrub and desert, or near desert. A land of undulating terrain, sandstone rocks, isolated dwellings, the occasional herd of goats, camels. Narrow

Mohenjo Daro, "Mound of the Dead," was one of the great settlements of the early Indus civilization.

Previous page: Village elder smoking a hookah in the northern Sindh.

animal tracks lead from nowhere to nowhere. The sun beating back from the pale brown earth creates a difficult glare.

Seen from the air, the Indus River glistening in the morning sun was a magnificent sight. However reduced in size, it is still immense and majestic. It is the real ruler of the country. The slow-moving green and green-brown water cuts a broad path through the desolate countryside. Most towns and cities are on one bank or the other. Mud from the river provides the brick for their dwellings. Beyond stretches an endless expanse of dust-covered scrub, broken here and there by the occasional palm tree.

The river, one of the world's longest, rises in the Himalayas of Tibet, crosses Kashmir and Pakistan, then empties into the Arabian Sea through its delta near Karachi. For millennia, those who know its ways have laboured to control the processes of silting and flooding it undergoes. It is a crucial resource for the Sindh.

During the plane ride, Dr. Mughal talked about our destination: "Mohenjo Daro has been a great find. We've hardly promoted it at all. There are very few tourists, even Pakistanis, who come to see this treasure. In fact, there are only 200 to 300 tourists a day in the season — mostly in the winter. The summer is too hot.

"In Mesopotamia they had only mud bricks. We here in Mohenjo Daro have baked bricks, millions of them, laid out with great symmetry. It was the largest known city of its time. And it is still only one-tenth excavated. An enormous job is still ahead of us."

Even mostly unexcavated it is an amazing architectural phenomenon. At the edge of the excavated part and overshadowing the other ruins lies the Buddhist stupa, or shrine, a round, domed building which is actually 2,000 years younger than the rest of the site. An intricate system of roads and alleys connected Mohenjo Daro's administrative and religious buildings, west of the stupa. Public baths, state granaries, a palace, an assembly hall, fortifications and a tower give a good idea of what the city must have been like 4,000 years ago and indicate that this was a highly sophisticated civilization. The richer citizens even had bathrooms with indoor plumbing, and garbage disposal units. There was also a municipal police force.

The noble Indus is the characteristic geographical feature of Sindh. It is at once the great fertilizer of the country, the medium of transit for merchandise, and the main line of communication for the inhabitants.

The general direction of the "Sweet-water Sea," as it is here termed, is nearly north and south.

SIR RICHARD F. BURTON, 1851
Sindh, and the Races That Inhabit the Valley of the Indus

Mohenjo Daro was originally about three miles in circumference and sat right on the river bank, with a mile-long embankment for flood control. Now, although the river has moved almost three miles farther east, the site is in danger of being destroyed by the rising water table, which is only a few yards below the surface. The original inhabitants, like all the people who lived along the Indus, were excellent managers of water, but poor irrigation and drainage practices in recent times have allowed the water to rise and increased its salinity. This is causing the bricks of Mohenjo Daro to disintegrate. Despite UNESCO funding to help save one of the world's great archaeological treasures, there has been considerable damage.

Our flying visit offered a rare glimpse into how the élite of Pakistan operate. Citibank had chartered the plane to take one of its Singapore executives to Mohenjo Daro. We landed at Larkhana airport and were met by an armed escort and a whole flock of assistants. A convoy of cars then drove us to the historic site. After the tour (guided by Dr. Mughal), we were treated to a lavish tea at the Dak Bungalow or "rest house." We also visited the Mohenjo Daro Museum.

Then we all climbed back into the Cessna 46 and flew to Hyderabad for the first time. It is the second-largest city in Sindh and the fifth-largest in Pakistan overall. When Muhammad bin Qasim conquered the Sindh in A.D. 712, Hyderabad was known as Neroon. It may be that Alexander the Great occupied it at one time. A Kalhora ruler laid out the present city in 1786, and under the Talpur amirs, or kings, it was the capital of Sindh from 1789 to 1843, when the British took control. When Napier arrived in the Sindh with only a small force of 2,800, he met the massed army of the amirs, numbering 22,000. Nevertheless, at the battle of Miani, Napier and the British were victorious. "We have no right to seize Sind," Napier confessed, "yet we shall do so, and a very advantageous, useful and humane piece of rascality it will be."

On landing, we were again met by a cavalcade of cars, all driven 150 kilometres from Karachi to meet us. From the airport we were driven to Bhit Shah Dak Bungalow, the site of the shrine of Syed Shah Abdul Latif Bhitai, or simply Bhit Shah or Shah Bhitai (1689-1752). This Sufi saint, poet and musician is best known for his *Risalo*, a collection of romantic — at times raunchy — poetry, reflecting the grass-roots culture of Sindh. Burton was the first foreigner to write about this Sufi saint, whom he called the Ha'fiz of Sindh, after the famous Iranian mystic poet. Later, Isabel Burton called him the Homer of Sindh. Bhit Shah, who was influenced by the Qur'an and by the poetry of Rumi, is today regarded as a symbol of Sindhi nationalism and resistance to the Punjabi domination of Pakistan.

At this site we were treated to an enormous lunch partially hosted by Citibank: chicken *qorma* (gravy), rack of lamb, fish, *roti*, pilau, millet *roti*, *daal*, and a whole array of exotic Sindhi desserts. Following the meal, we were shepherded out into the large courtyard-garden of the bungalow and given a command performance by the best and best-known folk musicians and

singers of the area. It was a wonderful session. Songs, dancing, instrumental
pieces.... It was impossible not to be caught up in the enthusiasm of these
talented artists, who obviously enjoyed performing for us — and particularly
for Hamid Akhund, the Secretary of Culture.

There were six "acts" in all, some by groups of musicians, some by solo
performers. I was greatly impressed by the talent and the high standards of
entertainment. However, Haroon Siddiqui thought that the star of the show
was not any one of the artists but Hamid Haroon, of Dawn Publications, a
rotund happy-go-lucky man with a clipped English accent and a quick
repartee. He was clearly the host, the patron and the man in charge. At lunch
he sat at the head of the table as though it were his natural right. In the plane
he automatically took the front seat with his guest, Mr. Talwar. His car always led the way. He seemed to be the head and to like being the head. "All
this," noted Haroon, "despite the presence of Hamid Akhund, the senior civil servant in charge of the occasion. Hamid Haroon issued orders easily:
'Chae lao' (Bring tea), 'Paani do' (Give me water), 'Faqir se gawao' (Let the
fakir sing). His orders were invariably carried out."

Nine men in saffron robes were the first group to sing. They were backed
by a *dhanbaro* — a five-stringed instrument. It was surprising to see the saffron robes, which are normally associated with the Hindu holy men of India,
not the Muslims. In this region we noticed many other details reminiscent
of Hindu culture. People greeted each other with folded hands, the Indian
or Hindu Namaste, even though they did not, like the Hindus, say "Na Most
Ta" when greeting each other. It was also difficult not to draw parallels between the rural Sindhi devotion to saints and their mausoleums and the
Hindu custom of grave worship.

A second group of performers played the *yak taro* — a single-stringed instrument. This group was followed by a soloist — a man who played the *sura-
no*, an old type of folk violin common in the Sindh, Iran and Kashmir and
often used in exorcism. The old maestro squeezed out a haunting melody
from the instrument, eliciting the phrases "Wah wah" and "Shabbash" (Well
done! Bravo!) from the audience. These traditional utterances of apprecia-
tion are offered spontaneously throughout a performance, rather than just
at the end of a piece. The practice creates a special bond between the performers and the audience. This rapport makes Eastern performances very
enjoyable — for both the audience and the artists, who, unlike their Western
counterparts, do not perceive such comments as an interruption or an irri-
tant, but are encouraged by them. It makes for a much more informal, less
rigid and more enjoyable show. Also, unlike Western classical musicians,
performers in India carry the "raga" or pattern of notes in their heads and
play without any musical score in front of them. This allows improvisation
and a certain spontaneity and independence within each piece. An individual artist — or a group — can prolong or repeat a raga or a couplet or verse on
popular demand from the audience, before proceeding with the rest of the
composition.

The next soloist — a singer — told us the story of being bitten by a scorpion. He performed in a soaring voice and with great dramatic flourish. The emphasis was on entertaining the audience, which he did by smiling mischievously, clapping his hands (he had bells attached to his wrists), and throwing his clay drum up in the air and catching it just as it was about to hit the ground.

The final musician to appear, and thus the most senior artist (in India and Pakistan, the junior artists must perform first), was Sohrab Faqir. A singer of Sufi songs — songs of praise to the saints of Sindh — he is one of Pakistan's best-known folk singers. A striking, charismatic man in his fifties, Sohrab Faqir had coloured his hair and beard red with henna. He wore a saffron-coloured shirt and pantaloons, a turban in the

Hamid Haroon, Chairman of the Dawn Group of Publications.

fashion of his northern tribe, and had a silver ring on each of the fingers of his harmonium-playing right hand. A wrist-band and a necklace of glass beads completed the ensemble.

He started his song with a long, soulful call to his Sufi saint. It was a moving moment. Everyone else maintained a reverential silence until he signalled to his drummers and other musicians to join him. He then broke into the vigorous beat of the *qawwali* — songs in praise of the Prophet Muhammad and others. He obviously enjoyed performing. At one point, he simply could not resist the beat and got up to do a dance turn with a member of the audience before resuming his song.

Finally, Sohrab Faqir extended the rare honour of asking all the lead singers of the other groups to join him. The evening sun was setting, and a cool breeze wafted over the garden, carrying the voices of the singers out into the night. It was sheer magic. "Burton couldn't have had it any better," said Hamid Akhund.

The idyllic session ended, as such music sessions often do, with a song of tribute to the most popular saint of all — Qalandar Lal Shahbaz, who is buried at Sehwan. The group sang "Dama Dum Mast Qalandar" (Intoxicated on Qalandar). We were indeed intoxicated with the music.

After the performance, the guests hung back a little. It seemed there was

The Sufi bard is, generally speaking, a profound student of the different branches of language and metaphysics; he is gifted with a musical ear, and fearlessly indulges in luxuriant imagery and description, which contain a simple sense agreeable to all....

SIR RICHARD F. BURTON, 1851
Sindh, and the Races That Inhabit the Valley of the Indus

another ritual to be performed. Hamid Akhund, who had organized the event, sat on a *charpai* — the cot of woven matting one sees everywhere in the Sindh — and distributed money to the artists in the time-honoured fashion of payday. All the cash was held in his lap, and he called the artists by name, paid them and made a note in his register. The artists thanked him with folded hands and backed out of his presence as a mark of respect. The traditions of Sindh that Burton wrote about live on!

At 6:00 p.m., with the sound of Sufi folk songs still ringing in our ears, we climbed into our Jeep and rode through the old city of Hyderabad and out into the country to the Moorish mansion of Senator Zulfiqar Ali Jamote — one of the most powerful and wealthy landowners of the Hyderabad area, and a great friend of Hamid Akhund. He was a wonderful host, welcomed us warmly, knew a lot and wanted to talk a lot.

Zulfiqar Jamote's sprawling villa, with corridors, arches, and parapets, was a hodgepodge of British, Mughal and Moorish architecture. Somehow it worked. It was spacious and comfortable and very well protected, with a ten-foot wall encircling the entire twenty-five-acre estate. Behind the *chabootra*, or terrace, spreading right across the front of the villa, was a wide, twelve-foot-deep veranda, its roof supported by four Moorish arches. We sat there with our host, looking down over a long stretch of lawn ending with an avenue of palm trees which gave an oasis effect. Beyond the trees was a thick, high, fir hedge. Everything was locked inside the wall, above which rose three watch towers — staffed around the clock with armed guards. This was a dangerous area, and a man of Zulfiqar Jamote's wealth and power needed this protection. I was glad I was inside the wall. There were gardens, more hedges and deer, peacocks and quail, which wandered happily around in their luxurious prison.

We sat for a while with Hamid Akhund, gazing out over this tranquil vista, getting to know one another, talking about Burton, talking about dacoits, talking about the musical performances we had just witnessed. We were treated as cherished guests. After being shown around the house, with its hardwood furniture made from the sheesham tree and its Sindhi vases and rugs, we cooled off with a thirst-quenching lime drink served to us out of an enormous glass pitcher.

My clothes were filthy, covered with the dust of the day. I excused myself when Hamid Akhund departed for Karachi, and was shown to my bedroom

The savouring of animal existence; the passive enjoyment of mere sense; the pleasant languor, the dreamy tranquillity, the airy castle-building, which in Asia stand in lieu of the vigorous, intensive, passionate life of Europe. It is the result of a lively, impressible, excitable nature, and exquisite sensibility of nerve....

SIR RICHARD F. BURTON, 1855
Personal Narrative of a Pilgrimage to El-Medinah and Meccah

at the back of the house, just behind a huge dining-room designed to seat at least twenty people. I could see that plans were underway for a tremendous feast. I washed and changed into another pair of trousers and a clean shirt. Everyone was dressed casually, thank God! No suits or ties in this desert or semi-desert existence.

Jamote, a member of the national Senate, is the local sardar or tribal leader, and his family has lived on farms in the area for generations. He is the principal landowner and landlord in the area, and farms more than 2,000 acres of sugar cane, mangos, guavas and other tropical fruit. Historically, sardars were the administrative heads of their areas. The Mughals and then the British relied on them to collect taxes and provide an infrastructure as well as to maintain law and order. Now, forty-five years after Independence, some of the sardars remain respected father-figures whom the locals depend on to intercede for them with the government. Senator Jamote has a house outside his compound where he holds monthly *autaq* or *kachehri* — which literally means "office," but refers to the audience a man of influence grants to people. He does this for hours, accepting petitions and listening to problems and other matters. He does more as a sardar than as a senator.

"I am a relatively inactive senator," he admitted. "I am in the opposition, belonging to the group headed by Pir Pagado," one of the influential Sufi saints of Pakistan, who, unlike other saints, has been active in national politics for many years. (In Muslim tradition, a holy person is deemed to be a saint by popular will.)

Later, Hamid Akhund told us, "Had Jamote been more active, or joined one of the main parties like Benazir Bhutto's People's Party, he would now have been a chief minister (premier) of Sindh. I have known him for a long time, and I really admire his integrity."

Senator Jamote really was a gracious and magnanimous host. There were other guests, among them Hamidullah Paracha, the falconer whom I had met in Karachi. He was a great friend and hunting companion of Senator Jamote's. We also met Sir Nicholas Barrington, the British high commissioner, who had come on a farewell visit before his return to London for retirement. The conversation was relaxed and easy. We sat around a blazing fire on a veranda that ran along one side of the house. As darkness fell, we were served drinks, dried fruits, sweetmeats. There were sometimes long silences. Conversation simply wasn't needed. We listened to the birds and the animals, and warmed ourselves in front of the fire, as the desert wind turned quite cold when the sun went down.

Sir Nicholas was in good form, and we talked about the problems of Kashmir. Both Muslims and Hindus inhabit the troubled state. Also, it is strategically significant, since it shares a border with China. A constant dispute rages between Pakistan and India about Kashmir's independence.

Sir Nicholas offered it as his personal opinion, not that of his government, that a new partition of Kashmir was needed, with the southern or Hindu part, Jammu, going to India, and the northern part, now under

Pakistani control, being awarded to Pakistan. The Vale of Kashmir, the real Kashmir, where Kashmiri is spoken and which is the centre of indigenous Kashmiri culture, he said, should be allowed to choose its own future, perhaps in a plebiscite, as called for by the United Nations in 1949 and 1951. The Kashmiris should be permitted to become independent. An unarmed Kashmir would not pose any security threat to anyone. The area, he said, could become a peaceful, economically vibrant tourist haven, as it used to be.

I expressed amazement at his views. I had never before heard any Western diplomat, senior or junior, even in private conversation, so openly discussing the possibility of an independent Kashmir. I feel that India would never allow this to happen. Kashmir is far too important to it, if for no other reason than as a source of water and a buffer with China.

"But what is the alternative?" Sir Nicholas asked.

The subject of Burton also came up. Sir Nicholas said: "Although everyone in England has heard of Burton, I don't think they know much about him. Certainly no one knows anything about his India years."

After referring to Burton as "a great character, a great explorer, and a brilliant man," Senator Jamote made some comments about the British legacy. "In all fairness, it must be said of the colonists of modern times, and by this I mean the British, that they were by and large the best. Far better than the French, the Italians and the Dutch. And they left behind a pretty good infrastructure. In fact, we can say that our entire infrastructure was laid down by them, and we have not improved it much. This is something we should be ashamed of. Take the irrigation system. Far from improving it, we have not even been able to maintain it, and we have mismanaged it. Now there is waterlogging and salinity everywhere. We've totally mismanaged our water resources. And we have deforested huge areas...."

It was late before we moved to the dining-room. I was very hungry. That was a good thing because there before us on the huge table was spread a feast fit for a king. Slowly and purposefully, we gorged our way through a seven-course meal. Rack of lamb, fried fish served with potatoes and vegetables, chicken *bhoona* (baked) served with bread, beef shish kabob, rice *roti* — a very Sindhi item — served with spinach cooked with onions and fresh garlic, and pilau or saffroned rice served with yogurt chutney. I politely tasted everything and ate what I could. Then the desserts: crème caramel and *halwa*. Very sweet and full of character. Then trays of fruit, coffee and tea.

It was all over at midnight. We moved briefly out again onto the veranda and towards the fire, and listened to the plaintive cries of jackals calling to one another in the darkness beyond the boundary walls, a whole chain reaction of pleas. I excused myself and went to bed. I was dog tired, and I knew the next day would also be hectic.

It had been a splendid day and a wonderful evening, but I had to reflect that all was not comfort and peace. Beneath the fine graciousness of Pakistani life lie serious problems. What role will China play in the future of

India and Pakistan? What will happen if American economic support to the region is not forthcoming? Will Pakistan and India go to war some day — and will it be over Kashmir? A frightening thought, given their nuclear capability.

As I drifted off, however, the last images were of the singers, the peacocks and the evening feast.

As I slept inside Senator Jamote's walled villa, I was suddenly startled awake by two shots in the night! Quite close by — though I could tell they came from outside the wall. Dacoit activities? We had been warned that there were bandits around the Hyderabad area. I listened for a while, but I was soon back asleep.

When I awoke next morning, it was quite cool, but dry. I watched the sunrise. Senator Jamote was up very early, in fact at 6:00 a.m., making sure that everybody had tea and coffee, biscuits and pound cake. Breakfast was served a little while later. Another huge affair: fried eggs, omelettes, toast, several jams, honey, fried *roti*, *paratha* (layered *roti*), curried chicken. Strong, strong coffee. And tea.

"Did anyone hear the shots?" someone asked.

"Oh yes. Dacoit activities go on all around here. We have to be quite careful."

This led to a discussion of the prevalent culture of guns and armed guards. Senator Jamote said, "As you probably noticed, guns are everywhere. This gun culture may be attributed to the Afghan war, and the flight of up to six million refugees into Pakistan, beginning in 1980. The Russians are gone from Afghanistan, but the Afghans have not gone from Pakistan. Millions still remain. Not all the rocket launchers and the guns imported from all over the world to help the mujahidin in their struggle went to the war. Some made their way into Pakistan."

Hundreds of thousand of Afghans poured out of refugee camps on the Afghanistan-Pakistan border to the southern cities. Karachi, as the commercial capital, attracted large numbers of them, especially to the trucking, transport and auto repair businesses (an Afghan speciality). They did a brisk business in guns as well. Soon the various criminal and political gangs were using these guns to settle intertribal and interethnic feuds: Afghans versus *Mohajirs* (Muslim immigrants who migrated to Pakistan in 1947 after Partition); *Mohajirs* versus Sindhis (the indigenous people, who resent immigrants).

The Afghans' guns thus became the tools of lawlessness and thuggery. Hostage-taking, kidnapping and armed robbery became so common that the federal government ordered the army to restore law and order, which it

Senator Zulfiqar Ali Jamote—one of the most powerful and influential landowners in the Hyderabad area of Sindh.

did at considerable political and social cost. At that time, the province of Sindh, for example, was paying the federal treasury one million rupees a month. Military check-posts had to be set up on main roads and highways — a jarring military presence in a nation trying desperately to avoid the return of military dictatorship and move on with democracy.

There is a general belief that while there is some order on main thorough-fares, thugs are just lurking around the corner, and one had better be pre-pared to protect oneself. Thus compound walls around homes, like Senator Jamote's, have gone higher and been fortified. The gates are always locked. Doors are always bolted. Windows are augmented with steel frames and lat-tices — as are even the first- and second-floor balconies of rented apartments and condominiums in Karachi. The rich have posted gun-toting guards at their gates around the clock.

"We just feel safer that way, even though I must say, in all fairness, that things have improved recently," said Hamidullah Paracha, the falconer, whom I had visited at his home in the secluded Defence Colony in Karachi. "In fact things were so bad that I took my family to Canada, to Vancouver. However, with the recession there and the situation improving slightly here, we came back. I posted the guards after we got attacked in October of 1992. Just outside Karachi, we were shot at coming back from a fishing trip. We barely escaped."

Paracha told us that rural Sindh has always been a rough place, especially in the now overgrown areas abandoned by the population over the ages as their settlements followed the shifting course of the Indus River. The forest provides an ideal hiding place for dacoits.

"We have known it, and we have grown up with it. We have got used to it, and we have learned how to avoid those areas," he said. "But what is happen-ing now is not the old style of petty dacoitery; it is anarchy in its worst sense. Now everyone is a dacoit. Anyone without a job and with a gun is a dacoit — primarily because there is no consequence to their banditry. There are prob-ably 1,400 to 1,700 such bandits in the Sindh alone!"

"Yes, of course it's dangerous," someone else offered. "One does not quite know where the dacoits are. The army is after them. They are after the army, settling scores. So you never know where there is trouble."

This conversation was one of the first in which it occurred to me strongly that there is a general lack of confidence in the ability of the state to keep or-der in the Sindh. Earlier, on our flight from Karachi to Larkhana near Mohenjo Daro, I had overheard a Citibank executive's comment about our armed escort: "It is good they are here. The going ransom for a senior bank executive is five million rupees!" (about U.S.$160,000).

Dacoitery has a long tradition in the Indian subcontinent. All hilly and forested areas have had dacoit gangs who live in the interior and loot cara-vans and individuals. Some take on the Robin Hood role, stealing from the rich and giving to the poor, becoming legendary figures. The 1980s saw the sensational case in central India of Phoolan Devi, a young woman who was

raped by some higher-caste Hindus in her village. She channelled her resulting anger into a ferocious and ruthless campaign of looting, mayhem and
killing, for the benefit of the lower castes. A few days after our conversation
at the villa of Senator Jamote, there was an article in *Dawn*, the national
English-language daily, stating that the Indian government had dropped
the charges—some dating back more than a decade — against Phoolan Devi,
the "Bandit Queen," who was in prison in New Delhi. The article said the offered amnesty would be effective only in Uttar Pradesh, where Devi was facing trial for the massacre of twenty high-caste villagers, killed thirteen years
before.

As we spoke of this unusual woman, the comment was made, "You see far
fewer women in Pakistan than in India, either in Karachi or in rural Sindh.
Many either observe the *purdah*, or just don't go out often. Those that do
generally wear a *chadar* (long shawl) around their shoulders and head, as
does Benazir Bhutto. Unlike women in India, the women you see on the
streets here are reluctant to be photographed. And their men frown when
they see a foreigner training a camera on their women. This attitude is not
much different from the attitude in Burton's day."

We left in our Jeep soon after breakfast. A perfect host to the very end,
Senator Jamote saw us right up to the gates of the villa, standing in the driveway, waving goodbye as we left the protection of the ten-foot walls and headed into the desert. No armed guards with us anymore. Just the driver.

We drove from there to the ancient city of Sehwan, the oldest inhabited
town in the Sindh. This is another place that Alexander the Great conquered. It is essentially a religious centre. It was difficult to imagine the
throng of pilgrims who would soon shatter the sleepy atmosphere of this
holy city. Normally it has a population of about 30,000, but this swells to
more than 600,000 during the urs, the death anniversary of the saint
Qalandar Lal Shahbaz. We planned to return for this religious festival about
a week later. Burton was certainly aware of Qalandar's importance among
the pirs of Sindh whom he wrote about.

In Sehwan we met Taj Sahrai from Dardu, which is just north of Sehwan.
He is the author of many books in English on the history of Sindh. His speciality is the period 4000 to 1500 B.C.

He told us that Sehwan is the most ancient living city of Pakistan.
"Tradition says that Alexander destroyed the fort and left his garrison here.
It was his soldiers who rebuilt the fort. Do you notice the clay houses? They
have been here for thousands of years. This is the oldest city on the banks of
the Indus. It used to trade in cotton, wool and wheat."

In Sehwan, as elsewhere, I noticed how many men wore the *ajrak*. This is a
length of cloth used as a scarf. It can cover the nose and mouth, to keep out the
ever-present dust. It can also serve as a turban or a bed cover. In its decoration,

natural vegetable dyes are used to form patterns, printed from designs carved on blocks of wood. There may be as many as 3,200 different patterns. I bought an *ajrak* from an old man in the Sehwan market. It was well used, musty smelling, of faded red cloth woven in a traditional pattern and evocative of the East. I had to buy the old man a new *ajrak* before he would sell me his old one. He was delighted. I wore my old *ajrak* immediately, wrapping it several times around my neck.

The ajrak, a length of cloth used as a scarf, can serve as a turban or even a bed cover.

Hyderabad and Miani,
Jherruck and Sondhan

I met a traveller from an antique land
Who said: Two vast and trunkless legs of stone
Stand in the desert. Near them, on the sand,
Half sunk, a shattered visage lies, whose frown,
And wrinkled lip, and sneer of cold command,
Tell that its sculptor well those passions read
Which yet survive, stamped on these lifeless things,
The hand that mocked them and the heart that fed:
And on the pedestal these words appear:
"My name is Ozymandias, king of kings:
Look on my works, ye Mighty, and despair!"
Nothing beside remains. Round the decay
Of that colossal wreck, boundless and bare
The lone and level sands stretch far away.

PERCY BYSSHE SHELLEY
"Ozymandias," 1818

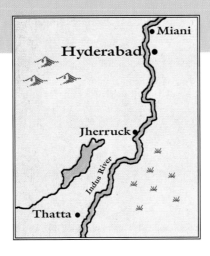

8

HYDERABAD AND MIANI, JHERRUCK AND SONDHAN

Hyderabad is about 150 kilometres northeast of Karachi, on the Indus River. As we approached it, I had the feeling that we were seeing the countryside almost as it had looked when Burton came this way.

We saw fields made green by irrigation provided by the canals off the Indus. All travel is along the narrow roads, edged with trees and scrub, that run beside the river and the canals. There were donkeys pulling carts and camels carrying loads. Suspicious stares followed us. We saw tent communities, and noticed women working in the fields, wresting a subsistence living from the land, their clothes colourful against the light-green foliage or the dry brown earth. There was a constant stream of traffic transporting merchandise: dried grass, bundles of sticks, vegetables, earthenware pots, sheep, goats. Always visible in the distance was a thin haze of brown dust — a fine powder that you hardly notice up close. Set down amid the arid countryside are gatherings of mud huts — whole villages of them. The telephone wires on the horizon seem incongruous in this primitive landscape.

Once in Hyderabad, we went straight to the campus of the University of Sindh, where we met Dr. N.A. Baloch, probably the best informed of all the people we interviewed. A stimulating conversationalist, he came to conclusions about Burton in an interesting way. Dr. Baloch is of medium build, dark, with black hair combed severely back and a small mustache. We found him polite, thoughtful, logical and of an inquiring mind. A great scholar with a tremendous knowledge of Sindh, he gave the impression that he had walked every inch of the province — which he probably had.

Hamid Akhund told us the following story about Dr. Baloch. Once, while he was waiting for a train, some local tribesmen were amusing themselves by trading riddles with one of their elders. No one could match the elder. Observing this, Dr. Baloch approached, answered one of the elder's riddles,

There are few districts in this part of Asia where the cultivators are not bankrupts, only prevented from failing, as it were, by its being the interest of the creditor not to ruin his debtor beyond a certain point. The peasant paid one-third and one-half the produce of his fields to the ruler, Amir, governor or collector....

SIR RICHARD F. BURTON, 1851

Previous page: Young girls carrying bundles of sticks near Dubba in Sindh.

and offered another in return. Surprised, the elder said, "Who is this stranger?" "Baloch," the professor replied. "N.A. Baloch?" the elder demanded. "Yes," said Dr. Baloch. "Ah," said the elder, "then the game is over. I could never match you!"

Working from memory, Dr. Baloch calculated the length of time that Burton spent in Sindh. He itemized Burton's activities as follows: "He arrived in January of 1844. It took only a few days by boat to get to Karachi. Then a month or so off to take a language exam in Bombay. In 1847, sick leave in Goa — six months. He returned late in the year, probably in November of 1847. Then on May 13, 1849, he left the Sindh again for Bombay. And then left Bombay for England. Roughly speaking, then, two and a half years plus one and a half years equals four years, less perhaps two

Dr. N.A. Baloch, a great scholar with a vast knowledge of Sindhi culture and history.

months for the Bombay exam. Therefore, excluding his 1876 trip, Burton probably spent in total no more than three years and ten months in the Sindh. Isn't it amazing? He must be given full credit for what he achieved in that time: ... reports, survey work, three books. And then a fourth one on Goa after he returned from sick leave.

"Now, about Burton's travels: when he describes his route from Karachi to Hyderabad — Karachi, Clifton, Gharo, Thatta, Dewal, Tando Muhammad Khan, Kinjur, Sondhan, Jherruck, Kotri, Hyderabad — he is describing the old route between the two cities.

"From Hyderabad to Sehwan, he travelled on the west side of the Indus; then to Larkhana and on to Sukkur. He may have been scouting for a railway line, because that's where the railway line did eventually go, and that's where they built a bridge to bring the rail line to the east.

"Then from Sukkur to Shikarpur and Jacobabad, this must be a separate trip, as an advance man for John Jacob, scouting it for him to conquer later.

"Then he goes off into Baloch territory on the edges of Sindh ... Kusmav, Rustam, Gehlpur ... maybe. Paving the way for boundary work, because that's the area where the boundary line for Sindh got drawn.

"I don't think there is any doubt about it. Burton was doing scout work for a railway line, for a boundary line, or else as an advance man for John Jacob."

I found the comments about the railway interesting. Perhaps it is only coincidence, but, in researching Burton's Nile journey of 1858, I discovered that there, too, the railway line closely matches the route taken by Burton; in fact, even today one could retrace much of the Nile journey simply by buying a train ticket!

"What was he doing during those years in Sindh?" Dr. Baloch asked rhetorically. "There are no records. Probably he was writing and learning for himself. Somewhere about this time, Burton realized that the army job was just that — a job. In addition to his reports, he also started writing for himself and for future publications. He was extremely industrious. Too ambitious. He was fascinated by almost everything. And he wrote about it all. His descriptions of people and their attitudes are very sensitive and observant. It is amazing that a stranger should be so observant. Read *Falconry in the Valley of the Indus* and his descriptions.

"Burton never lost his sense of wonder. He was really fascinated by Sindh. He talks of Sindh and Sindhis as though he knows every part of it and knows everyone. He was the first to write about Bhit Shah. He was the first to describe the curricula in use in the schools at that time. Studying and learning were a continuing process for him. In many respects, he was better than other Orientalists. His translation of *Alif Laila* [the *Arabian Nights*] is superb. I've compared it to the original, and Burton's translation is better than anyone else's. He knows the intricacies of the Arabic language, sidelights, suggestions, puns. He creates the same feeling in his translation as the original. His mastery of Arabic and mastery of English come through. He knew the psychology of both languages.

"I would put Burton's work, in overall quality and quantity, on a par with Professor Edward Browne's *Literary History of Persia* and Professor Reynold Nicholson's *Literary History of the Arabs*. Burton had extraordinary inquisitiveness to explore what deviates from the normal, an extreme kind of inquisitiveness to explore the forbidden, such as *Alif Laila*, where you get all sorts of abnormalities, not necessarily homosexuality, but dancing, music, sorcery, magic....

"I don't think Burton was a deviate. He was fascinated by women. He liked their company, spent a lot of time with them, was relaxed in their presence. He used them to get information. Even in his translation of *Alif Laila*, he is at his best when there is a woman present. He couldn't have been a deviate.

"He liked the Nautch girls, too. They were professional singers, not prostitutes. They had their own abode. They were not even dancers. Their tradition is of singing, not dancing. Burton used the world 'Nautch,' but it may not be accurate. Qambar is a country town in the district of Larkhana where Burton met 'Moonbeam,' the Nautch girl, whose sister, Nur Jan, became his mistress. You must go to Qambar.

"Burton spent four months in the Nautch girl's abode on the banks of the Phuleli River, which is actually a canal now, not a river. It was perfectly all right for him to go there. In fact, it was probably the only place he could go without criticism. It was a sort of guest house. He used the opportunity to learn the language and customs. He seemed to always use women. He was certainly curious about anything out of the ordinary, like pederasty, and even might have participated. But it is a little harsh to suggest he was a homosexual. He loved, was fascinated by, and was far too involved with women all his life."

We questioned Dr. Baloch about Burton and religion, and about why Burton never talked about Buddhism. He did, Dr. Baloch said, "But there

was not much Buddhism here then. He didn't have much opportunity to get involved.

"As I said, I think Burton was an advance scout, probably a surveyor for the railway that eventually went up the west bank of the Indus. Also, he surveyed and scouted Khanghar, which later became Jacobabad in honour of John Jacob — a much-revered East India Company commander. Burton seemed to go along the boundary of Sindh. A lot of what Burton did was a prelude to Jacob's work in the area."

After the long and interesting interview with Dr. Baloch, followed by lunch, we drove out of Hyderabad, towards the historic battlefields of Miani and Dubba. We were soon in lush countryside, evidence of the tenacity and drive of the Pakistani people. There was nothing here but desert when Pakistan was originally carved out of India in 1947 amid much bloodshed. Sindh was practically emptied of Hindus, as hundreds of thousands fled south, some by road, others by boat to Bombay; and hundreds of thousands of minority Muslims from India trekked north to the "Land of the Pure," a total of fourteen million people traversing the vast length and breadth of the northwest in what became the biggest mass movement of people in history.

The new immigrants to Sindh, who settled mostly in the two urban centres of Karachi and Hyderabad, started afresh with the zeal of new settlers. For such people, so preoccupied with the present, history and historical monuments do not matter much. No one around here seemed to know, or care, about the old battlefields of Miani and Dubba.

The good road we were on didn't last long. Soon we were on a rough, unkempt track full of potholes, with fields on either side. As we negotiated its ups and downs we left clouds of dust behind us, spoiling the idyllic scene. We saw little girls with bundles of sticks on their heads, carrying out the daily chore of gathering the family's fuel. The females wore bright, multicoloured dresses — a *choli* (top) and a *ghagra* (skirt to the knee) with bead and mirror work, the typical outfit of the Kolhi, a Hindu tribe.

When we stopped to photograph them, they started to shout "Police! Police!" We calmed them down and explained our innocent intent. The minorities are very aware that they are minorities. There are stories of persecution, bullying and rape. Everywhere we went, the Hindu minority seemed extremely uneasy.

Shortly afterwards we realized that we'd lost our way. No one seemed to

The Hindoo portion of the community occupies, in Sindh, the same social position that the Mussulmans do in India.

Sir Richard F. Burton, 1851
Sindh, and the Races That Inhabit the Valley of the Indus

know the way to Miani, not our driver or our guide or anyone we asked along the way. Finally, in the middle of nowhere, we saw rising out of the field and shrubs an oddly shaped obelisk about forty feet high. "A mean and ugly obelisk," Burton had called it. There were farms on three sides, a dusty road in front and, on a raised platform less than fifty yards square, the monument.

This was the first of the two battlegrounds where the Sindhis were slaughtered in General Napier's conquest of the Sindh. All that remains to identify the first bloody battleground is the memorial left behind by the British. It says, "Erected by Major General Sir C.J. Napier," and lists the number of soldiers from each regiment who died here from February 17 to 24, 1843, fighting "with the Ameers of the Sindh." I saw inscribed the 22nd Foot Ninth Regiment Bengal

In the middle of nowhere, we saw rising out of the field and shrubs the obelisk commemorating the battle of Miani.

Light Cavalry, 12th Regiment Bombay Native Infantry, 21st Regiment Bombay Native Infantry, 25th Regiment Bombay Native Infantry, Poona Irregular Horse, 1st or Leslie's Troop Horse Brigade Bombay Artillery, 3rd Regiment Bombay Native Cavalry.

Our guide, Abdul Ghani Patoli, curator of the Sindh provincial museum in Hyderabad, bemoaned the loss of the beautiful iron grille that surrounded the monument until three years ago. The battle on this site was a turning point in the history of the British in India. Napier's army of 2,800 (among them 500 English) was ranged against a Sindhi army of 22,000. Six thousand Sindhis were killed or wounded here. Twenty British officers and 250 of their troops also perished.

Dubba was not far away. This was the site of the second great battle. After getting reinforcements, Napier led a force of 5,000 on March 24, 1843, against a Sindhi army of 26,000, of whom 5,000 died. Napier lost only another 250 of his men. "Peccavi," — "I have sinned [Sindh]," was his supposed succinct pun and comment on his brutal victory.

The memorial at Dubba is even less imposing than the one at Miani — and also less visible, despite being very close to the dirt road. Sandwiched between a cluster of mangrove trees and a wheat field, it is hidden among wild shrubs. You have to struggle past thorn bushes (called *devi*, goddess, because of the power of their thorns to hurt you) to reach an area marked out by eight inverted cannons in the ground — twenty-pounders manufactured in London in 1799.

Both the Miani and Dubba battles were the culmination of a long history of British skulduggery and treachery in the region. The British engineered a phoney battle between members of the Talpur family. They even had an agent bribe some of the Sindhi forces not to put up resistance. Then, in the words of the chief political agent, E.B. Eastwick, they "slaughtered" the Sindhis. The tactics were openly opposed by General Outram, who thought Napier was too much after personal glory and the unbridled expansion of the Empire. "We have no right to seize Sind yet we shall do so...." Napier had declared. And he did. After Miani and Dubba, nine amirs of sovereign states were captured. Some were exiled to Bombay and later sent to Calcutta. These rulers did not return to Hyderabad until the 1860s. The British annexed 50,000 square miles of the Sindh from the amirs of Hyderabad, Khairpur and Mirpur, and were not to leave for another 104 years.

Quite near the monument at Miani is the village of Chandio. In fact, it is right on the Miani battlefield, just west of the obelisk. Here we witnessed a cockfight — as had Burton in numerous places in the countryside of Sindh. At least 100 Baloch tribespeople had gathered to see two professional cock trainers, Mohammed Nizam and Mohammed Souf, stage a fight between their prize birds. It was late in the afternoon, hot and dusty. The turbaned cock trainers proudly held their antagonists as the remaining villagers gathered in an excited, chattering circle to examine the two birds — one red and tan and the other mostly white with black feathers. I lay on the dusty ground on my stomach, the birds not ten feet in front of me, their two owners squatting on the ground holding on to them. Cruel scimitar-shaped spurs had been attached to each of the antagonists' feet.

Quite suddenly, the two cocks were released. They moved forward tentatively — eyeing each other, circling, feinting, necks outstretched, neck feathers raised. The crowd leaned into the circle, peering intently; the two owners were riveted, their necks outstretched too, like those of their fighters. The birds fluttered and rose about four feet into the air, then fell and rose again, wings outstretched, clawing at each other with their spurred feet. Alighting once more, they again circled each other, waiting for their chance. A second and a third attack would send up another cloud of dust and feathers.

Each time they went at each other, the birds pecked, clawed, fluttered and rose in the air. As the ritual progressed, I could see that the red and tan bird was getting the worst of it, with severe damage around the neck and head. However, the white bird, too, had been severely spurred under one of its wings. There was blood on the sand.

With the one bird badly injured, the trainers called a halt and retrieved their fighters to try to resuscitate them by blowing sprays of water on their heads and bodies. One trainer sucked the blood from his bird's wounds and from his comb. The fighter was seriously hurt and gasping for air. The trainers rubbed their birds down, exercised their wings, then set them on the dusty earth. Again the birds circled and circled each other, necks outstretched.

Another attack. They rose into the air in a flurry of feathers. Both birds

were clearly tired. They pecked feebly. The trainers looked at me and once more grasped their fighters to resuscitate them with water, blowing it in a fine spray over the heads and bodies of the birds. Into their beaks, onto their heads, under their wings.

The end was near. The crowd chattered excitedly. The owners looked worried. They kept glancing at me. The birds went at each other again, mauling each other with their sharp spurs. They had been fighting for at least eight minutes. I gave the signal, and the owners retrieved their fighting cocks in time to save one or perhaps both of them from death. Trained birds are valuable.

As the dust clouds subsided, the crowd circled the two owners and their birds again. Each was grooming and trying to save his fighter. Mohammed Souf sucked the blood out of the badly torn comb of his red and tan bird, then spat the blood on the ground. His treatment seemed to revive the bird. Mohammed Nizam applied a brown and foul-smelling ointment under the wounded right wing of his white-feathered bird. I was told both would

A Sindhi trainer carefully nurses his injured fighting cock.

survive. The trainers had been staging cockfights for more than ten years. They go on the road for the greater part of the year, participating in contests at the various *urs* celebrations, where crowds bet many thousands of rupees on the outcome of such fights. It was a colourful, exciting, but gruesome experience, and one of Richard Burton's favourite spectacles.

We drove late in the evening to Tando Allah Yar Khan. There were several checkpoints, and it was very obviously not a friendly area. Our guide, Abdul Ghani, who had shares in a cotton factory at Tando Allah Yar Khan, was insistent that we go to see his factory, where he served us tea and homemade biscuits. It was very dark, very silent and very ominous. I was quite uneasy. The tea had a strange taste. In that atmosphere, it didn't seem far-fetched to

Kukkur-bazi, or cock-fighting, is a common, but not a fashionable, amusement in Sindh. The birds are generally fought by Moslems at the Daira, or drinking houses, on Fridays, as was anciently the practice with our swains on Sundays. Formerly, no Hindoo dared to be present, as circumcision would probably have been the result; even in these days they are seldom seen at the cockpit. The game cock of Sindh is a very fine bird, distinguished by the bright yellow leg and a peculiar brilliancy and transparency of eye. The feeding and training very much resemble the Indian way, and require the greatest attention, as the use of steel and silver is unknown. There is no peculiarity in the mode of lifting or fighting the birds.

Sir Richard F. Burton, 1851
Sindh, and the Races That Inhabit the Valley of the Indus

wonder if it was drugged, but it was later explained to me that the tea had merely been brewed over an open fire — hence its smoky flavour.

At my insistence, after some discussion, we telephoned Hamid Akhund in Karachi. I was following his instructions to let him know where we were and what we were doing. It was 8:00 p.m., and he was still in his office. He was immediately concerned. There had been considerable dacoit activity in the area. Clearly irritated at our lack of caution, he instructed us not to stay in Tando Allah Yar Khan as we had intended, but to go immediately to Hyderabad and to stay with the university vice-chancellor, Dr. Allana. It was far too dangerous for us to stay where we were, he said. We were the government's responsibility! The situation in the province was tense, and even in Hyderabad our personal safety might be uncertain.

So, after a dark, anxious drive on narrow roads, past villages and open fields, we arrived at the university residence at its Jaamsharo campus on the outskirts of Hyderabad. It was after 10:00 p.m. Because of the stern warning, we were more than usually watchful as we drove in silence through the still busy villages. I was glad to be back near Hyderabad.

We were famished, but there was no dinner. In fact, the house was empty, and Dr. Allana was nowhere to be seen. Luckily, Haroon had brought two bananas, and we had one each. Haroon had learned the hard way, from his reporting days in Afghanistan and elsewhere, that you should always keep some food handy. You never knew where your next meal was coming from.

Very early, we were wakened by the bearer in charge. It was not yet light, and Dr. Allana was still nowhere to be seen. I could smell food. Somehow the bearer had conjured up eggs, toast, coffee and tea. And more bananas. We ate heartily before venturing out again to meet Abdul Ghani.

It was an interesting morning. Abdul Ghani was talkative, attentive and full of theories. He took us to the Hyderabad fort, and then inside the court of the Talpur rulers, who came from the hills in Baluchistan and overthrew the Kalhoras in 1787, after which they moved their capital to Hyderabad. It was these Talpurs whom the British defeated at the battle of Miani.

Hyderabad fort. The old fort door has been moved inside the city walls.

The court was an unusual square building, empty now, but still with its original decoration in very good condition. The old fort door had been moved to a safer place inside the walls and near the Talpur Court.

Burton wrote about his first visit to the court: "We reach the court-yard gate of the Talpur's dwelling. Three ragged rascals, with sheathed swords in their

Knives and daggers are omnipresent in Sindh. Here a man of the fields carries his working knife on his shoulder.

hands and daggers in their belts ... rush up to us as if their intention were to begin by cutting our throats. The young chief, seizing our hands, chatters forth a thousand congratulations, salutations and messages, nearly tears us from our saddles, and demands concerning our happiness, in tones which rise high above the whooping and yelling of his followers. One fellow rushes away to pass the word 'they come.' And out pours a whole rout to witness the event, and, by their presence, to communicate to it all possible importance."

We had no such welcome, but a small crowd had nevertheless gathered to witness our activities and my photography. I noticed and asked about the several tribal groups in and around Hyderabad: Baloch, Sindhi, Pathan, Jat, Afghan, Mohana — the people Burton wrote about. I asked Abdul Ghani if he knew of any old and unusual Sindhi knives that were available, and somehow he dug up an old Persian hunting knife with a silver sheath. It was interesting but in very bad condition. Nevertheless, eager to have some souvenir of Hyderabad, I paid the merchant what he asked and stuffed the knife into my camera bag.

The tombs of the Kalhora and Talpur amirs were only a short distance from the fort, in two adjacent walled compounds. They were enormous, beautifully decorated and bore witness to the huge wealth of the city and of the amirs in the late eighteenth and nineteenth centuries. Two tombs in particular interested me. They were Kalhora tombs — those of Ghulam Shah Kalhora, who died in 1772, and his brother Ghulam Nabi Kalhora, who died in 1776. They were the oldest and by far the most dramatic-looking of the tombs, one square and the other octagonal, decorated with cupolas and domes, and with frescos and blue-and-white tiles adding to their majesty and beauty. An elaborate Persian script on one panel in the older tomb was translated for us. "This is Ghulam Shah — the Emperor of the World. Before him the firmament kissed the earth."

A long drive to Sudderan's Column followed, through mostly dry, desert scrub, but with some patches that looked quite fertile and productive. Then, in what seemed a remote spot, we got out of our dust-covered Jeep and were ferried on a small, flat-bottomed boat across a shallow out-tributary of one of the Indus canals. After that we walked for about two miles over flat, dusty countryside, occasionally passing through a village settlement. We saw fields of sugar cane and villages of thatched huts surrounded by thorn fences. Also inside the fences were the villagers' buffaloes and goats. It was hot and dry, but we walked purposefully because I was anxious to see the column that Burton had romanticized in *Sind Revisited*.

"Before the time of the Rasúl (Apostle)," he informs us, "this plain was covered by a noble city which extended its limits over the distant fork of limestone-hills. And Rajah Rám, the ruler of that city, was a prince renowned (as many Eastern monarchs are in story-books) for valour, justice, and generosity...."

Burton goes on to recount, first, the death of Rajah Rám's favourite wife, the mother of Sudderan, the Rajah's oldest son, followed by the Rajah's marriage to "another of the fairest damsels in his dominions." The new Rani conceived a passionate affection for the young Prince Sudderan, but when he spurned her advances, she turned against him, denouncing him to his father "upon the false charge usual on such occasions, and insisted that his wickedness deserved the severest chastisement.

Sudderan's Column. The Thul *(pillar), continues to be a puzzle.*

"Like red-hot steel, as also might be expected, burned the uxorious old Rajah's wrath, which nothing but blood could extinguish. Hastily calling together a few trusty followers, he left his wife's apartment, determined ... upon the instant destruction of his son."

When Sudderan saw his father hurrying towards him with clearly hostile intent, he attempted to fly. As Burton narrates in his colourful conclusion to the story:

> *Rage winded the old Rajah's steps; already, sword in hand, he was close to his victim, when the good Sudderan, to save his sire from the sin of filicide, prayed for immediate death.*
>
> *He disappeared, and a pillar of earth rose from the spot, so near Rajah Rám that he ran against it, whilst a* Beth-Kol, *a loud and terrible voice, not the produce of human lungs, declared that Heaven had listened to the prayer of the innocent.*
>
> *The old king's mind was enlightened by the miracle. He returned home with a listless air; gave careless directions for the decapitation of his would-be Parisina; died shortly afterwards of want of appetite and that general derangement of the digestive organs popularly called a "broken heart," and was buried in yonder tomb, to be pelted and abused by many a generation of pilgrims.*

Actually, the *Thul* (pillar), continues to be a puzzle. It is a truncated cone about sixteen feet high, standing on a circular base or mound. It seems to be entirely constructed of the type of mud that is used in Sindhi buildings. It certainly stands out in the barren landscape, and seems to cover a natural platform of limestone rock. It also seems to be in the middle of what might have been an old river course. A young goat herder, in charge of a flock of about twenty animals, sat at the pillar's base.

The column was not difficult to climb. The rain had eroded the surface and created wide clefts in its side. I noticed a hole about four feet in diameter leading from the edge of the base downwards into the centre of the structure. This was something Burton saw, too. He wrote (in *Sind Revisited*), "I found a shaft sunk to the foundation. Below the base was a tunnel, into which I penetrated, despite the fiends and dragons, the cobras and scorpions, with which my native friends peopled it: it was about seven or eight feet in length, and it led nowhere. These diggings, I afterwards heard, were the work of Ghulám Ali Talpur, one of the late Princes, who, suspecting, as an Oriental always does, that treasure was to be found in, under, or somewhere about the mysterious erection, took the most energetic and useless steps to discover it."

I went into the tunnel, but found as Burton did that there was nothing there. It was dark, surprisingly cold and rather eerie. I was decidedly uncomfortable; in fact, I felt a strange presence there. I scrambled out on my hands and knees as soon as possible.

One would have thought that, with rain and other destructive natural elements, the pillar would have been eroded a long time ago. Either it is not very old, I concluded, or religious devotees preserve the ancient monument. Actually, only about three miles away from Sudderan's *Thul* there is another smaller tower, now almost completely destroyed. This smaller column, called *Kuttehar*, Abdul Ghani explained, is a tomb named after a dog who discovered the place where thieves had buried his master's valuable possessions.

Parched, we walked the two long, dry miles back to our river crossing and our Jeep, and then drove back to Hyderabad. From there we were to go to Jherruck, a town southwest of Hyderabad on the way to Karachi, about forty miles across the Kotri bridge.

> *We go to Sundan, to Jarak, to the Phuleli river, where he spent some time in his early days with a* moonshee, *and make a pilgrimage to the Indus river, and eventually to Hyderabad (Sind) and to Kotri the Fort, where, as he says, for the sake of "auld lang syne," he visits every place to right and left on his way, even the Agency and the old road. He says the changes take away his breath....*
>
> ISABEL BURTON,
> *The Life of Captain Sir Richd F. Burton, K.C.M.G., F.R.G.S.,* 1893

The historic town of Jherruck is located between the cities of Hyderabad and Thatta, and sits on a little hill near where the Indus River once flowed. It is an idyllic location and offers a wonderful view. To find it, we left the main Hyderabad to Karachi road, detouring over dusty plains and past villages, till we found ourselves among narrow streets lined with rows of mud houses. We drew up at last before a villa, very simple, with clean lines, simple arches, and a high roof. Completely surrounded by a seven-foot straw and mud wall, it was well preserved and kept very clean.

A tasteful sign above the front door declared that this was once the dwelling of the late Aga Hasan Ali Shah, the infamous "Persian Prince," who fought with the British in the First Afghan War and became their ally in conquering and controlling Sindh. It was this man who both fascinated and infuriated Burton, and whose brother became Burton's teacher and travelling companion.

Called Aga for Lord, and Khan for conqueror, this hereditary chieftain of the Iranian Ismaili Shiite Muslims gained ascendancy through interfamily intrigues and rebellion against the emperor Muhammad Shah. The Aga's dealings with the British, who were trying to keep both the Persians and the Czarists away from Afghanistan, were complex. John McNeil, the British

The Aga Khan's villa at Jherruck.

envoy in Persia, and Major Henry Rawlinson, posted to Persia from 1835 to 1839, were secretly negotiating with the Aga. In 1840, though ousted from Persia, he retained his close alliance with the British. By late 1841, he was busy, in his own words, "patrolling and gathering intelligence" for Rawlinson for a fee of 100 rupees a day.

The Aga Khan had not given up his hopes for a victorious return to Persia, and he offered himself as a token Persian governor of Herat in an attempt to bolster British claims to that historic Afghan city. Though the plan went awry and the British suffered great losses in the ensuing Afghan uprising, Rawlinson reported that the Aga Khan had "played a prominent part" in aiding the British on the battlefield when unrest spread farther south.

In the autumn of 1842, the Aga Khan had reached Sindh. General Charles Napier, eager to cap his military career with a spectacular victory before retirement, was plotting to dethrone the Sindhi amirs and annex their territories along the Indus. This was a situation from which the British and the Aga both stood to benefit. Placing himself and his cavalry at the service of James Outram, the British political agent, the Aga began gathering military intelligence against the amirs.

He also advised them to surrender to the British, but they refused. Napier then attacked without mercy and defeated them at Miani in February of 1843 and at Dubba a month later. It was then that the Aga came here to Jherruck, assigned by Napier both to guard the village and to keep an eye on the route to Karachi, on which British soldiers were being attacked by restless tribes based in Baluchistan.

The Aga again proved useful, reporting to Napier on the movements of the Balochis and offering them the same advice he'd given to the Sindhi amirs: surrender to the British. He dispatched his brother on missions into the interior of Baluchistan, but suffered a retaliatory raid, related tongue-in-cheek by Burton:

Some weeks the Agha spent in his new kingdom, leading a life after Sancho Panza's own heart; perhaps exceeding a little in the drinking and love-making lines. His followers ... "eat [sic], swilled, and played," till Jarak became another Nineveh on a very small scale. The Belochies, having nothing better to do, had threatened to attack it a dozen times or so, but the Agha laughed at their beards. Were they not hogs of Sunnis? Had he not dishonoured all their mothers? And had he not done the strangest possible things to their father's [sic] graves? Whose dogs were they that they should dare to face the death-dealing scimitar of the Iroonee?...

One evening the Agha had just finished his dinner, and was preparing for a game of backgammon or chess, which he was sure to win, as no man dared to win it from him; the drinking-cups and the bottles were ranged in a line before him; the musicians were twanging and howling in a corner of the room.... When all of

> *a sudden, half-mad with fear, rushed in an unfortunate Scindee,*
> *bringing the intelligence that a body of at least fifty thousand*
> *Belochies ... had arrived within a mile of Jherruk, that he himself*
> *had seen them, and hurried on to give the Agha warning, lest he*
> *and his heroes should be attacked unawares.*

The Aga ignored the warning, choosing instead to punish the bearer of
bad tidings. He had the messenger tied to a staff held by two of his men,
while others lashed his soles and toes. Eventually the messenger fainted
from loss of blood, and the Aga signalled his men to stop. But the messenger's warning was correct.

> *Scarcely had the wretched Sind's lacerated stumps been stuck in a*
> *neighbouring dunghill, the recognized treatment for the com-*
> *plaint under which he was suffering, when down came the Belochs*
> *upon Jarak in the most ferocious and rapacious of moods. Finding*
> *no arrangements made to oppose them, they scaled the puddle-*
> *parapet, dashed into the town, cut to pieces every beardless man*
> *they met; and although they failed to secure the august person of*
> *the Khan, they did not fail to appropriate the contents of his cellar*
> *and harem. The potentate lost much valuable property in wines*
> *and other liquors. It was some weeks afterwards that he recovered*
> *his wives; and when he did, he did not ... appreciate the value of the*
> *goods in question.*

Burton's description of this event is fanciful and exaggerated, obviously intended to entertain the English home audience. But the event itself was significant enough for Napier to write to Sher Muhammad on April 7, 1843, warning
him to "give back to the Agha Khan the plunder you took from Jerruck."

The Balochi attack may have taken place at this very villa that Haroon
and I discovered. Entering through the little door in the wall, we stepped
into a small veranda leading to the main room — a simple place of mud and
straw walls and dirt floor. Beyond it were several interconnected rooms, perhaps for the Aga Khan's *zenana* (women), who would have had their private
quarters and not been seen by outsiders visiting the Aga Khan in the main
living-room. The rooms shared a veranda that ran the length of the house
and gave onto a private courtyard. Wooden pillars supported the wooden
roof of the veranda. Mud steps led to the roof, where there was a small platform with a view over the entire valley of the Indus, which was visible about a
quarter of a mile away. When the house was built, the river must have run
right by it.

The villa is now the property of the present imam, Prince Karim Aga Khan,
the great-great grandson of Aga Hasan Ali Shah. The caretaker, Akbar Ali, informed us that some members of the Aga's family, and many of his followers,
have made a pilgrimage to this site, which is the first headquarters of an Ismaili

The magnificent, intricate gravestones of Sondhan silhouetted against the setting desert sun.

leader on Indian soil. Among the visitors has been Prince Karim himself.

Burton didn't much like the old Aga Khan, though it is not clear whether they ever met in the eight months that overlapped between Burton's posting at nearby Gharo in February 1844 and the Aga's departure from Sindh in October of that year. The Aga's brother, Abul Hasan, was one of his retinue who remained behind to continue the skirmishes against the Balochs, and it was he who became Burton's *munshee* (teacher/clerk). Abul Hasan not only taught Burton Persian, he also introduced him to Ismaili Islam, Sufism and Persian poetry, especially the work of the great poet-philosopher Rumi. Abul Hasan travelled with Burton through some of the most inhospitable territory in Sindh; he may have been the inspiration for Burton's useful disguise as a half-Arab, half-Persian.

Not surprisingly, Burton was secretive about his own mysterious espionage missions for Napier in Sindh and parts of Baluchistan. Neither did he reveal anything about the exact nature of his relationship with the Aga Khan. It is certainly reasonable to conclude that Burton was assigned to gather intelligence with Sindh surveyor Walter Scott in the territory of the same tribesmen whom the Aga's brother was subjugating with the continued support of the British. This seems far too strategic to be coincidence, despite Burton's light, humorous references to his "Moonshee." The arrangements Napier had made with the Aga Khan, the military exploits of Abul Hasan among the Balochs and Burton's own orders in Sindh were connected, and they were no laughing matter.

Burton was, on the one hand, making light of his association with Abul Hasan, while on the other appearing to offer sweeping condemnation of the

Aga Khan — a sure way to leave the type of mixed signal that makes for effective espionage. Because he was writing for the paying reader at home, Burton cannot, of course, be considered as giving the last word on the Aga Khan, nor does he attempt objectivity about the scheming and skulduggery that characterized both the Persians and the British.

Whatever the Aga's shortcomings, the Ismaili leader was clearly a very useful ally, as the record shows. Napier, despite occasional criticisms of the Aga, especially of his alleged monetary and sexual demands on his disciples and cruel treatment of some of them, called his ally "a good and brave soldier." For a considerable time after the Aga had left the military theatre of the north and reached the safety of Bombay, the British remained protective of him. They eventually conferred on him the title "His Highness" and arranged an audience with the visiting Prince of Wales, the future King Edward VII.

Burton's work seems to reflect a change either in attitude toward or in freedom to speak about the Aga. In *Scinde; or, the Unhappy Valley* (1851), he openly denounced the "Agha Kan, a Persian noble." But in *Sind Revisited* (1877) — by which time the British were openly solicitous of the Aga and his growing religious domain — Burton conceals his exact identity and elevates his position, calling him "Z___ Khan, a Persian pretender to the throne." He also avoided all subsequent references to the Aga — a minor change, but one hinting at the deeper complexities.

We left Jherruck, giving ourselves about an hour to reach Sondhan — not far away — before sunset. I was determined to see the sun setting over its gravestones — famous on account of their dramatic appearance. The experience was worth the rush. We savoured the sight of these magnificent structures silhouetted against the golden light of the sinking sun. A tribal herdsman adjusting his turban, also in silhouette, added a further exotic touch. Gravestones, hundreds of them, all carved in sandstone, covered the hillside. The carvings are remarkable: here a warrior on horseback, there a group of musicians. Away below us in the distance, I could hear sounds of children playing, goats bleating, and then, out of place amid the tranquillity of the scene, the single ominous crack of a rifle shot. No one seemed the least perturbed or concerned, however. It was all part of the scene. Living on the edge.

Another three and a half hours and we were back in Karachi. We had strict instructions to telephone Hamid Akhund and inform him of our safe arrival. After a rushed light dinner at the Sind Club, I stayed up late writing. It was so easy to imagine the young Burton scribbling away at the end of one of his days spent in the territory we'd just covered.

The next day we had lunch with F.S. Aijazuddin, the author of the best-selling *Historical Images of Pakistan*. After a lifetime of collecting old lithographs and etchings of Sindh and Pakistan, Faqir Aijazuddin had them published in a book in 1992. A highly cultivated gentleman, he had obviously been brought up in a very "Anglo" tradition. He was well versed in English history and culture. He agreed with us that Burton's gift to the culture and history of the Sindh was enormous. In recommending use of the Arabic script and documenting the tribes and their cultures, Burton had a lasting effect on the education of the country.

Mr. Aijazuddin had strong views on the "Karachi Papers": "Everyone who comes here working on Burton gets bogged down on the 'Karachi Papers.' They all ask where they can find the 'Karachi Papers.' But that's just a minor issue and not at all central to Burton. His years in India provided the crucible that formed his character. Yet it is strange that his biographers and most students of Burton skip over that period to study and analyse Burton the old man, without going to the source of what made the man, and influenced most of his writing.

"I really don't think Burton was a homosexual. What does it matter, anyway? The fact that he was so explicit and so clinical in his descriptions of pederasty does not prove that he was, as some Victorians may have concluded. He was a voyeur and an observer, not a participant."

In Mr. Aijazuddin's opinion, all the British were spies. They were trained observers and Burton was a product of his age. "All Britishers brought a keen inquiring mind. They would inquire and they would write. But he perfected the art. He was open-minded enough to see beyond the stereotypes, and he achieved what he achieved because he had the God-given talent to be a linguist. The moment he realized he could almost understand the language of birds, he knew he was on his way. You could just imagine him thinking, *I can sit among the Sindhis or any other people of India, and understand everything they are saying, and understand their world!* It's like the man who deciphered the hieroglyphics. The moment he broke the code, he was on his way to great discoveries."

But while Aijazuddin believed that most British were involved to some extent in intelligence gathering, he rejected the idea that it was all part of a master plan, the "Great Game": "The Great Game was a post-empire invention. There was no master plan. It just came about. This was all more local than we believe — British agents or officers making purely local arrangements, not as part of some great overall design."

What fascinated him, he said, was "the psychological mix of Burton. What drove the devil? He must have been a very tormented person. Railing against the army, his bosses, the empire. He was totally confident of intellectual superiority but found himself as no more than a two-bit lieutenant in the East India Company. Here was a man who was capable of finding, encompassing and interpreting a culture and reducing it to its durable essentials — accounts that do not ring false even today. But he remained an unrecognized, unlauded, two-bit lieutenant. That must have galled him."

That evening, Hamid Akhund took us to the office of Sirajul Haque, who wrote the introduction to the recent reissue of Burton's *Sind Revisited*, put out by the Department of Culture. He, too, had a new viewpoint about Burton and his contributions: "Burton's translation of the *Arabian Nights* is simply superb," he told us. "I've read four different translations, and his was the best. It was simply because he understood the language and the culture, and all its nuances.

"He did so much in India in so little time, possibly because he had no inhibitions, which is all the more remarkable because of the kind of restricted, structured society he came from. He tried *bhang* and *ganja* [two local intoxicants] and he visited the prostitutes. Only a man with no inhibitions could have done all that. Also, I think he went to the brothels for the experience ... simply to be able to write about them."

Mr. Haque found it difficult to believe that the "Karachi Papers" are not somewhere in the archives of the Foreign Office in England. But he also said, "Don't make a big deal out of the 'Karachi Papers.' Burton was fascinated with the forbidden. He saw it, wrote about it. That's why he went to the red light district, and probably why he went to the male brothels. It was a normal part of his curiosity, and his writing. There is plenty about it anyway in the 'Terminal Essay' [to Burton's translation of the *Arabian Nights*]. Certainly Burton practised it. He would have to in order to write about it — in the same way he drank, slept with native women, smoked hashish or ate opium. He was bent on experience, an adventurer looking for things to report and things to write about. It was the consequences of this curiosity that Isabel, his wife, tried to protect him from when she burned his diaries and his last writings."

Despite his admiration for Burton, Mr. Haque did not agree that Burton "went native" to the extent of relinquishing his essentially British outlook. "Burton was a Britisher who felt the British had a duty to 'civilize' the Indian 'savages.' At least he was honest. He used to file reports every month to Napier in the Sindh. And to the Bombay Presidency when he was in the south. He must have been a spy. Burton was a cog in the British machine here, in the tradition of other traveller-agents who took copious notes on key strategic information about people, about routes, river navigation, topography, ideal places for armies to camp — information of a purely military nature."

From some of Mr. Haque's other comments, I realized that his interest in Burton was part of an all-embracing love of his native province of Sindh, its future as well as its past. "I take a pungent Sindhi nationalistic approach in my preface to the reprint of *Sind Revisited* because I *am* a Sindhi nationalist. I would like to help my people avoid oppression in the future. I want to tell my people, 'Look, it can happen again.' That is my bias. Let's face it, tomorrow India and Pakistan may decide to fight over Kashmir. What if Pakistan fails? Pakistan then will break up, and Sindh will become independent. I hope Pakistan doesn't take on India. But I want my people to be cautious, to be prepared.

"Am I a Sindhi or a Pakistani? I am a Sindhi who has to live here as a Pakistani. But the Sindhi culture should not be submerged. And I am fundamentally opposed to the creation of a state solely on the basis of religion."

I was rather shocked to hear such strong Sindhi nationalistic sentiments so freely expressed. It is seldom that a prominent public figure states so boldly, "I am a Sindhi, not a Pakistani." Is this an omen?

The Affghans, or Pathans, are generally found about Hyderabad, and in the north of Sindh. Many of them have been settled in the country for some generations, and become possessed of considerable landed property. Some of the men are talented, and sufficiently educated to read, write, and speak four or five languages. In appearance they are a large and uncommonly handsome race of people, perfectly distinct from the common Sindhis, whom they regard as quite an inferior breed. The women are not inferior to the men in personal appearance, and display all the fondness for, and boldness in, carrying on intrigue that characterize them in their native land.

SIR RICHARD F. BURTON, 1851

Sukkur, Shikarpur, Jacobabad, Larkhana

Ah, make the most of what we yet may spend,
Before we too into the Dust Descend;
    Dust into Dust, and under Dust, to lie,
Sans Wine, sans Song, sangs Singer and — sans End!

The Rubaiyat of Omar Khayyam, 1859
EDWARD FITZGERALD (TRANSLATOR)

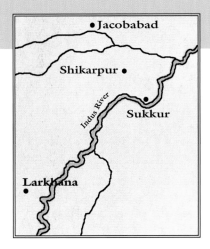

9

SUKKUR, SHIKARPUR, JACOBABAD, LARKHANA

The next day we caught an 8:30 a.m flight to Sukkur. We arrived at 10:00 a.m., our minds full of several different kinds of warnings: newspaper articles on Larkhana, where five women had been raped; word of the forced release of a Karachi drug lord for political reasons; the story of a heroin smuggler captured in a raid; a dacoit arms surrender in Hyderabad. I had to ask myself, *Where are we going?* This was a violent place, where life seemed cheap, where one regularly heard of feuds, jealousy, revenge, political leaders ousted or killed. Zulfiqar Bhutto hanged. Zia mysteriously blown up in a plane. Not much different from India, where Indira Gandhi was blown up by the Sikhs and Rajiv Gandhi assassinated by a Tamil.

As we moved farther north away from more travelled areas of the province and deeper into the Sindh, the sense of danger became more acute. Not that Karachi — a major drug centre — was exactly safe! As Burton had said in *Falconry in the Valley of the Indus*: "Nothing is more pernicious than the system of drugs, 'death's ceaseless fountain' to beast as well as man."

Sukkur is a town that Burton often travelled through on his various journeys to and from the city of Larkhana. It was from here that he travelled to Rohri to join his regiment, which he hoped was about to participate in the Punjab war, going all the way up to Bahawalpur, only to be disappointed that the Punjab campaign was over. The word Sukkur may be a distortion of the Arabic word *saqr* meaning "hell" — a reference to the extraordinary heat in the summer — as high as 125 degrees Fahrenheit.

The Sindh's third-largest city, Sukkur is a centre for commercial activity

The face of Benazir Bhutto, Prime Minister of Pakistan, stares out from a tattered poster in Larkhana.

The Mohana do not look like Sindhis. Their features are peculiar and the complexion very dark: some of the women are handsome when young, but hardship, exposure to the air, and other causes, soon deprive them of their charms.
SIR RICHARD F. BURTON, 1851
Sindh, and the Races That Inhabit the Valley of the Indus

Previous page: The Mohanas, or Boat People, live, fish and trade from flat-bottomed boats on the banks of the Indus.

not only for the Sindh but also for the Punjab and Baluchistan. Railways and highways go through the city, crossing over the Lloyd Barrage Canal — the longest bridge in Pakistan. Water from the Indus is diverted over canals to irrigate 5.5 million acres in the three provinces. Sukkur is also a centre for date cultivation, a huge industry which exports millions of dollars worth of produce each year.

Although things have improved a lot in the last few years, the region is still troubled by lawlessness. Taking no chances with our safety, Hamid Akhund had arranged for us to be met at the Sukkur airport by an escort consisting of a car with five armed military men. They had been ordered to travel with us wherever we went.

We made our way through the town, through streets crowded with camels, street vendors, motorbikes, scooters, other cars and the ubiquitous donkey carts laden with produce, to the banks of the Indus, where a boat was waiting to take us a few miles upriver towards the Punjab.

"Go up to the Lansdowne Bridge but not beyond," instructed Mohammed Ahsan Rana, the assistant commissioner and magistrate for Sukkur. "Beyond that point it is simply not safe. There are snipers on the river banks." With two armed guards and two guides, we cruised up the murky waters of the mighty Indus towards the Mohanas, or Boat People, also known as *Mir Bahr* — Masters of the Water. This is an extraordinary colony of people who transport wood and other produce up into the Punjab and back, trading by water. They live on flat-bottomed boats on the banks of the Indus, and some have houses, too, behind the boats, backing onto the water. I saw washermen, washerwomen, trained fishing birds — their legs tied to a pole with long pieces of string — storks and cranes, thatch and clay houses. Planks jutting out over the water and enclosed on three sides by colourful cloth screens were both latrines and washrooms. Women emerged, covered, from their baths. Islam does not allow them to expose their bodies. Public bathing, common on the rivers in India, Nepal and Sri Lanka, is not done in Pakistan. Even the Mohanas, many of whom are Hindus or have converted to Islam from Hinduism, still have the concept of *haya* (modesty) or *sharm* (shame), which requires them to keep covered.

Bathing is a very Eastern ritual. Despite all the filth around them, people have a sense of personal cleanliness. Hindus bathe in public in the Ganges in India. Muslims, too, have a complex concept of *paak* (clean) and *napaak* (unclean) and a rigorous regimen, washing after every latrine activity. If there is no water, a porous piece of rock or brick is used to dry the private parts as a temporary measure until water can be found to complete the cleansing.

Haroon explained to me that no Muslim can pray unless he is *paak* (clean), which is why the Faithful head straight to the tap or the tank upon entering a mosque to wash before proceeding to pray. The same applies to

A Mohana woman suspended over the Indus on a working platform.

Hindus, whose temples also have bathing tanks. Haroon commented, only half-jokingly, that in the West the surroundings are clean and spotless but the people may be filthy. In the East, however, the surroundings are filthy but the people are clean.

The Mohana boat people, often described by Burton, have enormous barges. Their giant bows rise out of the water, most with intricately carved hulls and huge rudders. The boats have low gunwales — to make it easy to load lumber, other produce, livestock, camels and so on. The flat bottoms of the boats allow navigation of the shallow parts of the river. Their lateen-rigged, wing-like sails are very similar to those of the dhow, a legacy of the Arab conquest of the valley.

We drew alongside the boats where the Mohanas live and work and, though I was somewhat embarrassed at our audacity, I nevertheless continued to take photographs. Seeing our armed guards and only too aware of their own lowly station in life, the people said nothing. The imbalance of class was right out of another century.

There are more than 7,000 Mohanas in this isolated colony, which stretches along the west bank of the Indus for about a mile. I don't think very much has changed in the 150 years since Burton was here.

We reached the Lansdowne Bridge and cruised under the giant overhang, but kept well to the south side as we had been warned to do. Returning, we stopped briefly on an island in the middle of the Indus where the Sadhu Bela Hindu Temple lies, a rare outpost of Hinduism in this Islamic country. It is a beautiful, small temple of pure white marble, with frescos and carvings around the outside. For what distant Mughal could this temple have been built? Flower patterns, jungle scenes, human figures, all tell some story or legend. There were no pilgrims, only an old keeper, who seemed very agitated by our visit. Inside the temple there were no Hindu idols or images. This was unusual. Was it a concession to the Islamic custom, or had some of the precepts of Islam — about not worshipping images — been incorporated into Hindu practice in the region?

We returned to the west bank of the Indus and our Jeep, then proceeded back through Sukkur to Rohri — a much smaller town, about a quarter of the size of Sukkur, but just as congested and busy. There were people everywhere, as well as cars, carts, donkeys and camels. And dust. We headed to Satvin Juwaastan (the Seven Sisters' Tomb). It is very similar to the tombs at Chaukundi and the Makli Hill, and commands a view over the two cities of Sukkur and Rohri. These burial places always seem to be on a hill.

"Yes. Graveyards are always on hills, never down in the valley or close to the water," for hygienic reasons, explained our guide. The graves had been built about 400 years ago. We deduced this from the tombstones that had the Islamic calendar years. Islamic tombs have little engraving and no carvings depicting stories or revealing the professions of the dead. No warriors or horsemen or clues as to whether a grave is that of a male or a female. Just simple slabs of reddish sandstone, with inscriptions from the Qur'an. The blue paint on the bricks was something Haroon had never seen before.

We toured the very old section of Rohri, right on the waterfront, across the river from Sukkur on the east side. Narrow lanes with an open drainage system alongside them separate the old houses of clay and carved wood. The irregular mass of mud walls that Burton described was still very much in evidence. The city is definitely in decay. The mud houses were crumbling, and there was an awful smell of human refuse. It was a scene right out of Burton's time, and he seemed to me to be there still. In this kind of town, among alleys like these, he met the people whose culture he tried to capture.

We were shown a saint's tomb, obviously a former temple, with thick columns, a Hindu-style carved door and a tell-tale oil lamp. Keeping lamps burning is a Hindu not a Muslim custom.

"But you still see them in the Sindh," Haroon noted. "This is a custom continued despite the sacking of temples in Islamic times." Next door to the saint's tomb is a *dharamshala* (caravan site). We saw pictures of *sadhus* (sages or holy men), but again no idols. Haroon surmised that any idols must have been removed, perhaps even voluntarily, in deference to, or in fear of, the strong Islamic injunctions against idol worship. One of the first acts of Muhammad and the early believers was to destroy all the idols of the Ka'aba in Mecca.

A few yards farther into the old town, with its maze of narrow lanes and its stench, we arrived at the mosque that Burton wrote about and that boasts a hair from the Prophet Muhammad's beard. What followed cannot have been very different from the experience Burton had 150 years ago.

After having told us that the hair was shown only on Fridays after the

Most towns with a Muslim population have an Eid Gah. *This is usually a large piece of high ground with a* mimbar *or raised platform from which the imam leads prayers.*

weekly communal prayers, the *mutawalli*, or keeper, nevertheless agreed to show it to us.

Opening a silver-plated door, he climbed dark stairs to the second floor, leaving us waiting in the main hall on the first floor. Minutes later we heard him reading verses from the Qur'an and invoking the Prophet's name: "Ya Muhammad, Ya Rasoolallah," "Oh, Muhammad, prophet of God." (Muslims resent the anglicized spellings of the name of the Prophet: Mehmet, Muhamet, Mohammed, and so on. The correct spelling—closest to the Arabic pronunciation — is Muhammad. Similarly, "Qur'an" comes closest to its Arabic equivalent, not "Koran.")

The *mutawalli* returned carrying a bundle a foot wide and maybe just as high. Seeing him, the knot of people attracted by our presence joined in the incantations. He proceeded to the centre of the prayer hall, where there was a four-foot-high platform — unusual in the middle of a mosque. Most mosques are big, empty halls where people line up for prayers behind the imam (priest), who sits up front, facing the wall. Obviously, the platform here had been specially built for showing the prized relic of the Prophet.

The keeper sat cross-legged on the platform, which had a glass enclosure around it, and was lit by fluorescent tubes on three sides and its roof, creating a halo-like effect. Chanting all the time, he began to unfold the cloth covers. There were many, many layers of them — green, red, saffron, yellow — some with Arabic inscriptions, others with golden threads, and some with beads dangling from the edges. He kept peeling them off until the bundle was reduced to no more than four inches, out of which he took an oblong gold box.

At this point, his voice rose a tone, and he pulled out two pieces of white cotton gauze and tied one around each hand. Then with great ceremony, he lifted the box and opened it carefully. We leaned forward for a glance at the holy object. He pulled out a small vial, which he held in mid-air, while increasing the incantations: "Ya Muhammad, Sallalla hu Alai hi Wassallam," "May the peace and blessings of God be upon Muhammad."

Others solemnly joined in. By now everyone's face was grave, as if in expectation of a miracle. And then, finally, the *mutawalli* unscrewed the lid of the little vial, while the chanting rose to a crescendo: "Subhannallah, ya Allah, ya Muhammad," "Oh God of mercy, oh God, oh Muhammad." Sticking out of a foam projection from the tube was a solitary hair three centimetres long, its colour iron-grey. Of course, we could not photograph it, the *mutawalli* had warned us ahead of time. Photographs would diminish the relic's rarity, its power to attract eyewitnesses who trek to the shrine to view a hair that has survived for 1,400 years.

There are two more pieces of the Prophet's hair in the Indian subconti-

The Prophet Muhammad's hair. The keeper sat cross-legged on a platform, which had a glass enclosure around it, and was lit by fluorescent tubes on three sides and its roof, creating a halo-like effect.

nent — in the Badshahi mosque in Lahore and the Hazratbal mosque in Indian-held Kashmir, where riots broke out in the 1960s when it was reported that the hair had been stolen.

According to Haroon Siddiqui, this sort of veneration is scoffed at by Islamic theologians. As well as thinking that the pieces of hair are frauds perpetrated on the illiterate masses, they note that veneration of such relics violates the fundamental spirit of Islam, which reserves all worship and praise for God alone and forbids the elevation of Muhammad to divine status.

It is a mark of Burton's knowledge of Muslims and Islam that when he visited this particular mosque of Sukkur in old Rohri — and he did this more than once — he raised doubts about the authenticity of the relic, noting that the Prophet's beard was black — not grey. In *Sind Revisited* Burton wrote: "When I first saw it, sir, the colour was certainly darker and the length was greater…. We know that the beard of the Apostle of Allah was black, and we have … a distinct tradition concerning its maximum length. But we refrain from these captious objections; we pay the fee, and we go our ways."

Our next stop was another hill — an *Eid Gah* (place of Eid). Most towns with a Muslim population have an *Eid Gah*. This is usually a large piece of high ground with a *mimbar* or raised platform from which the imam leads prayers. The *Eid Gah* is used twice a year for the two big religious festivals: *Eid al-Fitr*, which marks the end of the fasting month of Ramadan, and *Eid al-Adha*, which commemorates Abraham's willingness to sacrifice his son to the will of Allah, who substituted a ram instead. This later *Eid* coincides with Haj, the annual pilgrimage to Mecca, and includes a mass prayer at the *Eid Gah*, followed by the slaughtering of an animal. *Eid Gahs* are built because they are big enough to permit all the Muslims in town to say their *Eid* prayers together, as, by tradition, they are required to do. Cities with large enough mosques do not have *Eid Gahs*, which have no religious significance beyond providing a site for the occasion.

After a break from sightseeing to enjoy tea with Mohammed Mobin Khan, the assistant commissioner for Rohri, it was on to Bukkar Fort. As we approached the fort, just by the banks of the Indus, we heard the sound of drums and the unmistakable rumble of a gathering crowd. An *urs*. The fort

The Mohana, or fisherman caste, appear to be a tribe of converted Hindoos: … though depraved, they are by no means irreligious. They keep up regular mosques and places of worship, with Pirs, Mullas, and all the appurtenances of devotion. The river Indus is adored by them under the name of Khwajeh Khizr, and is periodically propitiated by a cast offering of rice, in earthen pots covered with red cloth.

SIR RICHARD F. BURTON, 1851
Sindh, and the Races That Inhabit the Valley of the Indus

As we approached Bukkar Fort, we heard the sound of drums and the unmistakable rumble of a crowd gathering at an urs.

houses the shrine of another saint, Pir Sadruddin Shah. This was the fort that Burton found to be "an admirable breeding ground for mosquitoes." This festival, which precedes the *urs* of Qalandar Lal Shahbaz at Sehwan farther south, had attracted many pilgrims making their way to Sehwan, as well as a whole host of musicians and dancers who perform at local fairs, weddings and celebrations at other, smaller shrines along the way. There were different groups of musicians, dancers and singers performing separately, each encircled by its own audience. We saw balancing acts, and trios of dancers tossing their long hair crazily in a circular fashion around their heads. Through all the activity was woven the persistent beat of the drums. We learned that the musicians were from Multan in the neighbouring province of Punjab. Some were resting, others cooking, others casually smoking hashish.

We made our way through the crowds, among the campers resting and enjoying the fair-like atmosphere, listening to the singers and their Sufi songs of praise. Beyond the old fort, we found a narrow, dusty lane that led down to the Indus. Here more of the Mohanas were anchored, perhaps as many as 100 boats. Some of the women wore the *buttu* or *bindi* on their forehead — the dot of Hindu women — reinforcing the Mohanas' Hindu traditions. A little way out, visible beyond the Mohanas' boats, was the island that houses the famous shrine of Khan Khawaja Khizr that Burton visited and wrote about. The saint is also referred to as Jenda Pir or Zinda Pir (Living Saint), and his shrine is revered by both Hindus and Muslims, especially those who earn a living by the river. As Burton noted, Jenda or Zinda is "the personification of the *Darya*," that is, the River Indus, whose name and spirit fishermen and others invoke for intercession with the gods in times of storms and floods, and whom they thank for the bounties of the river. The mausoleum-mosque-temple was almost wiped out in a flood in 1976. What remains is still an object of veneration, with a lamp burning twenty-four hours a day.

Devotees take the short ferry ride to the island shrine where Muslims read the Qur'an and a few Hindus light lamps — another sign of the once-strong Hindu presence here. A pervasive reverence for saints in the Sindh blurs religious distinctions and allows the two communities a relatively peaceful coexistence.

Our last visit of the day was to the beautiful Masum Minar minaret in Gharibabad. Burton wrote about this minaret. Leaning now, it was built by amir Masum Shah, a governor under Akbar the Great, and inaugurated by Akbar him

The beautiful Masum Minar minaret in Gharibabad.

self. It is 84 feet high, with 84 steps, and a base measuring 84 feet in circumference. Beautiful. I commented that it seemed like a phallic symbol or an enormous lingam. I was surprised to learn that Burton had made the same comment. Nearby were a grave and a dome built over an octagonal reception room, still with the original tiles in lovely colours of faded terra-cotta and blue.

There was a neem tree on the side of the street. This has great medicinal qualities that Burton wrote about. I photographed the tree, but was briskly rushed back to the Jeep. "This is a dangerous area!" the guard warned.

We spent the night at the Inter Pak Inn in Sukkur. The food at the inn was wonderful. *Murgh*: boneless chicken pieces marinated in lime juice, ginger, garlic, chili powder and salt. *Tandoori murgh*: chicken marinated in traditional *tandoori masala*. Chicken *kadahi*: chicken pieces cooked with tomatoes and garnished with ginger, garlic and chilies. *Muchli tikka*: cubes of fish marinated with Pakistani herbs. Fish *kofta* curry. *Jheenga masala*: jumbo prawns. *Murgh nargasi*: pieces of chicken cooked with spinach and eggs. Mutton *qorma*: goat cooked in the traditional way. Mutton *kadahi*: goat cooked with herbs. *Shahi jalfrazi*: boneless chicken with vegetables and beans, sautéed in fresh herbs and spices. Fish with ginger and onions. *Daal*: lentils. And for dessert: crème caramel, *shahi tukra*, pumpkin *halwa*. Green tea and *nan*, a wonderful grilled bread, completed most meals.

As it turned out, I didn't sleep much that night. I ended up walking up and down the corridor outside my room for most of the early hours of the morning. I woke up at 3:30 a.m. and didn't really go back to bed after that. I spent time writing until the *muezzin* called worshippers to prayer at about 6:20 a.m., ten minutes later than in Karachi. I never did find out why the time was different.

Over a breakfast of pancakes with thick honey and powerful coffee, we learned of dacoit operations in Khairpur and north of Jacobabad. People were being warned against going into the desert, and we remembered the reports about people being held for ransom. We were told that even an armed guard was no guarantee against attack.

Nonetheless, we proceeded. We had the assistance of Ravendra L. Jha, a young field guide for the Sindh Department of Culture. He was a Hindu. Hindus make up only 1.5 per cent of the estimated 113 million population of Pakistan. Other minorities make up another 1.5 per cent. Ravendra seemed convinced that hard work and ability could overcome any disadvantages faced by members of a minority group.

We set off for Shikarpur, farther to the north. There, we had an interesting time with Assistant Commissioner Tahir Khurshid Barar, whose office, behind a high wall and gate, was well guarded. There was an automatic machine-gun lying on his coffee table, and another on his desk. Haroon — ever curious — asked where they came from and where they were made. We were told they were Kalashnikov guns, made in Peshawar. Tahir Khurshid Barar was quite outspoken about the dangers of dacoitry in the area. A kidnapping had taken place only a week before, he told us. Several youths were being held for a high ransom, perhaps on one of the forested islands up the Indus. Negotiation under such circumstances is difficult. Abduction is simple; the arrangements for release are more complicated.

He took us to several places of interest in and around Shikarpur, particularly the old burial ground, the Lal Bungalow (Red Bungalow), the caravan site, and the old jail, which was incredibly crowded. We visited a Hindu temple that was also used by Sikh worshippers. There were both Sikh and Hindu icons in the temple. Finally, before leaving Shikarpur, we visited the *dhak* or enclosed bazaar, which was about a mile long and is more than 150 years old.

After Shikarpur, we made the forty-five-minute drive to Jacobabad (originally called Khanghar), directly north on the road to Baluchistan. We were warned that this was dangerous territory and that we were heading into an area where tribal law outweighed any other kind. Dacoit groups were active, and we were advised not to leave our Jeeps unless accompanied by our police escort.

We drove through level farm land, from time to time passing tribal villages. Although the settlements and their inhabitants looked quite different

The old jail in Shikarpur was incredibly crowded.

239

from one another, we were told that they were mostly Balochs.

The people didn't seem to be at all friendly; generally, in fact, they seemed quite resentful of our presence. I suppose the armed guards must have drawn attention to us. Actually, it was quite exciting. I knew we were going farther than Burton had gone, but I was determined to see Jacobabad and to learn something about General John Jacob, who was certainly one of the most extraordinary employees of the British East India Company.

The whole area around Khanghar was in a state of chaos when General Jacob arrived in 1847, and he not only created the town (and gave it his name), but also established systems of education, health, irrigation, housing, trade and, most important of all, law and order. He was a charismatic and revered figure, who, with his regiments of the Sindh Horse, is credited with bringing peace and prosperity to this desolate area. General Jacob died when he was only thirty-six, and achieved much in a mere seven years in the region. We visited his house, and we also saw the pagoda-like pigeon house that he designed, the clock that he invented and his tomb, which is still visited by those wishing to keep alive the memory of this most energetic man. General Jacob was a major when Burton was in Sindh; they overlapped for only a short period, in 1847. Burton mentions him, but I don't think they ever met.

Armed guards provided by Malik Asrar Hussain, deputy commissioner of the area around Jacobabad, drove us to the boundaries of the city at about 1:00 p.m. It was incredibly hot; but apparently Jacobabad gets much hotter than this later in the year. In the summer, it reaches temperatures exceeding 130 degrees Fahrenheit and is reputed to be the hottest place in the entire subcontinent. General Jacob died of heat stroke while working outside in the fields with his men.

When we got to the city limits, we had to wait a long time for our armed escort from Shikarpur. After several telephone calls to the commissioner's office in Shikarpur, we were fetched by a completely new batch of armed guards.

Our guide, Ravendra Jha, had invited us to have lunch with his parents in Shikarpur. Ravendra's father, an extremely intelligent and well-read man, was a former professor of English and lecturer at the local Shikarpur College. He and his wife gave us a sumptuous vegetarian lunch that included *sanghra* — a root unique to the Sindh — along with the more usual rice, chutney, *roti*, and pappadam.

Their house was off a narrow alley in a dark courtyard well protected from the sun and the outside world. It was cool and comfortable inside, sheltered by thick stone and brick walls. We were shown many old books

Outside Shikarpur. The people didn't seem to be at all friendly; generally, in fact, they seemed quite resentful of our presence.

Previous page: A tribal settlement on the northern road to Jacobabad.

and manuscripts, and conversation centred on history and religion in general and the difficulties experienced by a minority Hindu family in a predominantly Muslim state.

We left for Larkhana at about 4:00 p.m. and had a number of guard changes along the way. It seemed that the difficulty of combatting dacoit activity increased with the distance from Karachi. When we finally arrived at Larkhana at 6:30 p.m., we were met by yet another deputy commissioner and a new police guard.

Still accompanied by our armed guards, we checked in at the Sapna Hotel, right in the centre of town. I went up to my allotted room on the second floor. Outside my small window, I could see below me the rooftops of the poor quarter of the town. It stretched for miles. Also, just below my room was a mosque illuminated by lights strung across the roof line and around all the doors and windows.

I tried hard to get some hot water, but couldn't, and so had a cold shower. Outside, the *muezzin* called worshippers to prayer. I opened my window and looked out again, completely entranced by the magical atmosphere.

Larkhana is the fourth-largest city in the Sindh. Burton stayed here for quite a while, supposedly because he had met "Mahtab, the 'Moonbeam'" — the Nautch girl — and her sister, Nur Jan, who became his mistress. Moonbeam was said to have performed with her dancing troop and musicians and "a train of nine camels." Burton admitted that he was in danger of falling in love with Moonbeam, and lovingly described her beauty, her body, and her younger, even prettier sister. One hundred and fifty years ago Larkhana was famous for its Nautch girls, and Burton noted that the city was "celebrated for anything but morality."

Late that night, again with an armed police escort, we paid a visit to Larkhana's red light district. The bazaar atmosphere along the streets gave way to a quiet gloom on our arrival at the Baharpur District (the Place of Spring). This maze of alleys, clay walls, dust and smoke was the supposedly famous red light district, and we were surprised by its desolation and darkness. It turned out that the area had been practically closed down in the late 1970s. Police had raided the district so often that most of the women had left to ply their trade in other cities.

On two dimly lit streets there were a few rooms with flimsy muslin curtains screening the interior from the gaze of passersby. In an area that used to ring with the beats of *dholak* and *tabla* (Indian drums), and the rhythm of the harmonium, there was only depressing silence. The deserted streets now held only filth and odious smells and open drains carrying human waste. Occasionally, through the low windows and half-open doors we could see a woman hunched over a fire.

Our guide conjured out of somewhere a plumpish, middle-aged woman who was amazed to discover a senior police official translating for us. It didn't take her long to tell him off for ruining the area's business. A former dancer and singer, she was quite outspoken:

"I was born here and have lived here all my fifty years. This street had life, once. I used to sing and dance, and on some nights make as much as a thousand rupees. But once the police raids began, business disappeared. We would try and start again, but the bastards would come and raid again and again and again. Eventually, the younger girls just left for better places. Now, only the old hags like me are left behind. But we cannot even live a normal life. Once tainted we are tainted for life. Our name and our reputation are soiled forever. To the people, we are still loose women. So we retain the bad reputation but without a *paisa* (penny) of business. All we get now is the filth of the rich," she said, pointing to the sewers.

Masuma Begum, the "Innocent Lady."

"The only time anyone has anything to do with us anymore is during elections. They want our votes, about fifty of us. But once we cast our ballots, we are back to being treated as whores again.

"The ridiculous thing is that while the *sala bahenchod* cops have closed us down, business is booming. Not just in the big cities of Lahore and Karachi, but in Hyderabad and Nawabshah. I know because the *chokrees* (young flirts) tell me when they come back once or twice a year for Muharram (the holy annual celebration of Shia Muslims)."

"What's your name, madam?" Haroon asked.

"Masuma Begum." (Innocent Lady)

"*Sala bahenchod*," her name for the cops, means "sister-fucking bastard." It is the worst insult possible, and it carried an extra punch coming from a woman in a society that still expects its women to be polite and ladylike.

Larkhana is Benazir Bhutto's home town, and the next day included a look at various places associated with the Bhutto family. We saw the house of Nusrat Bhutto (Benazir's mother); the Prime Minister's ancestral home and constituency office; the grave of Zulfiqar Bhutto in the family graveyard where all the Bhutto family from Sir Shah Nawaz Bhutto (Benazir's grandfather) to Zulfiqar Bhutto are buried. There were political slogans all over the place: posters and graffiti. Zulfiqar Bhutto's grave had received the most attention.

Also in Larkhana, we were given a remarkable lesson in Islam. Quite by chance, we visited the Jamia Islamiya, Larkhana's Islamic seminary or *madarsah*. It had just moved to its new building, a mosque surrounded by a row of classrooms on three sides and with a courtyard in the middle. Most *madarsahs* are built on this plan, which is designed to afford a view of the

دنیا بھر کے محنت کشو

ایک ہو جاؤ!

تمہارے پاس کھونے کیلئے کچھ
نہیں سوائے تمہاری زنجیروں کے
اور پوری دنیا تسخیر کرنے کیلئے
پڑی ہے۔

ذوالفقار علی بھٹو

عبدالقادر شاہین   ملک شیر احمد   محمد امین بھٹی   ملک سیف الملوک

انچارج پیپلز لیبر ونگ   صدر   جنرل سیکرٹری   انچارج شعبہ نشرواشاعت
پنجاب

منجانب پیپلز لیبر بیورو پنجاب

entire school and encourage intermingling and easy access to the mosque for the five daily prayer sessions.

We were introduced to the resident principal and director, Dr. Khalid Mahmood Soomro, who trained as a medical doctor, then did an M.A. in Islamic culture at Sindh University, an Islamic preacher's course at Islamabad, and another in 1990 at Al-Azhar in Cairo — the oldest Islamic theological centre in the world. Dr. Soomro is also active in politics. In 1983-84 he spent nine months in jail for protesting against martial law as part of the Movement for the Restoration of Democracy (MRD). "They used to beat us with *lathis* (batons) and with rifle butts!" Dr. Soomro ran unsuccessfully in the 1993 federal election against Prime Minister Benazir Bhutto in this Larkhana riding on the Islami Jamhoori Mahaz ticket (Islamic Democratic Front). The Democratic Front elected only four members to the National Assembly. Dr. Soomro's father, who founded the academy, had also run unsuccessfully against the Bhutto family: in the 1988 election against Benazir, and in 1970 against Benazir Bhutto's uncle, Mumtaz Bhutto.

Dr. Soomro was of medium height and had the long beard, short hair, skullcap, *kurta* (shirt) to the knees and *shalwar* (pantaloons) of a Pakistani *moulvi* (a religious Muslim). He immediately made us feel very much at home. We sat on *charpais* (cots of soft coir matting) in the courtyard under a hot sun, sipping tea, while he talked with the ease of a seasoned preacher-politician. I felt that for the first time in my life I understood something of Islam.

The seminary was started by his father in 1970 in a small house in the older part of the city. It offers sixteen years of study, including the secular matriculation. All students are taught the 88,000-word Qur'an, the Muslim holy book, and some Arabic — the language of the Qur'an — Islamic history and the basic tenets of the religion.

Beyond that, the curriculum includes various branches of learning, one of which is the memorization of the entire holy book, known as *hifz*. Islam is the only religion that enjoins its followers not only to read the scripture but to commit it to memory. The process begins early, at age four or five, either at school or at home, and entails many hours of mostly rote learning, involving the reading of the Qur'an itself or the recitation of passages to the teacher while going about one's daily chores.

At Islamic schools, one usually sees children, their heads covered with a knitted white skullcap, sitting cross-legged on a carpet. The opened Qur'an sits on a *rehl*, a wooden bookstand that rests on the ground. The students recite in a sing-song, rhythmic manner, swaying the upper body forward and backward as they commit the words to memory. Burton found such scenes enormously appealing and wrote of them lovingly.

A good student normally takes two to three years to complete the task. It

A poster of Zulfiqar Bhutto. The grave of the late political leader continues to attract enormous crowds.

is mostly boys who become *hafiz* (one who knows the whole Qur'an by heart), but some women do undertake the study and, if successful, become *hafiza*. The test comes when the young *hafiz* is asked to lead the special evening prayers during the fasting month of Ramadan, when a *hafiz* would recite the entire Qur'an over a period of twenty-one to twenty-seven days, reciting about 3,000 to 3,500 words a day from memory. To ensure correctness, a senior *hafiz* would normally stand in the first row of the congregation and prompt the junior *hafiz* if he forgets a line or gets mixed up. The successful completion of the recitation of the whole book is celebrated with the distribution of sweetmeats, and much praise for the young *hafiz*, who is then assured the respect of fellow Muslims for the rest of his life.

Another area of study is *tajweed* — the correct pronunciation and recitation of the holy book and reading it with *qirat* (the art of modulating the voice for the formal recitation). A Muslim who is both a *hafiz* and a *qari* is doubly respected.

Yet another area of study is Hadith — the sayings, teachings and practices of the Prophet Muhammad, whose life became an open book for his companions. The detailed catalogue of these takes up several volumes. After the Qur'an, the Hadith forms the core of Islamic practices and the basis for Islamic law.

Then there is *fiqh* — Islamic jurisprudence, based on the Qur'an and Hadith and recorded in the works of four great scholars and jurists: Imam Hanafi, Imam Hambali, Imam Shafai, and Imam Maliki. Ninety-nine per cent of Muslims follow these four imams. (The rest, such as the Aga Khan Ismaili sect, follow other schools.)

Arabic is also studied. This is a straightforward course in the language of the Qur'an. (According to Dr. Soomro, "Burton made a most sharp observation which is still very much true: 'The people of Sindh pronounce Arabic in a most extraordinary manner....' Such a comment could only have been made by one familiar with the diction of Arabic and its correct pronunciation.")

Tafseer is the study of various scholarly commentaries on the Qur'an. They have a prominent place in the curricula of Islamic schools, including this one. They postulate different interpretations of the Qur'anic injunctions.

Mantiq — logic — is also studied. The course begins with the Arabic translations of Isagoga of Porphyry and proceeds to the dialectics of the poets Haafiz and Rumi (whom Burton also studied).

There is nothing more remarkable in Sindh than the number of holy men which it has produced, and the extent to which that modification of Pantheism, called Tasawwuf throughout the world of Islam, is spread among the body of the people.
SIR RICHARD F. BURTON, 1851
Sindh, and the Races That Inhabit the Valley of the Indus

Dr. Khalid Mahmood Soomro, director of the Jamia Islamiya, Larkhana's Islamic seminary or madarsah.

249

Hikmat (philosophy) and *munazirah* (rhetoric — for advanced students) complete the curriculum.

All of these subjects were taught in Burton's time, as he recorded in great detail in Chapter 6 of *Sindh, and the Races That Inhabit the Valley of the Indus*; some of the courses he listed — such as *khat* (calligraphy), *raml* (geomancy), *nujum* (astrology) and *jafr* (divining by numbers) — have now been dropped, except by specialized academies.

The graduates of schools such as this one staff the thousands of mosques in the Sindh and other Muslim societies, and lead the special Ramadan prayers or become *muezzins* and imams (prayer leaders).

The schools are funded, as they were in Burton's time, by private donations or local *waqf* (trusts). Burton noted that "the country swarms with Huffaz" (the plural of *hafiz*), and that is true to this day. He lamented that "the art of Qirat and Tajweed is little cultivated in our province," but that is less true today. Dr. Soomro noted that "Burton would surely have been affected by the Islamic influences all around him in the Sindh, which was still the great centre of Islamic learning. This whole area, from Thatta to Shikarpur and here in Larkhana, was bustling with Islamic *madarsah* or *khankhahs* (the centres of Sufis or religious scholars). Islam was everywhere around Burton — at the grass-roots level, as well as at the intellectual level. Muslims were a living example of Islam: simple, honest, straightforward, affectionate."

(Later, Haroon commented, "Read this as this gentlemen's supposition of what good Muslim Sindhis were during Burton's time. He displays little historic ethnographic knowledge, and is merely speculating. Even if Sindhis were that good, Burton remained unimpressed by them and called them crooks!" Though I took his point, I ribbed Haroon a little that his reporter's objectivity was making it hard for him to accept anything at face value.)

"Why," Dr. Soomro asked rhetorically, "would Burton move from Protestantism to Catholicism to a brush with Hinduism to Islam here in the Sindh? In addition to the influences I mentioned, Burton, or anybody, cannot help but be moved by the simplicity of the Islamic belief: one God; a human messenger who lives the life that he preached; and a message of equality before Allah, resistance to oppression, and earning a living by honest means. Once convinced of this Islamic message, Burton would have remained persuaded all his life.

"What is religion? It is the knowledge of who you are and of your relationship to your creator.

"Given the world's condition today, there is no path left other than Islam. Despite all the wealth of the West, it and its people do not have *sukoon*

It is by means of its peculiar rhythm that the Koran is so easily learned by heart, and probably it was composed in this form partly in order to assist the memory.

SIR RICHARD F. BURTON, 1851
Sindh, and the Races That Inhabit the Valley of the Indus

(peace, satisfaction, inner bliss). Those with the biggest wealth and material goods seem to be the biggest consumers of sleeping pills."

This seemed to provide the perfect opening for a question I wanted to ask him: "I am a man born in the East who went to the West and was successful in Western ways," I told him. "I am now back in the East studying the influence of religion, especially Islam, on Burton. What advice can you give to me?"

"Islam means submission to the will of God," Dr. Soomro replied. "*Iman* (faith) means *amn* (peace, tranquillity). Muslim means one who submits. *Momin* means one who does not inflict pain and suffering on others. So, one who follows Islam has *iman* (faith) and *amn* (peace) and is *momin* (just). My advice is simple: You must read the English translation of the Qur'an; read the life of Muhammad. You know, Muhammed was one man who really had no secrets, whose life was, and is, an open book; so read about him and his life; follow his example — make a *halal* (honest) living; side with the oppressed; help honest, hard-working people; serve those who are serving humanity. You cannot buy *sukoon* (inner peace). Only Allah has the prescription for it.

"Once you understand and establish a link, directly, with Allah, you don't bow to anyone else. That's what must have impressed Burton. That is the great quality of the Muslim, that he fears none but Allah.

"Burton went to Mecca and Medina. No one can go to the Ka'aba in Mecca and the prophet's grave in Medina and not come out of it without a lifelong imprint on one's mind and psyche and soul. You cannot listen to the Qur'an recited in the holy places of Mecca and Medina and not be moved by it. Even those who do not understand a word of it are moved by it, because it is the word of God."

There was much to ponder in this, but I wanted his response to something else I had long wondered about. I pressed on: "When Burton died, Isabel gave him the Last Rites, on his dead body, and proceeded to burn all his papers and his diaries. A devout Catholic herself, she never believed in the sincerity of his interest in Eastern religions, especially Islam. In one brutal act, she cut off from the world the wealth of his knowledge and all his observations and thoughts on Islam. Any chance we may have had of truly understanding his empathy and respect and love for Islam was lost forever. She really exemplifies the attitude of the whole Western world to Islam. It is difficult for the Western mind to comprehend the power of a religion like Islam and its hold on its believers. I think that is why the West continues to paint the stereotypical, cliched image of Islam as violent and fundamentalist."

"Ah, yes," he summed up for me. "Islam is so very powerful that the West is really afraid of it. Especially now."

My brain was spinning. Haroon and I had taken notes like mad. But both of us were relatively silent after this discussion. I was struck as never before by the vast gulf between East and West.

The three days in the Larkhana district had given me many new insights and experiences. I somehow felt I understood Burton much better now, had a clearer idea of why he was so drawn to Islam and its culture. The question of religion was the key.

Burton dabbled in many faiths, but none had greater fascination for him than Islam, and none held him longer. Burton was born into a Protestant family and married into a Catholic one. But he was neither Protestant nor Catholic. He was as much an adventurer in religion as in everything else. He claimed conversion to Hinduism, Sikhism and also Islam. For a man with exceptional powers of assimilating all that he encountered, conversion was a convenient and effective way to experience first hand the religious and cultural diversity of India, a country in which both polytheism and monotheism had co-existed for thousands of years.

In Burton's seven years in India he found an opportunity to study Islam more deeply than could be imagined for a non-Muslim. Nothing escaped his attention: theory and practice; differences in approach, such as those between Saudi fundamentalism and Indian ecumenism; modifications and cultural differences, such as the variations in the practices of Indians, Persians, Arabs and Africans. Burton delved into the mysteries of each of Islam's theological branches: the Sunnis (who were and are in the majority), the minority Shiites, the followers of the Aga Khan (the Ismailis), and the mystical Sufis whose practices have an appeal that cuts across sectarian barriers. Burton spoke the language of the Muslims and developed a life-long fascination and affection for them. For Burton, if a man was a Muslim, even his race was a secondary consideration, which was a startling attitude in an age of overwhelming racism, especially against black Africans. Burton was also intelligently critical of some practitioners of Islam, pointing out that their ways were theologically unsound and violated the spirit of Islam; in short, he was knowledgeable enough to distinguish between Islamic precepts and Islamic practices. He was also well aware of the most central truth of Islam: that it is only Allah who is worshipped, not his messenger, Muhummad, who, unlike Christ, does not participate in the divinity of Him whose message he brings.

The Crusades had left a legacy of fear of Islam, a prejudice common among Britons of Burton's time and one that lingers in the minds of many Westerners to this day. It was not a prejudice that Burton suffered from. He loved Islam. Of its great event, the Haj, he wrote, "I have seen the religious ceremonies of many lands, but never — nowhere — aught so solemn, so impressive as this."

He also wrote, "Islam approaches much nearer to the faith of Jesus than do the Pauline and Athanasian modifications which, in this our day, have divided the Indo-European mind into Catholic and Roman, Greek and Russian, Lutheran and Anglican"; and he admitted that he found the Muslim to be "more tolerant, more enlightened, more charitable than many

Muslim family travelling outside Larkhana.

societies of self-styled Christians."

Burton was a nineteenth-century man — a Victorian. It is startling to think of an English Victorian being a Muslim. *Was* Burton a Muslim?

I think Burton followed the dictates of Islam when he felt he was gaining anthropological data, even, perhaps, when he was seeking spiritual fulfilment. But I also think he could abandon Muslim practices blithely if they became an inconvenience. I have no difficulty in imagining him devoutly at prayer or fasting diligently from sunrise to sunset during Ramadan. But I know, too, that he could also put aside the strictures against alcohol in order to savour a good port, especially if there was no one around to notice the transgression. His participation in Islam never distracted him from his primary goal, which was not devotion but observation. He *was* distracted by other things, though: a pretty pilgrim, the interesting details of the other pilgrims' clothes.... A true believer on a sacred pilgrimage would not have been so easily diverted.

Whatever his anthropological or spiritual involvement in Islam, Burton's emotional involvement is unquestioned. Himself a romantic, he was drawn to Islam as an exotic and trance-like religion: "The melodious chant of the Muezzin — no evening bell can compare with it for solemnity and beauty...."

The romantic heroism of one important Muslim trait — that of accepting death with grace — was also clear to Isabel. In 1875, travelling with Burton to Bombay, she learned of twenty-three hajis who had died accepting their end in perfect peace. She found this acceptance profoundly admirable and said, "What a contrast in this quiet dropping to sleep with the horrors of the English death-bed, with the barbarous predilection for prolonging the agony."

Scholars of Burton differ in their estimation of another level of Burton's involvement with Islam — the amount of the Qur'an that he knew by heart.

Burton certainly memorized some of the holy book of Islam. It would have been unlike him not to. But I think that an excess of enthusiasm on the part of his biographers has led to the belief that he knew more than he really did. He himself may have contributed to this misperception. The careful scholar discovers that Burton's recorded public recitation of the Qur'an may well have been limited to a single instance in which his audience was an illiterate African tribe with little familiarity with the holy text.

There is no question, however, that his ability to assimilate the mannerisms of Islam was at the level of genius. He would have had to remember that when entering a mosque, the devout man puts his right foot first — but his left when entering a washroom. He would also have had to observe precise rituals of personal cleansing, of drinking water in a certain way, of saying each of the invocations to Allah in the right way at the right time. In these matters of etiquette which mark every aspect of the daily life of the believer, Burton almost never made a mistake.

I think that very probably Burton was not a Muslim, though his knowledge of Islam surpassed that of many who do fully embrace the faith.

It seems to me that biographers have missed the true significance of Burton's involvement with Islam. Though it is not a religion that baptizes its followers, his contact with Islam was like baptism for Burton. It introduced him to new life. Like so much else that he encountered in India, Islam played a role in changing him from the rather vague youth that he had been into the stunning man he was to become.

As Thomas Assad has pointed out, Burton wrote that Islam, in contrast to Christianity, exalts life:

> *Burton's notes make a valiant attempt to correct the erroneous view of Occidentals in matters of this nature by explaining tenets of the Moslem faith.... [Burton says that] by passing "over the 'Fall' with a light hand," by making man superior to the angels, and by acknowledging, "even in this world, the perfectability of mankind, including womankind," Mohammed did much to exalt human nature. Christianity suffers by comparison with Islam in this regard....*
>
> THOMAS J. ASSAD,
> *Three Victorian Travellers, 1964*

The return to Sehwan and Ranikot Fort

These "papers of some importance" must have been the most difficult Burton ever wrote. For the wrecking of his military career could not easily be explained to anyone.... The faint smell of brimstone — provoked and abhorred — would follow Burton everywhere from India....

FAWN BRODIE *The Devil Drives,* **1967**

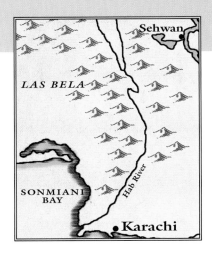

10

THE RETURN TO SEHWAN AND RANIKOT FORT

After many expressions of gratitude to Ravendra Jha and the armed police escort, we said our goodbyes and caught a 5:45 p.m. flight to Karachi. We arrived about 7:00, and were having dinner at the Sind Club by 9:00 p.m.

The following morning, a Sunday, I got up very early and had another of Mohammed Younus's scorching omelettes for breakfast, plus toast, plus coffee. I wanted to catch up on my notes. I also had some organizing to do for our heavy schedule during the last few days. Haroon and I planned to take one more side trip from Karachi to attend the *urs* in Sehwan. But before we left we wanted to hold a dinner for those who had helped us during our stay. This was to be my thank you to them.

Eight p.m. Dinner at the Sind Club. Twelve people — all of them introduced to us by Hamid Akhund — were eventually seated around table no. 11 at the Club. Everyone was involved in some way or another with the culture of Sindh, and everyone was knowledgeable — or at least opinionated — about Richard Burton.

It was a wonderful dinner. Everyone participated and everyone stayed late. We didn't try to cut it short despite the lateness of the hour. I knew that the end of the marvellous journey was in sight, and that the wonderfully cooperative people we had met were about to disappear back into their own culture, leaving me, the traveller with my own journey and my own curious mission.

Finally, however, the enjoyable occasion came to an end. As we were filing out onto the veranda of the Sind Club, one of the guests asked me, almost as an afterthought and perhaps jokingly, "Well, did you find the 'Karachi Papers'?"

The Sehwan urs *attracts an army of beggars — perhaps the biggest gathering of beggars ever seen in one place.*

Previous page:
... the Sindhis are by no means a bad people, as atrocity is rare among them, and consequently justice is not severe.

SIR RICHARD F. BURTON, 1851
Sindh, and the Races That Inhabit the Valley of the Indus

I smiled and answered evasively. "Actually," I said, "at one point, I thought I *had* located them."

"But now you're not so sure?"

"I *am* sure the papers did exist and that Burton did write them, but my opinion is that he wrote them not so much as an official report but as a private memorandum to General Napier. I know Burton refers to the report as 'official,' but I think he was using the term as a colloquialism. I don't believe the report was ever official at all. It was never intended for publication, and I doubt that it *was* ever published." Clearly, some sort of document was filed with Napier's other important correspondence, I told him, and unfortunately for Burton, information about the document and its contents was leaked after General Napier retired. I don't think Burton was a popular man, and Napier's successor saw to it that the report of its contents caused the virtual termination of Burton's military career. We certainly hadn't found a physical trace of any such papers, and I was becoming increasingly convinced that they had been destroyed.

Later that night, I once more pondered the question of the "Karachi Papers." The documents had clearly played a very important part in the moulding of Burton's life. They certainly put an end to any chance of his military advancement: forever after, he was pursued by the vague suspicion that there was something wrong with him, something twisted. No matter how scholarly the language in which he couched his discoveries about the mores and morals of the East — including the beauty of Eastern women — he remained suspect. It is a little hard to realize the magnitude of the issue in Burton's day because so much has changed. As Fawn Brodie says, "One should remember, however, that though the practice of homosexuality was probably no less common in England then than now, no one in his time wrote about it save to denounce it as a sin, and even the idea of describing it clinically was for most Englishmen profoundly shocking."

Burton did not write about pederasty or homosexuality for publication until almost forty years later. When he did, the boy brothels of Karachi were still on his mind. This was in 1884 when he tackled the subject again in his "Terminal Essay" of the *Arabian Nights*. And it is in this essay that I had been so sure I would find the contents of the Karachi papers.

Well, I didn't find them, and I did.

When I returned from my trip, I had the time to pore over the "Terminal Essay," examining every word of the notorious section on pederasty. After such careful examination, I was forced to the honest conclusion that what I had suspected was not totally true. I could not conclude that Burton had directly quoted his old report in the new work — in the way he so often quoted *Scinde; or, the Unhappy Valley* in *Sind Revisited*.

I was aware that Michael Hastings felt differently: "most of these notes made up the report he handed to Napier." And it is certainly true that the "Terminal Essay" offers graphic details that seem undimmed by memory: "He was presently placed on all fours and firmly held by the extremities; his bag-trousers were let down and a dozen peppercorns were inserted *ano suo*...." Yet these details are not presented by Burton as a description of Karachi *per se*; they are part of what can only be called a survey of widespread practices.

I decided that Burton certainly *had* retained his notes from the boy brothels of Karachi. And I also realized that what he had discovered there set him on a lifelong quest to understand what he had seen and to place it in as large a context as possible. It was almost as if he could not truly comprehend what he had observed in Karachi until he could apply to it the fullness of his many years of experience and study.

Burton was a prolific researcher and note maker. At the height of his fame, his Nile co-adventurer, John Hanning Speke, referred to Burton's "scribbling mania." He researched deeply and thoroughly and hoarded information. He kept everything — so much that he had to store it in a warehouse at one point. Although the "Karachi Papers" may have been destroyed, it is unlikely that Burton would have destroyed his own notes on which he based the papers. Fawn Brodie says, "the documentation for his courageous essay on pederasty in the 'Terminal Essay' of the *Arabian Nights* must surely have drawn upon his Indian experience. He seems then to have remembered everything...." Perhaps, but I don't think he relied on his memory alone. The amazingly detailed and provocative essay was more likely taken from the copious notes — still in his possession at the time — which he had garnered from personal investigation.

Burton, in fact, refers directly to his Indian experience. "Section D. — Pederasty" begins:

> The "execrabilis familia pathicorun" first came before me by a chance of earlier life. In 1845, when Sir Charles Napier had conquered and annexed Sind, despite a faction (mostly venal) which sought favour with the now defunct "Court of Directors to the Honourable East India Company," the veteran began to consider his conquest with a curious eye. It was reported to him that Karáchi, a townlet of some two thousand souls and distant not more than a mile from camp, supported no less than three lupanars or bordels, in which not women but boys and eunuchs, the former demanding nearly a double price, lay for hire. Being then the only British officer who could speak Sindi, I was asked indirectly to make enquiries and to report upon the subject; and I undertook the task on express condition that my report should not be forwarded to the Bombay Government, from whom supporters of the conqueror's policy could expect scant favour, mercy or justice. Accompanied by a Munshi, Mirza Mohammed Hosayn of Shiraz, and habited as a merchant, Mirza Abdullah Bushiri passed many an evening in the townlet, visited all the porneia and obtained the fullest details, which were duly dispatched to

*Government House. But the "Devil's Brother" presently quitted
Sind leaving in his office my unfortunate official: this found its
way with sundry other reports to Bombay and produced the expected result. A friend in the Secretariat informed me that my
summary dismissal from the service had been formally proposed
by one of Sir Charles Napier's successors....*

Burton then goes on to say, "Subsequent enquiries in many and distant
countries enabled me to arrive at the following conclusions...." and he offers
the results of years of research on the matter, research begun in the brothels
of Karachi so very long before.

The conclusion I finally came to was not that I had found the "Karachi
Papers," but that I had finally found how they had begun a forty-year
odyssey for Richard Burton as an anthropologist, a writer and a man deeply
interested in all aspects of human behaviour, including behaviour that others less brave than himself were afraid to examine with a clear eye.

Before I slept that night, I lay on my back staring blankly into the darkness of my room at the Sind Club. I had not yet crystallized my own opinions about the "Karachi Papers," but I was already profoundly impressed by
how patiently Burton had bided his time. Finally in 1884, when he translated and published his *Arabian Nights*, he was confident enough to bring up
the forbidden subject. No amount of unpopularity or inconvenience could
curb Burton's zeal for anthropological documentation. In him it was a passion far too strong to suppress.

The next day, Haroon and I were in good time for our early morning helicopter ride to Sehwan with Governor Mahmoud Haroon, the governor of
Sindh province. Hamid Akhund was with us. Just the four of us and two helicopter pilots. The flight took about an hour and a half.

Governor Haroon is from an old, established Karachi family. He owns
Dawn, the national English-language daily. An elderly gentleman with a very
aristocratic bearing, he had held office once before.

The helicopter ride was a novelty for me. We flew low over the Karachi
rooftops: first over the city, the roads, the busy traffic, then over tracts of
smaller and smaller houses, the slums and then finally the city outskirts.
Very quickly we reached arid, brown scrubland — almost desert. There
seemed no sign of life, not even a blade of grass. Brown earth, sandstone
rocks, bare hills, the occasional animal track, other tracks leading nowhere,
all shining back at us in the early morning sun. No sign of water. I could see
the shadow of the helicopter almost below us — a dark outline on the rust-
coloured desert floor. I sat by the window, forehead pressed against the
glass, looking down in an almost hypnotized state. The beat of the giant rotors made it too noisy for conversation.

And then, quite suddenly, the stone walls of a fort came into view in the distance. Endless walls seemed to appear out of nowhere, silhouetted against the desert horizon. This was Ranikot Fort. More walls. A tower. And then the complete outline — an irregular, almost triangular shape contouring the summit of a hill. Another watch tower. And below it another, smaller fort, Mir Garh (Fort of Mirs). The larger fortress, Sher Garh (Fort of the Lions), was now directly below us.

No one is certain of the origin of the fort or the great wall of Ranikot. Though in the middle of nowhere now, it must once have been on the trade route between Afghanistan and central Asia. There are valleys here, and the fort seems to be at the entry point to each of the valleys. Has the history of this place been totally forgotten? In all, the circumference of the great walls of Ranikot must be almost twenty miles. Why was it built? I had come across no reference to the fort in my reading, and Burton doesn't mention it either. He couldn't possibly have been here. The only mention in Sindhi history books was that the Talpur amirs spent a great deal of money repairing the fort when they were in power.

"It's part of our rich heritage," Governor Haroon shouted at us. "Yet we don't really know anything about it."

Fascinated, I made up my mind that somehow we would have to visit Ranikot before we left Pakistan.

Governor Mahmoud Haroon, the governor of Sindh province, at the tomb of Lal Shahbaz.

Holding red and green banners aloft, and with great shouts of "Mast Qalander," pilgrims dance to the music of single-stringed lutes.

About an hour later, we were over Sehwan. Below us flowed the mighty river Indus, the vegetation green along its banks. People looked up and stared. As we landed, our rotors caused a minor dust storm. Military police and guards cowered to protect themselves. The governor left the aircraft first, stepping onto a red carpet. The rest of us — Hamid Akhund, Haroon Siddiqui and I — fell in behind, keeping at a respectful distance.

Three cars were waiting, with armed guards, to take the governor and his entourage to Qalandar Lal Shahbaz's tomb, where the opening ceremonies of the *urs* were to be held.

When we got there, wreaths were laid and *ajraks* (scarves used as head coverings) were exchanged. Everywhere we went, we encountered crowds. We walked at least a mile with the Governor between the massed crowds that lined the streets. The Governor waved continually at the crowds — he was

Previous page: Quite suddenly, the stone walls of a fort came into view in the distance. Endless walls seemed to appear out of nowhere, silhouetted against the desert horizon. More walls. A tower. And then the irregular, triangular shape contouring the summit of a hill. Ranikot Fort.

clearly a populist — and they cheered enthusiastically. Eventually, we escaped to ride in a cool, quiet car that was part of an armed convoy. We were taken to the Sehwan fort, where we were offered cake and a refreshing drink made from apples.

This was the first time it had been quiet enough to talk. The Governor asked us where we were from, and what exactly our project on Richard Burton was. He seemed incredulous that anyone from as far away as Canada could be interested in such a Victorian figure and in the history of the East. However, after I explained that I had been born in Ceylon and that I had written a book about that country, his puzzlement vanished.

Our chat was short. The Governor was surrounded by aides, all of whom wanted to talk to him or to introduce him to various local dignitaries. He was soon fully occupied with his assistants, and eventually they hustled him back to Karachi in the helicopter. Haroon and I made our way down the dusty street from the fort, through the crowded town, to check into our rest-house room.

For the next three and a half hours, Haroon and I, and our guide, Nazakat Ali Fazlani, walked the streets of Sehwan and mingled with the enormous crowds. A town that is normally home to 30,000 had mushroomed with the arrival of more than 600,000 pilgrims. People of all types had come to the festival from all over Pakistan — some from as far as Bahawalpur and the northwest frontier. Many were camping, and there were tents everywhere— and cooking fires. We saw colourfully clad women and turbaned men with long, swarthy faces. People were dancing in front of the temple, hands held high. Drums beat continually. Here and there we glimpsed groups of flagellants with scarred bodies, beating themselves with their hands and crying out. As we pushed our way through the packed streets, we came upon three crazed-seeming dancers covered with blood, their arms aloft, their bodies glistening with sweat. They spun faster and faster, swaying with the beat of the drums. The crowd moved and swayed with them.

Haroon lost no time. He was soon interviewing people. He talked to a group from Punjab, some of whom had arrived that day, others the day before. We discovered that there was free food for the crowds. And the whole scene was food for thought. We saw people smoking *hookahs* and others smoking hashish, women in veils, *fakirs* and transvestites, goats for sacrifice. The crowd we had joined moved slowly through Sehwan, a vast, lethargic stream headed for the river, a canal offshoot of the Indus. There, bathers were washing themselves, their clothes, and their children — males in the river, women closeted in well-covered temporary washrooms of bamboo and coir matting.

We turned and took the long walk back to the resthouse. After a late, hasty lunch of mutton curry, rice and *nan*, with sweet saffron rice for dessert — along with quantities of water (our walk had made us thirsty) — we rested for half an hour. Outside, we could hear the crowds continuing to gather. The noise of drums, music, bells and excited laughter grew steadily in volume.

The Sehwan *urs*, I had been told, attracts an army of beggars — perhaps the biggest gathering of beggars ever seen in one place. Holding red and green banners aloft, and with great shouts of "Mast Qalandar," they danced to the odd music of single-stringed lutes. They sported white robes, colourful waistcoats, necklaces of shells, amulets and also an assortment of rags.

The Sehwan *urs* is celebrated every year in the first week of February, and it honours the Red Peregrine Falcon of the Valley of Sindh, Qalandar Lal Shahbaz, the patron saint of Sehwan. He was an amazing man. Born in the thirteenth century in Persia at Marwand, he was originally known as Shaikh Usman Marwandi. His father was a dervish (one who has taken a vow of poverty and austerity) of the Qalandar sect, and his mother a high-ranking princess of royal blood. Even when he was a very young boy, Shaikh Usman showed intense concentration and strong religious leanings. He knew the Qur'an by heart when he was seven; and soon after he was twenty he begged to be made a Qalandar *fakir*. Once initiated into the order, the young Shaikh Usman dressed in beggar's clothes and embraced poverty, wandering throughout all the countries of the Middle East. In 1263 he arrived at Multan, where the governor begged him to settle. He refused, and continued his journey, eventually arriving at Sehwan. There he took up residence in the trunk of a tree on the outskirts of town.

History says that the town's incumbent *fakirs* sent a messenger to the new saint, with a bowl of milk filled to the brim. The message was clear. The bowl could not hold a drop more, and there wasn't room in the city for another *fakir*. Undaunted, Shaikh Usman floated a single flower on the milk and asked the messenger to take the bowl back to the other *fakirs*. He could have made no better answer. He was a rare saint, and his legend grew.

History also says that Shaikh Usman had fallen in love with the daughter of his friend Baha-ud-din Zakariyya. His love was requited, and the girl's hand had been promised to him in marriage. She lived in Multan. Shaikh Usman returned to Multan to claim the hand of his promised bride. However, Shaikh Baha-ud-din Zakariyya had died in the meantime, and his son Sadr-ud-din refused to give his sister to Shaikh Usman in marriage. In a deep depression from which he never recovered, Shaikh Usman sadly returned to Sehwan and died there in 1274, a broken man.

The tragic story was retold year after year, and its dramatic appeal fanned the fire of Shaikh Usman's legend. On each morning of the three-day feast, the narrow lanes of Sehwan are packed to capacity as thousands and thousands of pilgrims, *fakirs* and other worshippers make their way to the shrine at the saint's grave.

Haroon explained: "Every *urs* turns into a carnival as well as being a religious festival. It's mostly rural folk, even though attendance is by no means restricted to poor illiterates. Some saints do have very educated and sophisticated followers. Many attract movie stars, and certainly singers and musicians, who are drawn naturally to the singing and dancing that goes on. But an *urs* is usually a rural fair where people go for spiritual uplift, as well as to shop and be entertained. Therefore, we must see the Sehwan *urs* in its full context.

"This particular *urs* is among the biggest in India and Pakistan because the saint has a massive following. This is the seven hundred and twentieth *urs* of this legendary figure — Hazrat Hafiz Haji Syed Muhammad Usman Marwandi Qalandar Lal Shahbaz of Sehwan Sharif. To the initiated, this long name tells us a lot:

"*Hazrat* (a saint); *Hafiz* (one who knew the entire Qur'an by heart); *Haji* (one who had performed the Haj, the pilgrimage to Mecca); *Syed Muhammad* (one who claimed direct descent from the Prophet Muhammad); *Marwandi* (one from the town of Marwand, in Iran); *Qalandar* (one who belonged to the Qalandar Sufi order). Also, he was known as *Lal* (Red) and *Shahbaz* (Peregrine Falcon); and was connected with Sehwan city, which is itself *Sharif* (noble).

"The word *urs* is drawn from an Arabic term meaning wedding, but is used in India and Pakistan to refer to the anniversary of a saint's death. A saint's death is believed to lead to his *wasl* (union or wedding) with God. An *urs* usually lasts three days, but the main feast is usually on the date of the anniversary of the saint's death."

Haroon explained that this particular Monday (January 31, 1994) was the start of a non-stop three-day trek by more than half a million people to the shrine for a *ziarat* (witnessing) of the saint's grave, with two objectives: (1) to offer *faatihah* (a reading of the first, very small chapter of the Qur'an) for the *eisal-e-sawab* (spiritual benefit) of the dead saint; and (2) to commune in silence with the saint, making a *mannat* or *minnat* (wish) telling him of their troubles, difficulties, desires and aspirations and pledging that if the wish is granted, they would do something in return — donate money for the upkeep of the shrine, perhaps, or vow to return to the *urs* each year for so many years, or feed so many poor people, and so on.

"Islamic theologians," Haroon continued, "have reservations about the *urs*. Islam prides itself on being a religion in which the believers have a direct relationship with Allah; they have been told they do *not* need intercessors to get to God, which is why, among the majority of Sunni Muslims, there is no priestly hierarchy, as in Roman Catholicism, and no papacy and certainly no equivalent of the Vatican. This last fact partly explains current Muslim resistance to Saudi claims to be more holy and religiously authoritative than others merely because they are the guardians of the holy cities of Mecca and Medina."

Lal Shahbaz's shrine, built in 1356, dazzles the eye with its Sindhi Kashi tile, mirror work and two gold-plated doors (one donated by the late Shah of Iran, the other by the late Prime Minister Zulfiqar Bhutto — both Shiites, as was the saint). However, as religious monuments go in India and Pakistan, it is not particularly distinguished architecturally. Nor is it especially large: the inner sanctum is no bigger than 100 square yards, with the silver-canopied grave in the middle.

On one side of the marble floor was a row of *rehls*, the collapsible, cross-legged, wooden stands, twelve inches high, on which are set copies of the Qur'an for devotees to read. On the other side, beside a bundle of burning incense sticks, were a row of *diyas* (oil lamps), obviously for the benefit of Hindu devotees who are used to lighting a *diya* in temples, or anointing themselves with its holy oil.

Around the grave there were seven big, green, wooden boxes, sealed and with a slot on top, to receive the devotees' offerings. Such boxes at shrines are a source of great controversy throughout India and Pakistan because the collections are substantial and are not always properly supervised or

In the East, man requires but rest and shade: upon the bank of a bubbling stream, or under the cool shelter of a perfumed tree, he is perfectly happy, smoking a pipe, or sipping a cup of coffee or drinking a glass of sherbet, but above all things deranging body and mind as little as possible; the trouble of conversations, the displeasures of memory, and the vanity of thought being the most unpleasant interruptions....

SIR RICHARD F. BURTON, 1855
Personal Narrative of a Pilgrimage to El-Medinah and Meccah

accounted for. In most places, they are supervised by trusts named by the government and by the *sajjada-nasheen* (those in charge of the shrines, usually descendants of the buried saints or families who have established a claim to the shrine). Rich devotees have been known to drop big bundles of cash into these boxes — sometimes "black money" from undeclared income. Pieces of rare jewellery have also been found in the boxes.

We watched the pilgrims file in, clutching, caressing, kissing, touching and feeling the grave, the railings, the doorposts — anything associated with the saint. They bowed and touched their eyelids to the grille; the lame raised themselves to rest their crippled limbs on it, praying for a miraculous cure. The most common wish is for the birth of a son — still the most desired outcome of a marriage. Most communicated with their hands folded — Hindu Namaste style — and eyes closed. Others were moved to tears at the sight of the shrine. Most brought flowers and a green *chadar* with Qur'anic inscriptions in silver or even gold threads, or Farsi or Urdu couplets in praise of the saint. The custom of the *chadar* is widespread in the subcontinent, especially in Pakistan. Some people parade them through the town with music and dancing before draping them over the grave. So many hundreds of *chadars* come, especially during the *urs* season, that the organizers have to keep clearing the piles. The ones with the holy inscriptions are saved for use on other religious occasions; the plain ones are distributed to the poor.

Was there a contradiction here? Haroon had explained that grave worship runs counter to the spirit and injunctions of Islam, which forbids even the making of permanent graves, let alone tomb worship. In Saudi Arabia, the kings are buried in unmarked graves. There is no grave for Ibn-e-Saud, the founder of modern Saudi Arabia, or for King Faisal, its most popular king so far. Despite theological warnings from some scholars, however, the practice survives, both in Shiite Iran — where people venerate the graves of their imams — and also in the Indian subcontinent, where the majority of Muslims are Sunnis. The practice has a hold on the masses, and politicians and film stars often pose for a "photo-op" beside the shrines, green *chadar* in hand, as a way of boosting their popularity.

Noon in Sehwan. The mass of worshippers crowded the narrow streets, spiralled out into the open spaces by the tributary of the Indus that flows by the town and continued up the hill to encircle the nearby hill fort built by Alexander the Great. The townsfolk welcomed the visitors by opening their doors. There are no real hotels here, so most visitors stay with friends or as paying guests or, if they are poor, as most of them are, simply camp on the sidewalks and the open ground as if at an open-air rock festival, rolling out their beds, lighting little fires for warmth and smoking their *hookahs* (standard big ones or small, cone-shaped, portable clay ones — filled not just with tobacco).

The smell of *bhang* (a local intoxicant) and *chars* (hashish) was pervasive. Some lucky ones had found places under makeshift bamboo-and-thatch halls put up and rented out by entrepreneurs. The encampment stretched all the way up to Lal Bagh (Red Garden), more than a mile from the shrine. The saint was said to have spent several years in spiritual exercises at Lal Bagh before settling in Sehwan, and many of the devotees began their pilgrimage there. They crawled under a fallen tree beneath which the saint had prayed, hoping for a cure for their physical ailments. They climbed three nearby hills to the shrines of three saints who were Lal Shahbaz's contemporaries. Then they started their trek towards the main shrine, alone, or with their families, or in groups, clutching their *chadars*. Some had come equipped with drums, to dance all the way. There was no escaping the beat of drums.

A group of professional dancers had come from Khanpur in the district of Rahim Jar Khan in the province of Punjab. Dressed in red, yellow and green, with *ghungroo* (dancing bells) tied to their ankles, they danced in the street. Their leader played a *chumta* (a two-foot-long steel tweezer that is usually used for picking up and arranging hot coals on a barbecue), while others played drums. The dancers swayed their heads from side to side, creating a whirl of their long hair.

Almost everyone wore a *gahna* (lei or garland of paper flowers, predominantly red), a symbol of their visit to the holy site. The pilgrims would wear it for several days. They were having their photographs taken in front of the shrine, for a lifelong memento of the pilgrimage. Professional cameramen with Polaroids did a brisk business.

The main street of Sehwan had become an enormous shopping bazaar. We saw high-piled mounds of nuts and dried fruit — raisins, almonds, pistachios, dates; also fresh orange and sugar cane juice for sale. There were *cha khanas* (tea houses), that speciality of the countryside, every few steps, with the tea kettle on an open pit, next to barbecued chicken and beef on skewers; sweet shops full of such Eastern desserts as *halwa, gulab jamun, jalebi* and sugared coconut rice; butchers selling live chickens and goats for slaughter on the spot. Also on offer were prayer beads, copper tablets with Qur'anic inscriptions and other tacky religious knick-knackery; silver jewellery and brightly coloured glass bangles by the thousands; and, as we got closer to the shrine, devotional music tapes, plus roses, rose garlands, rose water and *chadars* to put on the saint's grave.

There was a vast range of support services. The drinking-water man walked around with his leather water bag slung over his back. He sold water by the glass after buying it from a vendor with a large water barrel on a donkey cart. Sturdy young men offered a palanquin service to carry the old, the sick and the infirm through the crowds to the shrine. There were sidewalk shoeshine boys; barbers offering a shave and a haircut on street corners; and many *langars* (free soup kitchens) run by entrepreneur cooks whom the rich paid on the spot to feed a certain number of beggars, or to distribute food to the devotees camped everywhere. The big soup kitchen in one part of town was run on donations from Pathan truck drivers, the ones who like to decorate their trucks with hundreds of brightly coloured, painted designs, slogans and streamers. There was so much free food that a visitor could go through the three-day *urs* not paying a penny for meals. That's what all the *fakirs* did.

Fakirs were everywhere. Although *fakir* literally means "beggar," here the word takes on spiritual significance. Pakistan has hundreds of *fakirs*, the Muslim equivalent of the Hindu yogi or swami — people who, following in the footsteps of many saints and yogis, renounce worldly wealth and live off temples and shrines and offerings.

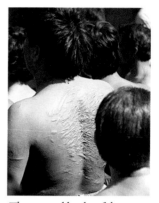

Fakirs wear red around Sehwan, the colour of Lal Shahbaz, but green elsewhere, the colour of Islam and of most other saints, much as Hindu ascetics wear saffron, the holy Hindu colour. They keep their hair long and wear long beards. They sport necklaces of *tasbeeh* (prayer beads). Others have small bells, or even gongs hanging around their necks. Some sling a *kisto* (begging bowl), usually made from the dried half-shell of a seaweed seed, around their necks. Many carry a musical instrument such as a *yak taro* (single-string Sindhi sitar), or they may accompany their hymn-singing and praise of the local saint on little cymbals or a conch shell. Some of the *fakirs* are

The scarred backs of the matamees — *too involved and in too much of a trance to care. They reminded me of Burton's observation that "the wonderful and the horrible are so closely connected that the former appears to lead directly to the latter."*

genuine holy men searching for spirituality; many, however, have chosen the life simply as one way to survive in a land where unemployment is so widespread that governments cannot calculate its real rate. A great deal of talent goes into devising ingenious ways of begging.

The *urs* had attracted hundreds of transvestites — or *hijras*, as they are called here — 1,500 to 2,000 by local estimates. They tend to have a good time at any *urs* because they are more tolerated and accepted here than anywhere else. Although mosques are off limits to *hijras*, they are allowed into saints' shrines.

The appeal of the saint Lal Shahbaz clearly cut across cultural, tribal and language divisions. Gathered together here were Sindhis, Punjabis, Pathans and Balochs. We heard at least five languages spoken: Urdu, Sindhi, Punjabi, Pashto and English. Both Hindus and Muslims were here.

Flagellants were here, too. The next procession that came by caused a considerable stir. There were wailing shouts of "Ya Ali, ya madad," and "Hasan, Husain," followed by a rhythmic thud. These were the *matamees* (mourners), minority Shiite Muslims who, in the Islamic lunar calendar month of Muharram, publicly mourn the anniversary of the deaths of Imams Hasan and Husain, the two sons of Caliph Ali, who died in the seventh century A.D.

battling Yazid, the personification of evil. Although this was not the death anniversary of Hasan and Husain, a good 200 of their mourners were here as a mark of respect for the local saint who also was a Shiite.

At least 100 of the flagellants were bare-chested. The lead crier called out "Ya Ali" (Oh Ali), and they swayed to the left, the left hand stretched out, shouted "Ya madad" (Oh help) and vigorously slapped their chests. Then they swung right, as the crier called out "Ya Ali," stretching out the right hand, shouted "Ya madad" and again slapped their chests, which had become quite red. Sweat glistened on their bodies in the bright sunshine. They were following a 1,400-year-old tradition that originated in Shia-majority Iran and is practised by Shias everywhere. The rhythmic chanting and beating continued, as the crier switched the call to "Ya Hasan" and the mourners responded with "Ya Husain."

As they made slow progress, they created a space in their midst for three young men carrying chains to step into the circle. Closer examination revealed the brutality of these instruments: from their oval-shaped hand grips dangled four to six chains, varying in length from ten to fifteen inches and ending in curved scimitar-shaped blades with sharp pointed ends. As the

Gory flagellant dancing in the Sehwan square

Solitary horn blower at the Sehwan urs.

others beat their chests, the chain carriers flagellated their backs with these contraptions, switching them from hand to hand and swinging them over alternate shoulders to strike first the left side of the back below the shoulder, then the right. Their backs were bleeding, but they were too involved and in too much of a trance to care. The backs of many others showed welts or gashes four to five inches long. They had obviously had their turn.

Haroon questioned one flagellant: "Yes, it hurts, but only a little," said Naeem Khan. Aged about twenty-five, he had been flagellating himself with the scimitar-shaped blades for ten minutes, and before that took part in the chest-beating *matam* for at least three hours. "We apply a special mud, and it works. In three days my back is okay."

His group had all come from Multan in the Punjab and would be at it for at least another three hours, wending their way to the shrine to arrive by 6:00 p.m., the appointed hour when the shrine's big drums would roll and every-one would dance and pay devotion to the saint.

We made our way to the open area at the front of the shrine where a spon-taneous *dhamal* (drums and dancing) was already going on. Haroon talked to Taer Paksh, twenty-five, who had come all the way from a little village in the Punjab with about 200 people from his village, including all his extend-ed family. He had been here two years ago, asking for a son. His wish was granted, and so he worked for two years to raise enough funds to bring his relatives with him, as he had pledged. He was now busy distributing sweet-meats to everyone in sight.

Before dusk, following the crowd, we moved slowly back to the shrine for the evening *dhamal*, the main collective spiritual event of the day. We shoved our way along with the rest of the crowd, part of a human river, towards another small shrine, that of Pir Batula Bahar, a contemporary of Qalandar Lal Shahbaz. Everyone entering the small shrine rang the gong hanging overhead. This is the Hindu custom when entering temples. Perhaps the saint buried here was a Hindu or perhaps this was a Hindu temple at one time, as Burton had noted about many shrines in the Sindh. We then joined another crowd moving slowly towards the main shrine and battled our way to the front. Several processions seemed to merge. The crowd inched slowly through the narrow streets. Lame beggars lay prostrate in our path, some on their stomachs, some on their backs, begging bowls held out. No one tripped or fell over them. It was difficult manoeuvring our way past the bodies. I found a few coins and put them into the begging bowls. So did most of the others in the crowd. It was expected, part of the ritual.

The entrance to the shrine was very narrow, and too many people were trying to squeeze through it at once. People were removing their shoes, as they must before entering a mosque or a shrine, and placing them with hundreds of others at the entrance, where there was a shoe attendant. Then the movement of the crowd took over. We were pushed right, then left, then squeezed slowly forward towards the narrow entrance. Our guide, Nazakat, was trying to protect us. He stretched out his arm as a buffer from the press of people, allowing us to rest for a few minutes against the wall. The crowd swelled still further, then thinned a little.

We took the opportunity and moved through the narrow arched entrance into the open courtyard, past an enormous three-foot gong. The courtyard was surrounded by a fifteen-foot-deep veranda with arched Moorish openings. Other pilgrims had taken their positions in these openings hours ahead of us. The courtyard itself was full, with everyone gathered around two leather drums at least three feet in diameter and three feet high. The drummer stood to play them, and four smaller drums were played by drummers sitting cross-legged on the floor of the courtyard.

There was an air of expectancy as the drums rolled. Women gathered in front of the drums. Some of the dancers were movie stars and attracted considerable attention. At the same time, groups of people continually passed through the courtyard into the shrine's inner sanctum to lay their *chadars* and move out through another door. There was an inherent order beneath the apparent chaos. No officials directed proceedings; no police. Instead, there was physical and spiritual camaraderie, a sense of togetherness and a willingness to accommodate others, despite — or perhaps because of — all the confusion.

In a little while the family of the *sajjada-nasheen* (resident in charge) of the shrine arrived bringing *mehndi*, a paste made from leaves and used to redden a bride or bridegroom's hands and feet. The *mehndi* for the dead saint symbolizes his role as the mystic groom of the evening. The family had brought a special *chadar* to drape around the drums, and rose petals to sprinkle on them. Incense sticks were lighted and rose water was sprinkled; then the gong in the entranceway sounded the signal for the giant drums to roll. The *naubat* (the traditional roll call of the drums) boomed, filling the courtyard with its great sound, and a murmur went through the crowd — now standing with eyes closed, hands folded, facing the entrance to the shrine's inner sanctum. A single *shehnai* (reed flute) player joined in, with the melody of the *naqqara* (the traditional music of major announcements). People began swaying slowly, and their feet began to shuffle.

An outsider could not help being moved by this grand spectacle of collective devotion and spirituality. The crowd swayed rhythmically, some people raising their index fingers to the heavens, others moving in semi-circles. We swayed too. We couldn't help it. The women untied their long hair in the manner of the ascetic *fakiranis* (feminine of *fakir*) and started swinging their heads in a circling motion, until all we saw was a blur of flying hair. Some were in a trance-like state; others still had the presence of mind to dig into their pockets for money to give to the drummers. Notes were passed from hand to hand over the heads of the crowd all the way to the drummers. There was no worry about theft. No one, not even the poorest of the poor, would steal what belongs to a holy servant of the shrine.

The lights went out halfway through the *dhamal*. Darkness enveloped the courtyard, but the constant drumbeat continued. People lighted matches to see by. Torches were turned on. The ceremony continued. Many now seemed in a trance-like state. Men were crying. People stretched their hands towards the shrine, beseeching their saint for some favour. Women took out their *chadars* or their *ajraks*, holding them out in the traditional pose of begging, as if asking the saint to throw some crumbs of favour and blessing towards them. Men held up the ends of the front portion of their long *kurtas* to symbolically receive the saint's favours. Many pressed each ear between their index fingers and thumbs in the age-old Indian sign of public *taubah* (admission of guilt and asking for forgiveness of sins).

The official *dhamal* wound down in an hour, although instant *dhamals* would occur spontaneously all night, all over town. Out in the town, at 10:00 p.m., thousands of people gathered in the open-air auditorium for a Sindhi poets' *quseeda khani* (a session of poetry-reading in praise of saints). In the streets, the *hijras* performed in makeshift shelters. Devotional and other music blared everywhere. Everyone was taking part.

In the tea stalls, the *lote walis* were singing. Another feature of local Sindhi rural sex life, the *lote walis* carry the *lota*, the small, all-purpose water pitcher used around the house for washing, doing the obligatory cleansing before prayer and taking to the washroom when there is no running water supply. Their name comes from the practice of using the *lota* as a drum while singing. They usually belong to a tribe, but are among those known as *khana badosh* (nomads), who, like the gypsies, keep moving according to the seasons.

As Haroon explained: "The *lote walis* are a step lower than *mujra* dancers, who sing and dance. The *lote walis* just perform in tea houses by the roadside or the main street of the village, singing bawdy songs of love, romance and

A young hijra, *curls falling over his/her forehead, shimmied over to our guide, Nazakat Ali Fazlani. Another danced in front of us. Slim, lithe and coquettish, he was an accomplished flirt.*

mirth and entertaining the rural menfolk. But they are not prostitutes."

As the *urs* continued, in a manner true to the spirit of Qalandar Lal Shahbaz — "I know nothing except love, intoxication and ecstasy" — we went to take a closer look at the *hijras*. They were doing a brisk business of two kinds: prostitution, and putting on dancing shows in tents for the titillation of rural men. There were at least four huge tents set up along the main street of Sehwan, where the late-night shows were in full swing. We visited two of them. There was an entrance fee of ten rupees, with a bouncer controlling traffic at the entrance. There was no stage, but dozens of chairs were set up in irregular rows. Loudspeakers belted out music, mostly popular Indian and Pakistani film songs, and the *hijras* danced between the rows. They wore heavy make-up — rouge and lipstick, with *kohl* around their eyes. Most had long hair, and all wore outrageously beautiful clothes: red satin, blue brocade, long skirts with bead or mirror work shimmering in the lights, and bright gold or silver party shoes. They swayed and gyrated and twirled, some looking convincingly feminine, others in an overtly sexual parody of women. They flirted with the men, holding their hands, even sitting on their laps. But there was no kissing Western-style, for that is not culturally acceptable here in public.

A young *hijra*, Madiya, curls falling over his/her forehead, shimmied over to our guide, Nazakat Ali Fazlani. Madiya was one of a group of fifteen who had come all the way from Lahore, 1,200 miles away.

"No, I definitely don't do sex," he declared emphatically. "People keep bugging me about it, though. All I want to do is dance and be with my *hijra* friends."

Haroon interviewed him in detail and at one point, to my surprise, asked: "Is your penis cut off?" Madiya gave him a blank stare and ambled away.

Another tent, a similar scene. Many of the cross-dressers appeared to have breasts. "Half-shells of coconuts," Nazakat explained to us. They all spoke in the feminine gender. The Urdu language consistently distinguishes between genders. Haroon explained to me:

"Mai Ja Rahee Hoon." (I am going – female.)

"Mai Ja Raha Hoon." (I am going – male.)

"Mai Aa Rahee Hoon." (I am coming – female.)

"Mai Aa Raha Hoon." (I am coming – male.)

Sanam was a young hijra from Larkhana. He danced in front of us. He was seventeen. Or at least he said he was seventeen, but he looked more like twenty or twenty-one. Slim, lithe and coquettish, he was an accomplished flirt.

"I knew at age six who I was going to be," he said. "By age eleven, I decided to be a *fakir*. I am now living with my friend, Mahbish. For about a year. In Jacobabad." Haroon again tried a question about whether he had been a victim of the beastly practice of having the *hijras*' penises cut off. He replied without hesitation: "Yes, our people have it cut off. Mine too. Six months ago. In a village. No, I won't tell you the name of the place. No, it didn't really hurt that much because I did it out of pleasure. We have people in the community who know how to do it. There was a ceremony. They applied herbs and a herbal ointment. I was all right in three days. No, I did not have to have drugs for it. As I said, I did it for my pleasure, by my choice. So, it didn't hurt."

Haroon explained that this was the first *hijra* he had ever met who would admit to the practice common in the *hijra* community in the Indian subcontinent.

It was getting cold now, but the crowds were as thick as ever. This town would not sleep. We returned to our resthouse. At midnight, I shoved earplugs into my ears. I covered my head with blankets and towels, trying to cut out the incessant noise. Muffled talking and music were still audible. Drums. The occasional firecracker.

Somehow I managed to sleep, though fitfully, until the *muezzin*'s call to prayer at 6:00 a.m. the next day.

Before breakfast, we picked up our guide for the trip to Ranikot Fort, and the armed guard, and headed out of town.

About an hour from Sehwan, we turned off the main road and drove along a desert track towards the mountain range about twenty-five miles distant. This was rough and desolate country: sand, scrub, rocks, dust and brush. Our armed guards rode in the Jeep ahead of us — three guards with rifles. One stood, openly displaying his weapon, looking nervously from side to side, keeping his finger on the trigger at all times.

"This is the heart of dacoit country," said Nazakat. "When the law and order was bad two to three years ago, most of the kidnappings took place on this very road. This is because the highway hugs the hills on the right, and that is the traditional route of the Balochs into the north. Few of the law-enforcement officers know this. And to the left, half a mile away, is the Indus, beyond which lies thick forest. Dacoits would either disappear into the hills on the right or take their hostages by ferry over the Indus into the forest. I would say about eighty per cent of all the abductions in the Sindh took place right here."

The road to Ranikot was quite deserted. On our right we saw the Phiggo Thorn hills — part of a long range that runs northwest through Baluchistan all the way to Iran.

"This area is called Buk," explained Mr. Haji Khan, an officer from the Revenue Department who collects rents on this government land from grazers. "The area is good only for sheep grazing, except in the rain-fed valley between the mountains or the two artificial *nalaas*, or tributaries, which have been created by digging a four-foot ditch. Only a few tribes live here, perhaps a dozen families. Farther up there are a few more, mostly where they can collect rainwater. They are a hardy people. One village of them, in the middle of the mountains, which you will see from the fort, has been there for more than 150 years. Their name was recorded by early British surveyors.

"Most of these people are different branches of the Baloch, mainly Khosa, tribe. They either have their own flock of goats or they graze them for the owners, who, of course, don't live here. They still operate on the old system —

An armed guard on the road to Ranikot — in the heart of dacoit country.

the landlord buys the goats, leaves them in their care, and they divide up the offspring. Some of them are very good agriculturalists; they know how to maximize the use of rainwater, which they divert into little ditches for four or five years to make that patch of land productive. They create a little new topsoil every year like that.

"They use the rainwater to sprout such plants as cantaloupe. We used to think cantaloupe needs a lot of watering. But these people know that cantaloupe needs a lot of water only until it sprouts, after which it doesn't. So they sprout them in the short rainy season. They are true environmentalists."

After half an hour over very rough terrain and a jarring track, we arrived at the entrance to Ranikot Fort.

It is possible that Ranikot is the largest stone fort in the world. It is about twenty miles in circumference, and some parts of the great wall date back to the Stone Age.

On the west bank of the Indus, Ranikot is about nineteen miles southwest of Sann in the Dadu district and about forty-seven miles from Hyderabad. The entrance to the fort is impressively grand. Some historians believe the fort was built before the arrival of Alexander the Great in the Sindh in 326 B.C. And many scholars feel that the Neron Kot, purportedly conquered by the Arab general Muhammad bin Qasim in A.D. 712, was in fact Ranikot. As I mentioned earlier, there are records showing that the fort was repaired early in the nineteenth century by the Talpur rulers.

Inside the great fort are two other small forts. Mir Kot, also called Mir Garh, is built on a cliff about 500 feet above sea level, while the other, Sher Garh (Fort of Lions), is built 1,000 feet higher. The dressed sandstone walls of the fort stretch in three directions: east, south and west, while a sheer wall of natural limestone runs along the northern perimeter. The walls of Ranikot are twelve feet thick and thirty feet high. There are sixty towers rising above the fort. The whole complex is situated on an ancient route connecting Sindh with Afghanistan, central Asia and the West.

Ranikot is deserted, although the government has built a little resthouse in the centre of the smaller fort. Some fifteen minutes after our arrival, the *chowkidar*, or resthouse keeper, arrived from the village in the valley, bringing nuts and bananas for lunch.

We could hear the sound of a camel bell coming from the nearby village. We made our way down the narrow path leading from the fort. But the village, too, appeared to be deserted, except for the solitary camel, a mangy

The vast heaps of ruins which cover the face of the country, the traces of great and important works, the concurrence of tradition, historians, and travellers, in describing its ancient glories, are so many proofs that the province was not always what it is now.

SIR RICHARD F. BURTON, 1851
Sindh, and the Races That Inhabit the Valley of the Indus

beast, trying to graze in the arid landscape. From the valley we looked up at the higher fort, Sher Garh, 1,500 feet above us.

We drove slowly away from Ranikot and the great wall of Sindh. The guard again stood with rifle at the ready, his eyes raking the landscape for signs of trouble. There was no sign of anyone until, almost at the main road, we encountered another camel, a bad-tempered beast. We cadged a ride. My first camel ride.

Then we said goodbye to our armed guards and left. Hyderabad, our first stop, was an hour and a half away; Karachi, two hours more. I passed the time in speculating about why Burton never got to Ranikot. If he had made the journey, we certainly would have known. He could not have resisted setting down his impressions of such an extraordinary place.

Mr. Mohammed Kasim was the brother of the owner of Abid Jewellers in Karachi. I heard that he had three interesting Sindh daggers: two Talpur ivory-handled weapons with gold filigree work on the spine and base of the handles; and a very old *fakir* crutch with a slender dagger fitted into the top part of the crutch. Making any sort of purchase from him wasn't easy, however. There were a lot of questions. Who was I? How had I been referred to Mr. Kasim? Finally he agreed to show me the daggers. But they weren't on the premises. I had to walk two blocks down a dark street. *Is this a kidnapping?* I wondered. Through an alleyway, up one flight of stairs, and then a lift to a fourth-floor flat. The iron gate was locked behind me. Then an iron grille. This too was locked behind me. Would I ever get out? I was shown into a side room. The door was locked again. Where was the threat: on the inside, or the outside?

Mr. Kasim proved to be a gentle, humorous man, however. Eventually, he became quite talkative. He produced the two daggers: The Talpur daggers, one large and one of medium size, had obviously belonged to a rich family. The other, the crutch of a *fakir*, would have belonged to a poor man with some need to protect himself. Mr. Kasim was asking far too much money, but they were rare items. I really wanted the daggers. I wanted the *fakir*'s crutch, too, but thought I would never get it out of Pakistan.

Then there was a problem about paying. He would not accept traveller's cheques, so I had to find a money changer, then a bank. Still no luck, so I took a taxi to the American Express office. I queued endlessly to get my signature authorized. At last, the purchase was completed, and I took my treasures back to the Sind Club.

When I returned to Canada, I learned that the two Sindhi daggers were Peshkabz daggers. Both have hilts of walrus ivory and watered blades of dark steel. The hilts have enamelled gold enrichments intricately carved on both sides. There are no sheaths, which in the olden days would have been of leather embroidered with silk and enriched with gold or silver enamelled mounts.

It is the character of their ornamentation rather than their shape that indicates that the two Sindhi daggers were more Persian than Afghan. The intricate engraving was also much more ornate than is usually found in India. Although my daggers had no precious stones, a great part of the treasure of the amirs consisted in the rubies, diamonds, pearls and emeralds with which their daggers, swords and matchlocks were adorned. Persian goldsmiths were engaged at court in enamelling and damascening, and were renowned for their artistry.

There is a peculiar Sindhi custom alluded to by Sir Henry Elliot, and mentioned in the *Táríkh-i-Sind* (*History of Sind*): namely, that the practice of dismounting before coming to close combat is common among many of the border tribes between Sindh and Rajputana. The Sindhis, unlike most Asiatic warriors, found it repugnant to fight on horseback, and prided themselves more on being foot soldiers than calvary.

The *Táríkh-i-Sind* says, "When they saw the army of the Moghals, they dismounted from their horses, took their turbans from off their heads, and, binding the corners of their mantles or outer garments to one another, they engaged in battle; for it is the custom of the people of Hind and Sind, whenever they devote themselves to death, to descend from their horses...."

Finally, the time came for our last dinner with Hamid Akhund. As a farewell gift, he gave me a bound copy of *Sind Revisited*, the one reprinted by his department, at his initiative. "Burton's books carry a lot of information on Sindh in the mid-nineteenth century," he said. "It is essential that the record be brought out and made widely available, even if much of what Burton had to say about Sindhis was not complimentary."

He had been looking for a first edition of *Sind Revisited* for many years. He finally found one in the Sindhi Adabi (literary) Board five years ago, but its first ten pages were missing. He ordered it reset and printed anyway, hoping to find the missing ten pages somewhere else. He didn't. The book was run off from page eleven on. It was not until the summer of 1992 that he laid his hands on another copy from a friend in Lahore. "That's why you will find a different paper stock at the beginning — the title, the dedication to General Walter Scott, the preface by Burton, the Table of Contents, and the first ten pages." The reprint was officially released in Karachi in January while we were there.

He continued to ruminate about Burton, and made a most telling point, one that has escaped most Western scholars: "I know what he wrote is true about *one segment* of Sindhi society. He recorded street life and the life of ordinary people. He obviously had no access to the aristocracy or to our intellectuals or writers or our poets or our theologians or our nawabs or our *syed*s, the nobility and the scholarly classes — most of whom were involved in anti-British activity and would not have even talked to a Brit, even if he was posing as a Sindhi Muslim. But the ordinary people would have been, and

287

clearly were, fascinated by a white man who took the trouble to learn their languages and who wore the same clothes they did; they welcomed him amid their ranks and they spoke to him. Those are the types of people Burton had access to, and he wrote about them — generally very well, especially when I get the sense that he was giving an eyewitness account. So, Burton's was not a complete record of the Sindh. It was a partial record of what was easily accessible to him, but it's a very good partial record. It's so good I wish he had had access to the Sindh society he did not see, or could not see.

"What I don't like, the only thing I resent, is that he called Sindh the 'Unhappy Valley.' It was not. It was then a happy valley. Maybe it's an unhappy valley today, given our political problems. But it certainly was not an unhappy valley then."

Sehwan—a procession during the urs. A town that is normally home to 30,000 people mushrooms with the arrival of more than 600,000 pilgrims.

Goa, and the Blue Mountains

In these latitudes, man lives only between the hours of seven P.M. and midnight. The breeze gives strength to smoke and converse; our languid minds almost feel disposed to admire the beauty of the moonlit sea, the serenity of the air, and the varying tints of the misty coast.

RICHARD F. BURTON
***Goa, and the Blue Mountains*, 1851**

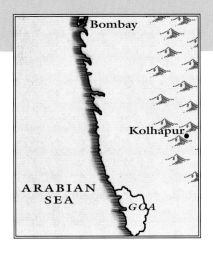

11

GOA, AND THE BLUE MOUNTAINS

At 6:00 a.m., the *muezzin* call to prayer. It was my last morning in the Sindh. For once our driver, Gul Hassan, was on time. He would get a good tip. He had been exasperating but loyal. I liked him.

The station wagon that was to take us to the Karachi airport refused to start. However, with the help of two bearers at the Sind Club, we pushed the van in the darkness across the parking lot and somehow managed to get the thing going. A last hug for Mohammed Younus, who had wakened me and looked after me for my entire stay at the Sind Club. He is an old man and was quivering with emotion. Probably I would never see him again.

We arrived at the Karachi airport in good time, and I said goodbye to Haroon Siddiqui. He had been fabulous. I couldn't have done the Sindh trip without him.

I arrived in Bombay at about 11:00 a.m., half an hour ahead of Karachi time, to find a note waiting for me from Mahnoor Yar Khan, Haroon's gracious sister-in-law, to say that she had organized the trip to Goa and to the Nilgiris, and that I should pick her up at 8:30 a.m. on Sunday, February sixth, at her sister's apartment just down from the Royal Bombay Yacht Club. She was involved in the Indian Film Festival until then, but would be filling in for Haroon on this important last leg of the journey. This was good news. I would certainly need a translator — a vital part of the journey.

Generally a Nath or large gold or silver ring worn by married women only in the right or left nostril. Secondly, a Bulo or small ring inserted in the cartilage between the nostrils, and allowed to hang over the upper lip. Among the wealthy it is set with coral, pearls or precious stones. The poor content themselves with a bit of silver made in the form of a drop, and called a "Paro." Thirdly, a Mundhi, or finger ring of gold, with a ruby, turquoise or diamond inserted into it. The less expensive ones are enameled, the cheapest are of plain metal.

The number of jewels depends, of course, upon the wealth of the parties; among the very rich, large sums of money are thus expended.

SIR RICHARD F. BURTON, 1851
Sindh, and the Races That Inhabit the Valley of the Indus

Previous page: Fort Aguada in Goa. Fishing boats coming in with their day's catch and fishermen mending their nets, silhouetted against the setting sun.

The next day — the day before I was to leave for Goa — I went out to the Elephanta Caves in the morning. This was my last chance to see one of Bombay's major attractions, a reminder of one era of India's past glory. I left Apollo Bunder by boat at about 9:00 a.m. and, after an hour's journey out from Bombay into the Arabian Sea, arrived at the island of Elephanta — six miles from the shore, but still inside the harbour.

Elephanta Caves sculpture on an island in Bombay Harbour.

Very little is known about the history of the Elephanta Caves. The name is derived from a colossal stone elephant which was found on the island and which now stands near the museum in the Victoria Gardens in Bombay. The local name of the island is Gharapuri, derived probably from the ancient Agrahara-Puri, but the name was changed by the Portuguese when they discovered the large stone elephant near the landing place.

Some time between the sixth and eighth centuries A.D., Bombay experienced the Golden Age of the late Guptas, and it is probable that the talented Gupta artists created these beautiful sculptures of stone carved out of the caves—all devoted to the worship of Shiva. The facial expressions on the stone carvings show strength, love and peace beautifully and powerfully. The carvings are enormous and fit perfectly into the natural relief of the caves and their structure. I felt both moved and calmed by my encounter with the art of the caves.

Maharashtrian fisherwomen inhabit the island and tend the boats. They wear colourful sari dress, with part of the skirt tucked up between the legs so as to get the hem out of the way.

One hundred steps lead up to the Elephanta Caves. All along the side of the steep climb vendors and entertainers provided a bazaar-like atmosphere, which included some rather aggressive monkeys! In all, my visit took about two hours, and I found it an absorbing and relaxing way to spend a morning.

I spent the afternoon walking and driving around Burton's Bombay. Bombay's architecture is so British that the walk from the docks to the old fort, to the Horniman Circle, past the Asiatic Society Library to Watson's Hotel and then Elphinstone College was like taking a walk in Victorian England — except for the Indian faces! It all seemed so different from when I had first seen Bombay a few weeks before. I felt much more at home, and also as if I was in fact walking in Burton's footsteps.

I knew quite a bit about where the Burtons went in 1876 and what they saw. They stayed at Watson's Hotel. They took a trip to the Elephanta Caves. They saw the Malabar Hills and the Valkeshwar Temple, the one with the tank, which we had visited on our first day in Bombay. They also went to the

Parsee Tower of Silence and the Bhindi Bazaar; but I really doubt that Burton took Isabel to see the red light district!

I decided to go there for one more look. This *was* on Burton's itinerary in the 1840s, if not 1876. One of the first things he discovered here was how well and conveniently and without hypocrisy prostitution in India mixes with commerce and the daily life of the neighbourhood. The bodies are for sale, along with the other commodities in this bustling, commercial centre adjacent to the Bhindi Bazaar, in the heart of old Bombay. Unlike many North American cities, the population centres of India have always had red light districts against which neighbours wage no campaigns. And unlike European centres, where municipal authorities feel the need to define and zone and regulate activities in the red light districts, the cities, towns and villages of India just let the prostitutes alone. This absence of moral posturing would have appealed to a man like Burton, who scoffed at Victorian prudery.

India offered Burton a range of sexuality unimaginable to Victorian England or even today's liberated Western world — a session of romantic, suggestive, Urdu or Persian poetry by a singing girl, in a palace or at a middle-class party; the pornographic verses of a *lote wali* at a country fair; an evening of flirtation with a scented, flower-bedecked *mujra* dancer at her *kotha* (brothel); a whole menu of homosexuality, with young boys or manicured men or a bevy of *hijras*; the straightforward sex of a quick visit to a prostitute in the red light district; the semi-permanent arrangement of a Shiite Muslim *muta* marriage; or the mutually beneficial relationship with a *bubu*.

India understands the truth about sex far better than the West: it is the bedrock of human relations; it is natural; and there is no point in hiding it, let alone trying to control it in the name of religion or social mores. For a man of Burton's energy and appetite, this was paradise on earth, to be enjoyed fully!

Just as important to him was another central tenet of Indian life: erotica co-exists easily with two other essential elements in society — commerce and spirituality. In fact, a range of spirituality — Hinduism, Islam, Sikhism, Christianity, Zoroastrianism, Judaism....

This Indian genius for creating a seamless web of religion, sexuality, and the day-to-day business of earning a living is to be found right in the red light district of Bombay: semi-nude prostitutes beckoning customers into their tiny hovels that abut the sidewalk, next door to busy shops filled with the sacred iconography of all of India's religions — incense burning by framed pictures of this or that deity in the pantheon of Hindu gods or the oil lamp burning in the business of the fire-worshipping Parsee, or the sign decorating the shop of a Muslim: "Everything is in the hands of God!"

On Sunday, as arranged, Mahnoor Yar Khan and I flew to Goa, arriving at about noon. I instantly noticed how much cleaner the air was. What a relief

it was to breathe fresh, pure air again. I could see at once why Goa and the Nilgiris were chosen for convalescent leave.

By the mid-nineteenth century, Goa was little more than a backwater, an imperial remnant. The Portuguese had conquered it in 1510. It was a vibrant place then, but its fortunes declined.

During the Napoleonic wars, British forces occupied Goa. The Portuguese refused an offer from the British government to purchase the colony for half a million pounds in 1839, maintaining possession of the territory until India annexed the state in 1961, more than 100 years after Burton arrived there.

The six months that Burton spent in Goa and the Nilgiris in 1847 were official sick leave. A cholera epidemic had swept through the Sindh, and Burton became seriously ill.

He travelled in a light, lateen-rigged transport boat down the west coast of India from Bombay to Goa, then to Calicut and other areas on the coast of Malabar. He also learned of and made a journey to the village of Seroda, which was famous in those days for its *bayaderes*, or dancing girls. The writer Mario Cabral e Sa, whom I was to meet at the end of my visit to Goa, had something to say about this visit, suggesting that Burton's curiosity cost him a bad beating on the one night he spent in the town.

With car and driver we drove first to the old City of Goa, on the way passing Fort Aguada, which Burton sailed past, beside the Mandovi River, along which Burton journeyed to Panaji (or Panjim, as he called it) when he first arrived, and eventually to Betim village. Bordering the river were many mangrove swamps, and Betim village itself presented a very picturesque scene of fishermen mending their blue nets. There was a strong smell of fish in the air. There were also many pigs wandering among the village houses.

We continued on to the Old City of Goa, where the Portuguese poet Luis de Camoëns had spent some time. Burton was enthralled by adventurers and had read widely on Portugal's golden age of discovery. Camoëns's poem *The Lusiads*, about the Portuguese voyages of exploration and discovery, profoundly influenced Burton.

We stopped outside the Convent of Santa Monica, where we knew Burton had tried to abduct a young nun. Burton told the story as if it had happened to someone else, a young British lieutenant "who knew everything," who could "talk to each man of a multitude in his own language...."

As Burton recalls the tale — which he says was related to him by Salvador, his Portuguese guide — the young lieutenant came across a pretty white

Fisherwomen in Goa wear colourful sari dress, with part of the skirt tucked up between the legs to get the hem out of the way.

Old photograph of the Convent of Santa Monica.

nun, a teacher, with "large black eyes, a modest figure and a darling of a smile." He convinced her, after several surreptitious meetings, to abscond with him and leave the convent, which she obviously hated; but the carefully planned abduction went awry. With the Portuguese guide tending the get-away boat, the young officer, heavily disguised and in black-face, stealthily entered the convent in the dead of night to capture his affectionate prize. Unfortunately, in the darkness the young officer entered the wrong room and instead carried away the sub-prioress. While effecting his getaway, the officer "lingered for a few minutes ... crept out of the room, closed the door outside, passed through the garden, carefully locked the gate, whose key he threw away, and ran towards the place where he had appointed to meet Khudadad [his accomplice], and his lovely burthen. But imagine his horror and disgust when, instead of the expected large black eyes and the pretty little rose-bud of a mouth, a pair of rolling yellow balls glared fearfully in his face, and two big black lips, at first shut with terror, began to shout and scream and abuse him with all their might...."

"'Khudadad, we have eaten filth,' said my master, 'how are we to lay this she-devil?'

"'Cut her throat?' replied the ruffian.

"'No, that won't do. Pinion her arms, gag her with your handkerchief, and leave her — we must be off instantly.'"

And thus ended the romantic adventure. There is little doubt that the story was about Burton's own personal experience.

The wall he was supposed to have climbed over was still there. It would

In appearance these fishermen are an uncommonly ill-favoured race; dark, with ugly features.... Their characters, in some points, show to advantage. They are said to be industrious, peaceful, and honest as can be expected.

Sir Richard F. Burton, 1851
Goa, and the Blue Mountains

have been quite a climb, as the wall was a good twelve feet high. There were nuns in blue habits in the foreground. Not far away was the St. Augustine Tower brilliantly silhouetted against the afternoon sun.

Our next stop was at the Bom Jesus Basilica, almost certainly the richest church in all of Goa. The Basilica, built in the sixteenth century, receives many visitors, not so much because it is sacred to the Infant Jesus, but because inside the Basilica is the tomb of St. Francis

Old photograph of the Bom Jesus Basilica — almost certainly the richest church in all Goa.

Xavier, whose body had survived many moves and other indignities: a toe was once bitten off by a female worshipper, and on another occasion an arm was severed and taken to Rome. Eventually, he came to his extravagant resting place here. Close by is the Se Cathedral — an enormous, white building from the late sixteenth century, by far the largest church in Goa. At one point, Burton checked out the accommodations in a refurbished "prison," visiting it by moonlight and continuing his moonlit walk in the neighbourhood of the cathedral.

Although Goa is approximately 70 per cent Hindu and only 30 per cent Christian, it has far more Christian churches than Hindu temples. This, I learned later, was because the Portuguese destroyed many temples when they first arrived in Goa.

Goa is a melting pot. Most people visualize Goa as a land with a predominantly Catholic population, with more churches than sinners. However, the truth is far different. Goa is unique. It is very un-Indian (as distinct from anti-Indian). It is a blend of East and West, but an East which is much more ancient than Hinduism, and a West much less profligate than that of the marauding mariners of the Renaissance.

Before we drove back along the coast to Panaji, we passed Viceroy's Arch, which Burton certainly would have entered, and the Church of St. Cajeton, which was built in the style of St. Peter's Basilica in Rome. We also walked around the Secretariat Building, once a Muslim palace and later a Portuguese fort.

Panaji is a sleepy, pleasant town, entirely Portuguese-speaking. Its best view is from the Church of Our Lady of the Immaculate Conception — another white building. Down below the town flows the wide Mandovi River, cutting

Nomadic women, heavily ornamented. They move up and down the Goan coast with the seasons, trading and telling fortunes.

through lush countryside with palm trees, paddy fields of rice and groves of mango, papaya and jackfruit. The old Portuguese section of Panaji with its windows, churches, wells, balconies and porches was very quaint. There were crosses everywhere, one in a niche in a wall with flowers — almost like a shrine.

We drove back to Fort Aguada in time to see the sunset over the Arabian Sea. Fishing boats coming in with their day's catch and fishermen mending their nets were silhouetted against the setting sun.

We had dinner that night on a stone patio overlooking the Arabian Sea. The sound of the heavy surf below us was mesmerizing, and the cool breezes reminded us that we were far, far away from pollution and traffic. Here there were only fishermen, outrigger canoes, and the occasional Banjaran woman carrying water to some unknown spot beyond Fort Aguada. Dinner was grilled squid, garlic and fried onions, washed down with *feni* — first the cashew-flavoured and then the coconut drink. For dessert *bi bink*, a Portuguese speciality. Lots of eggs! Very rich. I poured myself into bed quite early. The coolness of the air-conditioned room came as something of a shock. I hadn't slept in air-conditioning for some time and wasn't used to it. I turned it off.

After a 7:30 a.m. breakfast of papaya, toast, honey and two cups of coffee, we drove the forty-five or so kilometres to Seroda through the Old City of Goa, Banastrim, Kundai, Mardol, Ponda and Borim. We visited the Malm fish market on the banks of the Mandovi River opposite Panaji and saw there the Konkani fishermen and women, who move from place to place according to the season. Pigs were very much part of the scene. They are a moving sanitary disposal unit for excrement and refuse. Burton noticed them, too: "That Panjim is a Christian town appears instantly from the multitude and variety of the filthy feeding hogs, that infest the streets. The pig here occupies the social position that he does in Ireland, only he is never eaten when his sucking days are past."

His description of this area, though not particularly pleasant, was very vivid: "Panjim loses much by close inspection. The streets are dusty and dirty, of a most disagreeable brick colour, and where they are paved, the pavement is old and bad. The doors and window-frames of almost all the houses are painted green, and none but the very richest admit light through anything more civilized than oyster-shells. The balcony is a prominent feature, but it presents none of the gay scenes for which it is famous in Italy and Spain."

He tells us how he and his fellow officers came to be interested in visiting Seroda:

> *Now it so happened that all three of us had been reading and digesting a rich account of Seroda, which had just appeared in one of*

the English periodicals. We remembered glowing descriptions of a village, inhabited by beautiful Bayaderes, governed by a lady of the same class — Eastern Amazons, who permitted none of the rougher sex to dwell beneath the shadow of their roof-trees — high caste maidens, who, having been compelled to eat beef by the "tyrannical Portuguese in the olden time," had forfeited the blessings of Hindooism, without acquiring those of Christianity, — lovely patriots, whom no filthy lucre could induce to quit their peaceful homes: with many and many etceteras, equally enchanting to novelty-hunters and excitement-mongers.

We unanimously resolved to visit, without loss of time, a spot so deservedly renowned. Having been informed ... that we should find everything in the best style at Seroda, we hired a canoe, cursorily put up a few cigars, a change of raiment, and a bottle of Cognac to keep out the cold; and, a little after sunset, we started for our Fool's Paradise.

We arrived in Seroda by car, not by boat as Burton did. It didn't seem much of a town, but by all accounts it was famous 150 years ago for its Nautch girls and entertainment houses. Burton seemed to have had a good experience here with the Nautch girls, and made some interesting observations on the colour, caste and creed of his entertainers. He and his companions stayed the night, complained about being fleeced and eventually visited the house of a certain Major G___, an Englishman who had married a Nautch girl and had died a Hindu. He visited the Major's tomb too.

We were shown his tomb, or rather the small pile of masonry which marks the spot where his body was reduced to ashes — a favour granted to him by the Hindoos on account of his pious munificence. It is always a melancholy spectacle, the last resting-place of a fellow-countryman in some remote nook of a foreign land, far from the dust of his forefathers — in a grave prepared by strangers, around which no mourners ever stood, and over which no friendly hand raised a tribute to the memory of the lamented dead. The wanderer's heart yearns at the sight. How soon may not such fate be his own?

Burton seems to have been fascinated with the deaths and burial places of Englishmen who had come to the East before him and who had either "gone native" or become scholars and given themselves, as he did, to the local culture.

We drove to the other side of the Mandovi River and to Margao. This was a much bigger town and much busier. For a little while we walked around its busy streets. I was determined to do this because I wanted a photo of the nine-foot-high, bronze statue of Camoëns, which I discovered had been moved in 1982 from outside the cathedral to the safety of the local museum.

Burton was obsessed with Camoëns, and I feel he must have identified with the Portuguese poet's adventurous life. Burton himself stated that Camoëns was "one of the most romantic and adventurous of an age of adventure and romance." Burton would have loved to have lived Camoëns's life: "exposed in manhood to the extremes of vicissitudes, to intense enjoyment and 'terrible abysses'; lapsing about middle age into the weariness of baffled hope: and ending comparatively early in the deepest gloom of disappointment, distress, and destitution, the Student, the Soldier, the Traveller, the Patriot, the Poet, the Mighty Man of Genius, thus crowded into a single career, the efforts, the purpose, the events of half a dozen...."

Camoëns did have a romantic, tragic and extraordinary life. It is easy to see why Burton was so captivated by his story. He was born near Lisbon in 1524. As a young man, he fell in love with a thirteen-year-old, Caterina de Ataide, a romance which eventually led to a duel with Caterina's brother. Camoëns was exiled. He returned two years later, fought again and was exiled again. He lost his right eye in a skirmish in Africa and returned to Portugal. A street fight six years later put him in prison, but he was pardoned on the condition that he go into exile again, this time to India. He saw Caterina only once more, then embarked on his six-month voyage to India in 1553, during which trip he began work on *Os Lusiadas* (*The Lusiads*), a romantic story dramatizing the conquests of the Portuguese in the Indies. He hated India, and the wealth that he sought eluded him. He was sent to China but returned to India in 1558, after being shipwrecked off Cambodia on the way. It continued to be a tale of tragedy. He learned of Caterina's death, and when he finally reached Goa he was imprisoned on a technicality—yet another of the many prison terms the poet was to endure. He hated Goa, and his fortunes varied as did his private life. After nearly seventeen years of frustration, Camoëns decided to return to Portugal, but when he reached Mozambique he was imprisoned again, this time for debt. Eventually in 1750, he reached Lisbon, where his talents were spurned by his home country. He was reduced to begging. A decade later, in 1580, he died a pauper. Only now is Camoëns acknowledged as being one of Portugal's greatest poets.

Burton was certainly influenced by Camoëns and his writings, and later translated *The Lusiads*. In reading Burton's translation it is easy to see parallels to his own life of adventure.

Goa is a palimpsest upon which the vagaries of history have been traced, erased and rewritten time and time again. Kingdoms rose and fell in a baffling sequence. The vanished capitals have long since yielded place to ghosts and jackals; but history, myth and legend are alive.

MARIO CABRAL E SA,
Goa

On my last morning in Goa, I had an interview with the journalist and writer Mario Cabral e Sa. He lived on the small island of Diva, a short ferry ride from the town of Ribandar. We had agreed to meet soon after breakfast, as early as I could get there.

Excited and impatient, I checked out immediately after breakfast and headed for Ribandar, along the river bank, up the palm-fringed road and to the ferry platform. The ferry leaves every hour for the island. Diva is in the middle of the Mandovi River overlooking the Old City of Goa. Its people mainly farm and fish for a living.

Some of the oldest houses in Goa are on the island. Mario Cabral e Sa's house, on the corner of a quiet street, was very Portuguese in style. His father's house was opposite his and was at least 200 years old. This was quaint, suburban Goan living. Mario Cabral's house, probably built at the turn of the century, was spacious, roomy and cool, with high ceilings and a stone floor. It was un-

Mario Cabral e Sa, journalist, author and opinionated historian.

cluttered, furnished with old furniture and a few antiques. Old Portuguese glass lamps hung from the beams of the ceiling. Outside, magenta and white bougainvillaea covered the front of the house.

Mario himself — bearded, greying and enthusiastic about Goa and its people — welcomed us warmly. He was well-read, particularly about the Portuguese. He was also very critical of other writers, particularly the British. I could see that he wasn't really happy about the British involvement in Goa. He also claimed to know a lot about Burton and was certainly very opinionated about him

"You know Burton's story about the nun at the Santa Monica Convent? I think it is completely made up. He made several other attempts to abduct nuns from convents here. These might be true. But certainly the story related to him about the Santa Monica Convent is all made up. Burton recounts it in the third person as if it is told to him about a young English officer — presumably himself. Why he adopted the third person I have no idea. There certainly was some hanky-panky going on between the nuns and the friars opposite at St. John of God. There was actually a passage under the road between the buildings. The nuns won't admit it, but there was. Tiny skeletons have been found in the passage."

Mario Cabral also commented on Burton's trip to Seroda. "Burton definitely went to Seroda. He would go a long way for female intrigue and companionship. I'm sure his story is true. There is a folktale here in Seroda that a *farangi* (foreigner), a Britisher, was beaten up for intruding and interfering with a local seraglio or house of the temple dancers. If you read between the lines of Burton's account, he mentions a 'very unsavoury experience.' I think it was Burton who was beaten up. He was always asking questions and interfering. If you compare his experience here with that later on [in 1860] with the Mormons when he tried to find out about polygamy you will discover that he had exactly the same treatment. He was beaten up for interfering.

"He didn't have a good attitude towards the people of Goa. He never seemed to be as sensitive about the people as he was in the Sindh. Perhaps he didn't like the climate. It was hot and humid, and I suppose he was sick. He doesn't say anything good about the people or the houses.

"In his writing Burton was very precise, almost clinical, about his voyage. He was very good at documentation. But he appeared to have a superiority complex toward the Portuguese and Spaniards. Perhaps he believed the old adage: 'Europe ends at the Pyrenees.'"

Some time after noon, in brilliant sunshine, we left the island of Diva and crossed over to the mainland on the Mandovi River ferry. We were in a rush to get to the Goa airport in time to catch the 2:30 Indian Airlines flight to Bangalore.

We got to the airport in time, mainly because the plane left half an hour late. Below us, as we left Goa, we could see the long golden beaches and the palm-fringed coast. No wonder Goa is becoming one of the most popular tourist resorts in the southern hemisphere.

We had originally scheduled a night in Bangalore, but were anxious to get on with our journey up to the Nilgiris, so we hired a car and driver and drove the eighty-five miles to Mysore, first through a strangely rocky countryside, and then, as darkness fell, through the hazards of night driving in India. What an experience! It was a well-built road, but oncoming drivers blinded us with their high beams, which they seldom dimmed; and the larger lorries, enjoying their dominant position on the narrow roads, paid little or no attention to the central white line as they approached us. Our driver seemed quite used to this, however, and swerved off the road onto the shoulder as if it was quite a normal part of Indian driving.

The roads were lined with trees: rain trees, tamarind, mango, and the occasional banyan tree — with its roots cut about ten feet above the road and just out of reach of the trucks and lorries, which passed us in both directions belching black, foul-smelling, diesel fumes. The drive took more than four hours and was tense going for most of that time.

I remembered the trees particularly — a British legacy. Umbrellas over the roads. This was the India I remembered. Town after town after town. Busy, bustling.

We reached Mysore at about 9:30 p.m. Although no longer the official capital of Karnataka, Mysore is still the principal residence of the head of the former royal family, the Maharaja of Mysore. This is a city of palaces, gardens and oriental splendour, but there was little we could see in the darkness. The next day I planned to see the Maharaja's palace, an enormous late-nineteenth-century building that took more than fifteen years to build. The Maharaja still lives in part of the palace; the other part is now a hotel and open to the public.

The next day we would also make the five-hour winding drive uphill to Ootacamund, now called Udhamangalam. I felt strange. All this was getting very close to my own childhood again—my personal history in India. I had lived in Ooty. I was eleven years old when I went to Breeks Memorial School in Ootacamund, in 1946. Almost fifty years had passed. How would it feel to see it all again?

It really is odd that Burton didn't write much about Mysore, particularly as the British had such a strong presence there. He must have been here some time, as he comments in his Goa book that, "After the dusty flats of Mysore," the feelings inspired by the view of the ravine separating the Oolacul from the Coonoor Range up in the Nilgiris were like those "with which you first gazed upon the 'castled crag of Drachenfels,' when you visited it en route from monotonous France, uninteresting Holland, or unpicturesque Belgium."

This is the town where Hyder Ali (1728-82), a Muslim, deposed the Raja in 1761 to become the ruler of Mysore. Later, when the British refused to support him against his Indian enemies, Hyder Ali invaded British territory and was narrowly defeated near Madras, coming closer than any other Indian ruler to ousting the British from southern India. His son, Tipu Sahib (1749-99), was Sultan of Mysore from 1782 to 1799. An excellent administrator in his own state, Tipu Sultan was a determined opponent of British power in India and entered into a tentative alliance with the French. Though defeated by Cornwallis in 1792, he continued his opposition and was eventually killed by the British while defending his capital, Seringapatam.

Today Mysore is a major city with a population of almost a million. Industrial expansion has created a varied texture in the personality of the town, in which thick traffic clogs streets still rich with the remnants of the royal past.

We had a quick breakfast at 7:00 a.m and were off again along the tree-lined, British-built road to the hill town of Ootacamund. We stopped first, though, for a brief look at the Maharaja's palace, which I had seen only once before as an eleven-year-old. It is immense, an Indo-Saracenic mixture of Hindu and Islamic architecture where the architect's imagination has run wild, creating a monument to a whole array of Eastern styles. A gilded dome dominates a profusion of gateways, courtyards, lesser domes, arches, turrets, canopies, balconies, cloisters and pavilions — all intricately decorated and laid out to ensure a wide and magnificent perspective. It was beautiful in its way, and we lingered for several minutes to marvel at its splendour.

The Maharaja of Mysore's immense palace, an Indo-Saracenic mixture of Hindu and Islamic architecture.

From Goa, carried by palanquin almost all the way because he was sick, Burton travelled to the Nilgiris — the highlands — and eventually arrived at Ootacamund, the British hill station. But the English and the lifestyle in the hill station were not to his taste. He soon grew to hate "snooty Ooty," and was much more interested in visiting the bazaars and the villages of the Todas, the local tribe, and delving into native life. Two months in Goa, and about four months in the Nilgiris. That was all. Burton couldn't stand it anymore. He was bored; his health had hardly improved; and he had a serious eye infection, which he described as "rheumatic ophthalmia." His eye problems never left him, and despite another term of surveying — and perhaps spying — in the Sindh, he once again received extended convalescent leave and left for England in 1849. His Indian army career was over.

The road to Ooty is uphill all the way — 100 miles of winding effort and strain for our old Ambassador car. Zufiq, our intense and very silent driver, concentrated at the wheel, straining and urging his ancient car through the highway's tortuous twists and turns, sounding the horn on the many blind bends. Several times a downhill lorry almost sent us over the steep drop on our side of the road. Bigger was definitely better — or safer, at least! But we did reach Ooty, at about 11:00 a.m., having made better time than we expected.

Ooty is an anachronism. With its rather Scottish-appearing scenery, and its range of architecture, it still seems very British, a relic of the Raj. As you approach town there is a sign, "Welcome to Ootacamund, Queen of the Hill Stations." Kipling said Simla wore the crown. But can there be two queens?

Where does the name Ootacamund come from? Perhaps the Tamil *whotai* — a species of dwarf bamboo that grows in nearby forests; *kai* — meaning fruit or green stuff; and the Toda word *mund* — meaning hut. Therefore *who-tai-kai-mund* — Ootacamund. Anyway, everyone still calls it "Ooty." The British used to come here to Ootacamund to get away from the malaria. Walter Campbell, a spirited young highlander who described his ride up to Ooty in 1833, referring to cholera and malaria and the untimely deaths both caused, said that coming to Ooty was "like passing through the Valley of Death to Paradise!"

This queen of southern India's hill stations is much more built up now than I remember it, but it has the same old character. "Snooty Ooty" is almost at the highest point of the Nilgiris (*nila* means "blue" and *giri* means "hill"), at the very northern edge of Tamil Nadu. It was noticeably cooler than anywhere I had been in India or Pakistan. It was as a refuge from the blistering heat of the Indian summer that the town was chosen, as early as 1819, by John Sullivan. Sullivan was the first European to build a house in Ooty, and a few years later the English — and a number of Indian maharajas — followed suit. British historian Thomas Babington Macauley came to Ootacamund in 1834, and the "nonsense" poet Edward Lear forty years later. One of the governors of Madras, the Duke of Buckingham, built his

Government House here and, in about 1870, began one of the finest botanical gardens in all of India. Lord Lytton also came here when he was Viceroy of India from 1876 to 1880. All sent back glowing accounts. But clearly John Sullivan was by far the most important figure in the history of the town. By 1829 he held five times as much land in the area as all the other Europeans put together. In 1830 a military commandant was appointed to run the settlement, and eventually, in 1845, John Sullivan sold his house to Mac Murdo, the military commandant at the time.

The centre of town is dominated by an enormous artificial lake, also built by John Sullivan. British houses, British clubs and British schools. The British took advantage of the superb climate to introduce practically every conceivable type of sport and recreation: fishing, hunting, cricket, tennis, boating and horse racing. Ooty *is* a "queen."

Breeks Memorial School was still the same — a Victorian-style, red-brick building set on a hill near the centre of town. Even the spire was the same. There were kids playing in the front playground, some girls among them. That was different. But not the school. The science lab was still on the ground floor, the junior school on the second. Then up one flight of stairs to the headmaster's office. "Do you want to see the headmaster?" "No, no, no — it's all right." A kind boy gave me his Breeks Memorial School button. I thanked him. I was quite touched by the gift. The kids are very nice. They are mostly all Indian now, although they were practically all white when I was there in the mid-1940s. Then it was a school for the children of missionaries, civil servants, government officials, army officers, planters and other business people. I know it was expensive. The new, somewhat more modern buildings on the slopes around the school have changed the atmosphere a bit but not a lot. It was thrilling to be back.

We then walked up to Lushington Hall, built by another governor of Madras, right next to the Botanical Gardens. It is built on a wooded hill, a spacious English mansion at the top of a winding driveway. I remembered it well. When I was here, Lushington Hall was where students at Breeks Memorial School boarded. It is now a school in its own right, called Hebron. I walked around nostalgically. A few students had gathered outside the buildings with their parents. Was this some kind of visiting day? I didn't ask, happy to be wandering around in a semi-daze trying to remember all the schoolboy experiences I had when I was boarded here with my cousins. Strangely enough, unlike at Breeks, all the students at Hebron seemed to be European. Perhaps it was now a school for the children of diplomats.

Up over the hill behind Lushington Hall, beyond the trees, I remembered, there was a Toda village. Ootacamund began as a settlement of aboriginal Todas, sitting on the green hills with their buffalo. Now the tribe is greatly diminished in numbers. The Toda village had been absolutely out of bounds to us schoolboys, but I remember being fascinated by these people who claimed to be the original settlers of the Nilgiris. Their features were different from those of the Tamil inhabitants of Ootacamund, and they seemed lighter in colour. They lived an isolated existence with their herds of buffalo and dome-shaped thatched *munds* (or huts) strategically placed inside a low encircling stone wall. I used to sneak up to the Toda settlement for a glimpse of a different world that seemed highly exotic to me then. Where did they come from? Burton, when he was in India 100 years before me, must have been similarly fascinated, as he spent considerable time studying Telegu and Toda, both southern Indian languages, and in researching and writing about this extraordinary tribe.

Although we attempted to walk up from Lushington Hall to see the Toda village, it was now impossible to do so. The path running through the woods to the settlement was blocked by an imposing barbed-wire fence, on the other side of which was an impenetrable hedge. The only access now was through the Botanical Gardens at the base of the Lushington compound and then up the steep slope from the other side of the hill. We set out, but just as we got to the bottom of the hill the mists poured in, as they often do in the Nilgiris, and there was a heavy downpour. We were absolutely drenched by the time we found shelter under a broad umbrella tree in the Botanical Gardens. It grew strangely dark before the rain, and the mist crawled in and hung ominously over the hills behind Government House.

It was almost noon, so after retreating to our car and driver, we drove around the Ootacamund lake, through the busy market where the ever-present crowds now huddled together under bobbing umbrellas. The rain

Breeks Memorial School was still the same—a Victorian-style, red-brick building set on a hill near the centre of town. Even the spire was the same. There were kids playing in the front playground, some girls among them.

had created a small flood on the narrow market road. On the steps of the nearby Hindu temple, a young boy, his face whitened with chalk and a long skewer placed through his extended tongue, stood in the rain, begging.

We made our way up to the old Fernhill Palace for lunch. Again I remembered being brought up here as a boy. Fernhill Palace belonged to the Maharaja of Mysore, who used it as his summer retreat. I don't think it has changed very much in the last fifty years. The gardens are still the same — laid out in a formal design and overlooking the Ootacamund valley. Inside, the small summer palace has an aura of old prosperity: dark corridors, spacious rooms, hunt photographs and stuffed animals, including a large male tiger. The very polite waiters served us an English meal in English surroundings. I might well have been sitting in a country house in Devon with a magnificent view over a misty green valley.

After the rain had stopped, we headed back to the Botanical Gardens. This time we were able to walk up to the Toda settlement, and I witnessed a very different scene from what I remembered when I was a boarder at Lushington Hall. The domed, thatched huts had been replaced by concrete ones — evidently a local government donation to the Todas. Only the church or temple, in its small compound, with its original thatched roof, simple wooden fence and mud walls, looked the same. I was very disappointed, but my spirits rose again when I was told that there was a newer Toda settlement about twenty miles outside of Ootacamund near the town of Avalanche. This name rang a bell. I seemed to remember that Burton mentioned Avalanche in his writings. Before we left the Toda settlement I photographed a young chieftain in front of the temple and paid him. He looked quite regal in his white robe, but I was sad that commerce had crept into even this protected remnant of the tribal past.

We went back to the Ootacamund Market again. The sun had come out now, and we saw a completely different scene: long rows of vendors seated on the pavement selling fruit, vegetables and other produce from laden baskets. Both women and men were colourfully garbed, as Tamils generally are. The children were laughing, having fun, chasing each other and darting through the busy crowd, enjoying the clean cool air that follows a heavy rain. The streets and pavement glistened in the afternoon sun. We walked up the hill to the old Silver Market, where I hunted for knives. I found one old Mysore dagger with a silver handle; but what really fascinated me was the Tamil Nadu jewellery. Unique craftsmanship of the very highest calibre had

The "mild Hundu" as we shall miscall him.... He is remarkable for passive courage, in suffering braver than any woman: he will inflict injuries upon himself with the sang froid of a Leaena, provided you hold out to him the one inducement, wealth.

SIR RICHARD F. BURTON, 1851
Scinde; or, the Unhappy Valley

315

moulded necklaces, earrings and bangles in twenty-four-karat gold. I looked for and eventually found some I wanted to buy and set about haggling for a good price. I suppose this was expected. *I* expected it, anyway. I love poking around in these markets, mingling with the people, looking for symbols of my heritage. I had to be dragged away.

We had a lot of places of historical interest to visit before heading out of town to the Wellington Club where we were staying. Burton had referred to a number of buildings in his account: the library in the Victoria Hotel, the Roman Catholic chapel, Fernhill School, the Union Hotel, the Nilgiris Church Missionary Hall, Woodcock Hall, Stone House, the Commander's Bungalow, St. Stephen's Church. Where was Maleemund Meyni — Burton's favourite picnic spot? We drove around aimlessly, looking for landmarks. Many of the names had been changed. Where was St. Hilda's? And the Hobart School? We didn't get very far and only managed to take down a lot of names, a lot of possibilities and some questionable directions. It was getting late, however, and we had an eighteen-mile drive to Wellington and the Club.

We took the steep, twisting road down towards Coonoor and the small town of Wellington. Mahnoor Yar Khan's kindness and patience, as well as her knowledge, had assisted me greatly in Goa and Ooty, and she had also asked her uncle, a retired manager of a tea plantation and now a tea executive in Coonoor, to sign us into the Wellington Club. The club is still a very military establishment. Flanking the front door were two enormous, Victorian brass cannon, and symbols of the British military presence were everywhere — with regimental plaques, banners, lists of officers, mementos of significant

The Ootacamund Market: long rows of vendors seated on the pavement selling fruit, vegetables and other produce from laden baskets.

historical events and, of course, old rifles and swords decorating the corridors, anterooms and bar. The skins and stuffed heads of animals shot by the British and other members of the club were also still prominently displayed. It was easy to step back in time here — both mentally and physically.

It was getting dark, but I could see that the clubhouse was right on the edge of a golf course. A little farther away, past the fairway, slopes planted with tea bushes stretched up to the horizon — a very up-country atmosphere.

Two attentive bearers took my bags to my room just across the compound, and I settled down to some research and writing. Burton didn't like Ootacamund or the life here and didn't seem to have much in common with the well-heeled English army officers who were his compatriots: "You dress like an Englishman, and lead a quiet gentlemanly life — doing nothing."

No wonder he flung himself into ethnological observations and descriptions of the area. Burton actually stayed in Coonoor just two miles down the road, "Not, however, at the government bungalow—that long rambling thing perched on the hill above the little bazaar, and renowned for broken windows, fire less rooms, and dirty comfortless meals, prepared by a native of 'heathen caste.' We will patronize the hotel kept, in true English style, by Mr. Davidson, where we may enjoy the luxuries of an excellent dinner, a comfortable sitting-room, and a clean bed."

The cantonement of Ootacamund, or, as it is familiarly and affectionately termed by the abbreviating Saxon, "Ooty," is built in a punch bowl, formed by the range of hills which composes the central crest of the Neilgherries....

In August, 1847, there were a hundred and four officers on sick leave, besides visitors and those residing on the Neilgherries. The total number of Europeans, children included, was between five and six hundred. It is extremely difficult to estimate the number of the hill people. Some authorities give as many as fifteen thousand; others as few as six thousand.

RICHARD F. BURTON,
Goa, and the Blue Mountains, 1851

Burton was fascinated by the Todas. They took his mind off Ooty. Turning his attention to language studies and the inhabitants of the Nilgiris, he became engrossed with this pastoral community found only in the Nilgiri Hills. They had a strange language, looked very different from the other southern Indian inhabitants and had a curious religion and customs. Where did they come from? Were they the descendants of Scythians, Druids, Jews and Romans? Or were they merely remnants of Tamils who had migrated up from the plains of southern India? In *Goa, and the Blue Mountains*, Burton mocked the former theory, concluded that the Todas were, in fact, a southern

Indian race and described their character and customs, among them female infanticide, alcoholism, begging and prostitution.

> The Todas, as we have said before, assert a right to the soil of the Neilgherries.... Their lordly position was most probably the originator of their polyandry and infanticide: disdaining agriculture, it is their object to limit the number of the tribe....
>
> The appearance of this extraordinary race is peculiarly striking to the eye accustomed to the smooth delicate limbs of India. The colour is a light chocolate, like that of a Beeloch mountaineer. The features are often extraordinarily regular and handsome; the figure is muscular, straight, manly, and well-knit, without any of that fineness of hand and wrist, foot and ankle, which now distinguishes the Hindoo family, and the stature is remarkably tall. They wear the beard long, and allow their bushy, curly locks to lie clustering over the forehead — a custom which communicates to the countenance a wild and fierce expression, which by no means belongs to it. The women may be described as very fine large animals; we never saw a pretty one amongst them. Both sexes anoint the hair and skin with butter, probably as a protection against the external air; a blanket wound loosely around their body being their only garment. Ablution is religiously avoided.
>
> There is nothing that is not peculiar in the manners and customs of the Todas. Ladies are not allowed to become mothers in the huts: they are taken to the nearest wood, and a few bushes are heaped up around them, as a protection against rain and wind. Female children are either drowned in milk, or placed at the entrance of the cattle-pen to be trampled to death by buffaloes. The few preserved to perpetuate the breed, are married to all the brothers of a family; besides their three or four husbands, they are allowed the privilege of a cicisbeo. The religion of the Toda is still sub judice, the general opinion being that they are imperfect Monotheists, who respect, but who do not adore, the sun and fire that warm them, the rocks and hills over which they roam, and the trees and spots which they connect with their various superstitions. When a Toda dies, a number of buffaloes are collected, and bar-

The Todas are merely a remnant of the old Tamulian tribes originally inhabiting the plains, and subsequently driven up to the mountains by some event, respecting which history is silent. Our opinion is built upon the rock of language. It has been proved that the Toda tongue is an old and obsolete dialect of the Tamul, containing many vocables directly derived from Sanscrit.

SIR RICHARD F. BURTON, 1851,
Goa, and the Blue Mountains

*barously beaten to death with huge pointed clubs, by the young
men of the tribe. The custom, it is said, arose from the importu-
nate demands of a Toda ghost; most probably, from the usual savage idea that the animal which is useful in this world will be
equally so in the next.*

*The Toda spends life in grazing his cattle, snoring in his cot-
tage, and churning butter. The villages belonging to this people
consist of, generally speaking, three huts, made with rough
planking and thatch; a fourth, surrounded by a low wall, stands
a little apart from, and forms a right angle with the others. This
is the celebrated Lactarium, or dairy, a most uninteresting structure, but ennobled and dignified by the variety of assertions that
have been made about it, and the mystery with which the savages have been taught to invest it. Some suppose it to be a species
of temple, where the Deity is worshipped in the shape of a black
stone, and a black stone, we all know, tells a very long tale,
when interpreted by even a second rate antiquary. Others declared that it is a masonic lodge, the strong ground for such opinion being, that females are never allowed to enter it, and that
sundry mystic symbols, such as circles, squares, and others of the
same kind, are roughly cut into the side wall where the monolith
stands. We entered several of these huts that were in a half-ru-
inous state, but were not fortunate or imaginative enough to
find either stone or symbols. The former might have been removed, the latter could not; so we must believe that many of our
wonder-loving compatriots have been deceived by the artistic attempts made by some tasteful savage, to decorate his dairy in an
unusual style of splendour. Near each village is a kraal, or cattle-
pen, a low line of rough stones, as often oval as circular, and as
often polygonal as oval. The different settlements are inhabited,
deserted, and reinhabited, according as the neighbouring lands
afford scant or plentiful pasturage.*

Burton noted that when he encountered the Todas, the practice of
polyandry was on the decline. He also thought that infanticide had fallen
out of favour, except in remote areas, but he did say, "Old women are by no
means common."

***Even in India, the land of ethnologic marvels, there are few races so strange and re-
markable in their customs...***

SIR RICHARD F. BURTON, 1851
Goa, and the Blue Mountains

The next day, we hired a guide, Alphonse, from the local YWCA, who was reputed to have some knowledge of the rural settlements around Ootacamund.

Our driver, Zufiq, was still with us, and we drove first through Palada village, then to Ithalar, Emerald and the Forest Rest House in Avalanche, through some forests and then into open farm country with unusually red soil.

All the women seemed to be doing heavy labour. We stopped and walked away from the village road for about a mile and a half, along the banks of a river up onto some open hills where there were two Toda settlements.

There were a few domed Toda dwellings, but of these no more than three or four were thatched. However, these were the original houses: a low opening in the front for entrance, and a hole in the roof for smoke; a cow entrance at one end; and a circular compound for buffalo. The government has tried to introduce changes, including more modern brick and cement domed houses to replace the original dwellings. These efforts have not proved popular. Todas have been known to remain in their old dwellings and to house their buffalo in the new constructions.

There seem to be two principal gods worshipped by the Todas, a brother and a sister called On and Tiekirzi, who rule the worlds of the dead and the living respectively. But Todas also believe there are 600 gods who live on top of hills, like immortal herdsmen who keep watch over men and buffalo. A typical Toda god is a being who is distinctly anthropomorphic. One such god is called Teu. He lives much the same kind of life as the mortal Todas, having his dairies and his buffalo. There are various ceremonies and rituals of the dairy in which the buffalo plays an important role. The gods who inhabit the summits of hills are never seen by mortals, but Teikirzi doesn't live on a hill like the other deities. She is everywhere.

As Burton mentioned, the Todas have polyandrous habits, postulating the sexual amorality of women. In the old days, the missionaries found this shocking. Current sterility among the Todas may be caused by syphilis and inbreeding. There are clearly far fewer women than men, and infanticide may still occur, although the practice of having female babies trampled to death by buffalo was stopped by the British government in 1856.

Back in Ootacamund we saw the old Post Office — now surrounded by modern buildings. We also saw Woodcock Hall, now the Brindaban Hotel, on top of the hill overlooking the Ootacamund valley. Also, the Nilgiri Library, a tall, rather austere-looking red-brick building with windows of ecclesiastical design. It was built in 1868. The library is private, for members only, but we talked our way in and were astonished to see three volumes of Burton's *Arabian Nights* prominently displayed in the reading room.

I found there Sir Frederick Price's *Ootacamund: A History*. Prices notes that Richard Burton gave some amusing accounts of how visitors spent their time at Ootacamund when he was there. He adds, however, that Burton's comments should be taken with the proverbial pinch of salt, as "Burton had nothing good to say of the Nilgiris."

In further explorations around town, we failed to find Stone House (the first house built by John Sullivan, the founder of Ootacamund), although we eventually were informed that it was at the top of Sullivan Hill. We did, however, get to Maleemund Meyni, the picnic spot mentioned as Burton's favourite. It is not as quiet or as idyllic now as it must have been then, being on a road with a lot of traffic. Nevertheless, it is still a beautiful spot, with a panoramic view over the farms in the valley. A very tranquil up-country scene.

Back in town we dropped in to the Ootacamund or "Ooty" Club. A beautifully proportioned, low, white building, the Ooty Club sits gracefully on a steep knoll at the top of an avenue of venerable trees. It was built as a private home in 1831 by Sir William Rumbold. Sir William was a bad businessman, and extravagances caused a decline in his health. He was dead at age forty-six. The house then became, first, the temporary headquarters of the governor general, and later the home of the visiting governors of Madras, who started coming to Ootacamund regularly: Lord Elphinstone was one of the first to do so. In 1841, ten years after it was built, the house became the Ootacamund Club.

The Ooty Club is famous for the Ootacamund Hunt. At first foxes were hunted, but later jackals were the quarry of choice. The Ooty Hunt began hunting "jacks" with fox hounds in 1846, five years after the club was founded. They say the Club still hunts, but no one knows what they hunt, although the new plantations are helpful in attracting jackals.

The exclusive Ooty Club still sits gracefully on a steep knoll at the top of an avenue of venerable trees.

Our host at the Club, Colonel Povayya, instructed one of the bearers to show me around. Among many historic details, he pointed out the Billiard Room, where Neville Chamberlain invented snooker. It was all beautifully kept in the old tradition. The walls were adorned with many prints, paintings and a host of ancient photographs, and also with the skins and heads of tigers, leopards, one lion, an ibex and a bison. Suddenly, and quite by chance, I came across the tawny head and skin of what I thought was a jackal, snarling at me from above a doorway in the Main Lounge. Horrified, I asked my guide what the animal was. "Ah, sir," he replied with pride, "that is a fox!"

Although it was still early afternoon, there were two patrons drinking at the bar. Rumour had it that the Indian gin that they served there was the best; the Indian Scotch, however, was looked at very doubtfully.

> *As for the poor in Ooty, who can afford nothing, they drink as much as anybody. It's cold for them up here, poor devils.... They must have a nip of something.*

> MOLLIE PANTER-DOWNES,
> *Ooty Preserved*, 1967

It had been a busy day trying to pick up pieces of Ooty history and relics of Burton. I was beginning to feel that Burton certainly didn't do justice to either Ooty or Goa in his writings. *Goa* might have been his first book, but it wasn't until a little later that his curiosity and his poignant observations achieved the level evident in the Sindh books. *Goa* is a flawed but interesting book. It is interesting mainly because of what Burton achieved later on. He wasn't really at home here as he was in the Sindh. Conversely, I was far more at home here than in the Sindh!

The next day, after breakfast, we drove a few miles out of Ooty to Doda Betta, the highest hill in Ooty on the eastern outskirts of the town. What a spectacle! There was a glorious view down over the valley and the town of Ootacamund. The only other people at this stupendous lookout point were two young men belonging to the Anandmargi sect, a sect started in Bhangor, whose adherents believe in universal brotherhood. Their colourful orange garb stood out prominently against the tranquil blues and greens of the Nilgiri countryside.

Eventually, on our return to town, we found Stone House. It *was* on top of Sullivan Hill, and is now the residence of the principal of the government art college. It was indeed made mostly of stone, but was much smaller than I had thought it would be and looked strangely out of place, although in a very prominent position overlooking the town and the valleys surrounding Ootacamund. There were two very old oak trees nearby. Legend has it they were planted by John Sullivan himself.

Though we had spent quite a bit of time searching for sites that were elusive, I felt that I had got a lot out of the visit to Ootacamund. Here, more than anywhere else, it was easy to understand that Burton was a loner who could never really fit in. Idle pursuits were a waste of time for him, and he couldn't afford the social activities anyway. He was far more interested in the Todas and the other local people. As soon as he thought he was fit enough, despite his bad eye infection, Burton went back to the Sindh where his heart had remained.

Kotagherry, or more correctly, Kothurgherry, stands about six thousand six hundred feet above the level of the sea, on the top of the Sreemoorga Pass, upon a range of hills which may be called the commencement of the Neilgherries. The station contains twelve houses, most of them occupied by the proprietors: The air of Kotagherry is moister than that of Ootacamund, and the nights and mornings are not so cool.

SIR RICHARD F. BURTON, 1851
Goa, and the Blue Mountains

I was dwarfed by the fading opulence that surrounded me. The remnants of an imperial past. It was my past, and it was not. Beyond the walls of the Wellington Club, the jungle waited as it has always waited.

Outside in the heavy dark, the air threatened rain. There was a sinister feeling to the atmosphere — a feeling of mystery, perhaps even doom. I was alone; the club was empty, the night watchman nowhere to be seen. Perhaps he had taken off to one of the local bars in the town up the hill. The doors of the club were wide open. It was very quiet; nothing moved.

Except me. I was energetic with busy purpose — writing. My pen flew over the page. There was so much to write about. My trip was almost over. It had been long and tiring, but rich in insights. I simply had to get it all down: so much about Burton; about the East; about the narrow, constrictive Victorian world he fled from in the early 1840s and the 10,000-year-old civilization he fled to.

The discovery of an exotic, seductive civilization entirely different from one's own can profoundly alter one's outlook — Burton's and my own. In trying to follow in Burton's footsteps in India I had experienced two journeys: the journey of my mind through years of research, and the physical journey over thousands of miles. Two journeys — one truth.

Hanging on the wall in front of me, high above where I sat, was the skin of a black leopard. Sinister, snarling, evoking images of an evil, enigmatic, curious, self-destructive, solitary, elusive creature. But dead now. Contained, captured and tamed. I kept looking at that skin.

The lights of the Wellington Club were flickering and burning low: the generator was probably on the blink. I had a torch to find my way in the darkness to my cabin outside the main club building. But I was still writing, my thoughts full of Burton.

I glanced up. The skin of the black leopard hanging above me on the wall seemed to move in the thickening shadows. As if life had somehow been breathed into it.

Rain! Cool rain. Green hills around the Wellington Club — tea, jungle and the eighteenth hole. For my last breakfast here I had two fried eggs and one last look at the black leopard skin hanging in the Wellington Club bar.

We packed and drove off into the rain, up, up, the twenty-five kilometres to Kotagiri, along a wet, slippery, winding road. Far below us, the valleys were shrouded in thick mist. We passed occasional settlements, tea plantations and jungle. Finally, we reached the small village of Kotagiri (*kota* means fort; *giri* means rock). We drove through the village. People, mostly tea labourers, huddled together under sheets of coloured plastic.

We turned off at Aravandu for five kilometres, and then drove one kilometre down a steep, winding, dirt road to the Bairpu Estate — past the occasional tea plucker. The mist was much thicker down here. Finally, near some small sheds, we parked, then walked the remaining fifty yards to a steep overhang. The sound of water came to us. There was supposed to be a giant waterfall here, but we could see nothing. Somewhere under all this mist I had hoped to find Catherine Falls, of which Burton wrote.

I would be disappointed to see only mist instead of Catherine Falls, but some things are beyond the control of even the most determined traveller. I nearly turned away.

But then, quite suddenly, the mist cleared a little. Beneath me I saw grey swirls and glimpsed the long, thin line of water cascading far below me, falling and falling from a high, precipitous hill. It was spectacular. Magic.

Then, just as suddenly, the mists closed. The falls disappeared, leaving only the sound somewhere in the distant depths.

I stood for a moment longer on the small promontory of rock, where Burton certainly would have stood. Below me, the water roared at the bottom of the deep chasm. Around me swirled the mist. On the wet slopes above stretched miles of neatly trimmed tea bushes glistening in the rain. A hundred and fifty years ago, this would have been jungle.

Burton did return to the Sindh he loved after his sick leave in Goa and the Nilgiris. He was fading fast, however, his ophthalmia worse, and his nerves tightly stretched. He was dillusioned with the prospect of "desert districts, dusty roads, tamarisk jungles, mud mausolea, lean Hindoos, puny Scindians, mosques, bazaars, and clay towns with tumbled-down walls." He worked, but with little zest, and eventually his writing and research dwindled to almost nothing. When he was finally sent back to Bombay for his trip home, many of his friends thought that he was dying and would not see England again. It is lucky that he did, because he was one of the most versatile and remarkable men of his age — an adventurer in the intellectual and spiritual world, as well as the physical world.

In the next forty years, he conquered many other worlds, both as an explorer and a writer. The most vivid exploits of this unique Victorian explorer, soldier, poet, anthropologist and diplomat still lay before him. But I had found, in those seven years in India, the seeds of the legend that was still to come.

Conclusion

The facts of history prove nothing more conclusively than this: a race either progresses or retrogrades, either increases or diminishes: The children of Time, like their sire, cannot stand still.

RICHARD BURTON
First Footsteps in East Africa,
1856

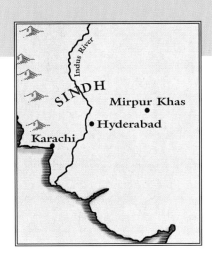

12

CONCLUSION

Returning to Bombay, and then to Canada, I completed my physical, historical and philosophical trek. It remained to try to express what I thought I had learned. Speculation about Burton from the vantage point of 150 years later seems to lead naturally to reflections about the fate of empires, the cycles of power, the position in history in which a man finds himself, especially an exceptional man such as Burton. Intelligent, ambitious, adventurous, he was a renegade, but he was always acutely aware of the confines of the historical context.

Burton's personal history is almost a microcosm of the history of the British Empire. He was by profession a soldier of commerce. The East India Company was an essential element of the imperial commercial expansion that followed Britain's Romantic fascination with the East. Britain's insatiable urge to move into new territory eventually met with diminished success. In many ways, Burton's enigmatic career paralleled the cycle of the Empire. In the end, dispatched to a meagre diplomatic posting in Trieste, the aging adventurer could not help but notice that the British Empire itself was beginning to decay and would soon start on the downward course that led to its ultimate decline.

Burton was always an outsider, in some ways a throwback to the earlier Romantic age that idealized the dream-like East as an enticing realm of mystery and splendour. As the British Empire spread, Burton's life and career developed, but his role in Britain's imperialist project was secondary to his own interests, so that, in essence, he remained apart from his own times.

Burton *was* a tool of the British Empire, but he was far above his task as an imperial pawn. His travels in the Sindh had effects greater and more long-lasting than the deeds of many supposedly more eminent men. As a soldier of the British East India Company, Burton's official mission was to assist

The insecurity of existence and property in the East, and the every-day dangers of an Oriental life are too real for the mind to take any interest in the fine-drawn distress and the puny horrors which are found sufficiently exciting by the European...
SIR RICHARD F. BURTON, 1851,
Sindh, and the Races That Inhabit the Valley of the Indus

Previous page: The children of Sindh. Richard Burton's legacy lives on. Sindh, and the Races That Inhabit the Valley of the Indus, *published in 1851, is still studied in schools today.*

Britain in consolidating its control over Sindh. Perhaps he did; but he also absorbed what the Sindh had to teach him and gave it back to its own people, filtered through his own, unique way of seeing. One hundred and fifty years later, all that remains of Napier are the crumbling ruins of old monuments and a few notes in the history books. What remains of Burton is a lasting legacy of the Sindhi language and history, safely in the hands of the Sindhis themselves. Studied and revered, Burton's books and documents live on — a tribute to the man and a lexicon of anthropological discovery. His contribution transcended the limited achievements of the average imperialist. He rose above them. Both Burton and the empire he served are dead. But in a larger sense, this mystical and mercurial adventurer has eluded the fate of empires.

I have studied the phenomenon of the cycles of power for a long time. In the mid-1970s I read an article entitled "The Fate of Empires" by Sir John Glubb, better known as "Glubb Pasha." He was born in 1897, fought in France in the First World War, then left the regular army to serve the government of Iraq. From 1939 to 1956, he commanded the famous Jordan Arab Legion. Glubb's article had a profound effect on me, and I felt that his observations and analysis could be helpful in interpreting Burton's career. Burton's seven years in India 150 years ago put him there almost in the middle of a particular cycle of power — a cycle that ended relatively recently.

We live according to cycles: from the intricate physiological cycles within the body to the much longer cycle of the stages of human aging from birth to death. Great cyclical waves and patterns in the sciences have been detailed by writers such as Thomas Kuhn. Sometimes a turning point in a cycle comes from one startling idea, such as Einstein's Theory of Relativity. There are cycles in economic theory, too: classical economic thought giving way to Keynesianism, and more recently to monetarism. Each period of change results in turmoil, since the old belief system has to be destroyed for the new system to establish itself. Over very long periods of time, the new becomes old and the old becomes new again. In the world of business, cycles cannot be avoided. To attempt to alter or suppress them can sometimes delay the inevitable — but may hasten it, too.

The longest cycles appear to be the cycles of empire. An entire civilization, with all its attendant complexities, can be seen to move as simply from life to death as a human moves through his or her much shorter cycle. In recent years, popular understanding of this concept has come through the work of authors such as Alvin Toffler, though Glubb recognized it long ago.

Those who analyse the behaviour patterns of civilizations often identify three large phases: the ages of Agriculture, of Industry and of Intellect or Information. England had entered the Age of Industry in the mid-1700s. The new era dispensed with agrarian-feudal society and its rulers, and industrialization created a rich, many-sided social system in Europe and North America. Increases in productivity which altered the balance of power throughout the world eventually led to the rise of two great empires: the British Empire and the American superpower. The Western nations came to

Portrait of Richard Burton, circa *1872, about the time of his final posting as British consul at Trieste.*

dominate the world both economically and militarily. The culmination of this industrial phase was marked by the two world wars in the twentieth century, a consequence of the fight for world dominance by the industrial powers, with the United States emerging as the winner — which it remained for most of the rest of the century.

Now, however, we appear to be at the end of that cycle of power and we are almost certainly facing the dawn of a new cycle. Living as he did from 1821 to 1890, Burton saw Britain's imperial power increase and then begin to wane. When he was in India in the 1840s, Britain was approaching the zenith of its might. It would take another hundred years for the empire to crumble.

According to Sir John Glubb, the only thing we learn from history is that men never learn from history. He shows us how to learn from the lives of empires. He points out that most empires in history have been large land blocks, almost without overseas possessions. (The British Empire was an obvious exception.) He also lists some of the empires recorded in history, and the lengths of their lives:

The Nation	Dates of rise and fall	Duration in years
Assyria	859-612 B.C.	247
Persia (Cyrus and his descendants)	538-330 B.C.	208
Greece (Alexander and his successors)	331-100 B.C.	231
Roman Republic	260-27 B.C.	233
Roman Empire	27 B.C.-A.D. 180	207
Arab Empire	A.D. 634-880	246
Mameluke Empire	1250-1517	267
Ottoman Empire	1320-1570	250
Spain	1500-1750	250
Romanov Russia	1682-1916	234
Britain	1700-1950	250

The life cycles of these empires are strikingly similar. Empires, like stars, are born in sudden outbursts of immense energy. Courageous new conquerors are normally poor, hardy and enterprising, but above all aggressive. The decaying empires that they overthrow are wealthy but defensive. Fearless initiative characterizes this first phase. As the empire grows and passes through the various stages of its 250-year life, the sovereign people has time to spread its values and peculiarities far and wide. On its decline, another people with different values and attributes becomes dominant, and its peculiarities are likewise disseminated. If the same nation were to retain its influence indefinitely, its peculiar qualities would come to characterize the whole human race. But history does not allow this to happen.

On a nation's way to imperial greatness, the battle fought by pioneers in pursuit of freedom is followed often by conquests and commercial expansion. Spurred on at first by a struggle with Spain, Britain built the most powerful navy in the world, commanded the oceans of the world from 1588 till 1914, colonized and conquered vast areas of the globe and grew rich.

Following the heyday of the pioneer and the period of conquest, there is a period in which the empire basks in its glory and honour, and to do so, for a time, remains its principal objective. Inevitably, this ambition gives way to the merchant ideal, which fosters the commercial growth and development of the nation. The East India Company both stimulated and benefited from the commercial ambitions of Britain in India. The commercial phase was a grand era. Art, architecture and other forms of luxury found rich patrons. Palaces were built, money was invested in communications, highways, bridges, railways and hotels. Victorian England was proud, united and full of self-confidence. Duty and patriotism were key words. Boldness and initiative were shown in the search for profitable enterprises in the far corners of the earth. This risk-taking commercial spirit exemplified the Victorian world after 1840. It was the prevalent mood when Burton went to the East, which was, not coincidentally, the centre of one of Britain's most daring and profitable commercial ventures: the opium trade.

The expansion of commerce is followed by greatly increased affluence. A surfeit of money causes the decline of a strong, brave and self-confident people. However, the decline in courage and enterprise is gradual. Money replaces honour and adventure as an objective. Gradually, affluence kills the voice of duty. Immensely rich nations are no longer interested in glory or duty, but only in the preservation of wealth and luxury. The military aggressiveness so necessary to conquest — both physical and commercial — becomes redundant. The newly sophisticated empire now denounces militarism as primitive and immoral, ignoring the danger of pacifism. History has showed that great nations do not normally disarm from motives of conscience but because of a weakening of a sense of duty in the citizens, and an increase in selfishness and the desire for wealth and ease. Spending money on defence seems wasteful to such citizens.

The next stage of empire is one in which striving is replaced by thought, and action is replaced by talk: the Age of Intellect. Burton being the very model of the powerful intellect could not help but be drawn into the intellectual fray. He came to maturity during Britain's Age of Intellect. Today we are experiencing North America's Age of Intellect, with its endless discussion and debate, endless interviews on television and in the press, incessant talking. The dedication to discussion seems to destroy the power of action, however.

Decadence is a moral and spiritual disease, resulting from too long a period of wealth and power, producing cynicism, pessimism, frivolity and the decline of religion. But decadence is the disintegration of a system, not of its individual members. Transported elsewhere, members of a decadent society soon discard their decadent ways of thought and prove themselves equal to the other citizens of their adopted country.

Burton was never content with intellectual endeavour alone. India was the springboard that launched him into a physical as well as intellectual adventure that lasted throughout his life. India provided the spark that lighted the fire. It was typical of Burton to be in his time rather than of it. Instead of retreating from physical exploration, he moved farther and farther into it. Even as an older man, his intellectualism was melded to action. Rather than just reminisce about the old days in India, he returned in 1876. The trip was rigorous physically, taking him — and the faithful Isabel — far and wide. It was also rigorous intellectually. At each step of the journey, he reflected on the changes that thirty years had brought to the outposts of Britain's empire. Burton looked at history and understood it.

Sir John Glubb's notion of the cyclical nature of history was heavily influenced by the thinking of the great Arab historian Ibn Khaldūn (1332-1406), whose work *Muqaddimah* outlines one of the earliest non-religious philosophies of history.

Ibn Khaldūn's work is a brilliant analysis of what he sees as the social cohesion that links history, politics, economics, education.... Social cohesion is spontaneous in limited kinship groups, such as tribes. When combined with a sufficiently strong religious ideology, it can motivate a ruling group to take power over its own and other tribes. Eventually, though, the ruling group weakens because of the complex interaction of developing sociopolitical factors. The dynasty declines, giving way to a new one, ruled by a new group with a stronger cohesive ideology. Classical Islamic theology and philosophy are at the base of Khaldūn's theory. For him, history was a continuous loop, with no essential progress, just constant movement from the primitive state to civilized society. He visualized the turning of the great circle of history, recognizing that: "there is a general change of conditions ... as if it were a new and repeated creation, a world brought into existence anew."

In our own times, two analysts who look at the complexities of modern life as the inevitable result of our place on the curve of the cycle of empire are James Dale Davidson and William Rees-Mogg. Their book, *The Great Reckoning*, considers the possibility of a cycle of centuries, pointing out that every five hundred years an event seems to take place that changes the course of history for the next half-millennium: events of the stature of the invention of gunpowder, the fall of Rome, the birth of Christ. Critical turning points are often marked by stunning advances in technology. *The Great Reckoning* suggests that our present period of great technological change is bringing about an upheaval analogous to the change in worldview caused by the "Gunpowder Revolution," in which it suddenly became possible to conquer by killing from afar.

These writers speculate that our world today, with its congested demography and uncertain economy, will become increasingly troubled as the 500-year cycle that began with Columbus comes to an end. They see debt-ridden countries collapsing under the weight of the welfare state. To them, the end of the postwar period is signalled not merely by the collapse of one superpower (the United States) and the takeover of its manufacturing-based strength by a rival (Japan), but rather by a fundamental shift in the underlying principles of progress itself.

Any man in his lifetime can observe only a small segment of the vast cycle in progress around him. A clever man, however, will deduce far more than a less clever man. Though a man of Burton's understanding would not be surprised to see that 150 years have wrought enormous changes, he would be fascinated by what he would see today. Particularly in India. An outburst of creative, entrepreneurial spirit and a sense of national purpose has created a new, wealthy society that dominates Asia. China and India appear to be the latest Asian nations to experience such entrepreneurial fervour and explosive growth. The smaller nations in Asia are also showing signs of burgeoning energy. What is missing are the formal trade and political alliances that would result in the birth of a true empire.

Burton would certainly have speculated at this point on the development of the new Asian empire. He would have questioned whether Japan or China would be able to prevail politically. And, perhaps most important of all, he would have had questions about the role of Islam.

Ibn Khaldūn pointed out long ago that an empire needs an imperial religion. The imperial religion of both Britain and the United States has been Christianity, with its easy relationship to the concepts of democracy and capitalism. The state religion of the USSR — atheism — did not prove as powerful as Christianity. It was capable of sustaining Communism for a limited time, but atheism, unlike Christianity — or Islam — seldom captures the heart.

When Burton returned to the East in 1876, he saw that the world of 1841 had disappeared. The attitude to the imperial religion of the British Empire had also changed. By 1876, it must have been evident that, missionary efforts notwithstanding, there was never the slightest chance that India would become a Christian land. Burton probably also understood that though its time had not yet come, Islam offered a religious ideology capable of forging the social cohesion needed to build a new empire.

Burton realized how compelling Islam is, and in my travels so did I. In his time, unlike our own, the cycles of power were not such that Islam could be asserted as a powerful world religion; so, for Burton, devotion to Islam remained a personal not a political involvement. Today I think he would see it differently. Islam is by far the most vital of the religions of pre-modern, traditional societies. It is a crusading faith, and its energy now appears to be renewed and militant. As the twentieth century draws to an end, religions — and Islam in particular — will seem increasingly attractive as an antidote to incompetent governments and unstable societies.

The reassertion of the power of religion will not be a mere revival of Islam. It is probable that Islam will come to define the terms of conflict between North and South. After all, Islam is the world religion that historically has posed the gravest threat to the Judaeo-Christian tradition. Had Burton been alive today, he would not have been surprised at this rising tide of Islam, and might even have welcomed it. It is the religion of the front-line states that for a time confronted Israel and opposed the aspiration of the Jewish people for a homeland in the Middle East. And it is the faith of those who control the world's oil wealth. Islam may be better suited to the economic world of the late 1900s than it was to the world of the late 1800s. As Burton would certainly have noticed, today's megapolitical conditions of devolution and the breakdown of order heighten the appeal of Islamic doctrines. It is well known that a handful of militant political groups have taken to terrorism. These Islamic militants, reared in poor economies and a climate of domestic and geopolitical frustration, are willing to fight and die for their cause.

Today, there are five counter-powers in proximity to the main areas of Islamic ferment: Russia, Turkey, India, the secular and pro-Western regimes of the Middle East and the Zionist state of Israel. Of these, India is by far the most interesting. Like the former Soviet Union, India is a multi-ethnic empire forged in the time of colonialism. The animosities between its Islamic populations and the Hindu majority led to the fissuring of the British India that Burton knew. Now, as the forces of devolution gather strength, India faces internal pressures to split apart.

As the journey progressed and I became better informed, I saw increasingly clearly that cracks are showing in the provinces of Jammu and Kashmir. The Indian authorities blame Pakistan for Islamic ferment; the Pakistani authorities blame India for an upsurge in Hindu militancy. As domestic protest movements in both countries become more violent, it may well be that the two countries will go to war in this decade. It is a dangerous situation, and Burton would certainly have been saddened by it.

One hundred and fifty years ago, at the beginning of the great Victorian era, Richard Francis Burton responded to the challenge and allure of the East. He was one of the most remarkable adventurers in an age of adventurers. Staunchly patriotic, he nevertheless realized the failings and potential dangers of British imperialism. He loved the East, and the East provided the young adventurer with the world in which he could pursue his zest for life and satisfy his inquisitive mind — a world of sympathy, mystery and melancholy; of tenderness mixed with earthy coarseness; of excitement; and of intriguing cultural and religious complexity.

Today we face the twilight and demise of the great American age of prosperity. The East will rise again. The domination of India by the West that Burton witnessed and participated in will give way to a new era — fuelled by economic and technological change and religious influence.

Burton embraced his future by leaving the confines of conventional Victorian society in the mid-nineteenth century and discovering for himself a 10,000-year-old civilization on another continent. We, too, can embrace our future. But we cannot do so by living an isolated provincial existence with all the protection that an affluent society affords us. We must see for ourselves, find for ourselves, learn the ways of the new frontiers. As Burton did. As I tried to do.

In making the journey, I found that my fascination with the past became a fascination with the future. My obsession with the extraordinarily industrious and inquisitive Victorian adventurer Richard Burton led me to try to follow in his footsteps. It was a remarkable experience, often mixed with anguish and frustration, and fuelled by curiosity, restlessness and wanderlust. There is much to be learned from books; but the trials of physical effort, intimate involvement and personal experience add a dimension of understanding that cannot be gained from literature alone. There is danger, too. But as the Persians say, "Death is a Festival." This sense of danger heightens the intellect, makes keen the powers of observation and, as Burton himself pointed out, invests the scene of travel with an added interest.

There is enjoyment, too, from animal existence.

> *Though your mouth glows, and your skin is parched, yet you feel no languor, the effect of humid heat; your lungs are lightened, your sight brightens, your memory recovers its tone, and your spirits become exuberant; your fancy and imagination are powerfully aroused, and the wildness and sublimity of the scenes around you stir up all the energies of your soul — whether for exertion, danger, or strife. Your morale improves; you become frank and cordial, hospitable, and single-minded: the hypocritical politeness and the slavery of civilization are left behind you in the city. Your senses are quickened: they require no stimulants but air and exercise, — in the Desert spirituous liquors excite only disgust....*

RICHARD F. BURTON,
Personal Narrative of a Pilgrimage to El-Medinah and Meccah, 1855-57

In a way, it is the journey not the arrival that matters. There is the affinity of the traveller with the traveller — my active, sympathetic understanding of Burton's curiosity and craving for the strange and exotic. And a sadness, too. It is sad to contemplate the murder of this man's ambition, an ambition almost certainly killed because no superior could ever manage Burton's quixotic character, could ever be sure that at some crucial moment Burton might not prefer his own opinion over somebody else's order, as an anonymous contemporary pointed out. An insolent want of tact both in official and social matters curtailed first his army and later his diplomatic career; but frustration did not curtail genius, and the demon of his curiosity drove him insatiably towards knowledge and experience. Discipline and obedience were ignored in the pursuit of adventure, wisdom and the meaning of life. This, and his single-minded romanticism, dictated his personality and all he did. Burton remains a mysterious genius without the poet's gift of expression and eloquence, but nevertheless possessed of majesty in discovery and insight in interpreting what he discovered.

Assad tells us that Frank Harris, Burton's contemporary, reported that "Burton's laughter, even, deep chested as it was, had in it something of sadness." Perverse and passionate, Burton was both imaginative and destructive, humane and blasé, understanding and temperamental. And always a romantic. His romanticism is the key to Burton and his love of the East. The romantic is a person capable of being alone, capable of heroism, willing to look beyond the obvious to seek the hidden.

I am a different man now. Following in Burton's footsteps has changed me. In many ways he is still a mystery, but sometimes the mists lifted to allow me some insight into the man and the process he was part of. Still, there is much to be learned, and more roads to travel. The finding is important, but so is the journey. I realize that more vividly now that the journey is over. I had a dream, but now that dream is ended. I am the richer for the journey and the poorer for its having ended. Tired — and yet with an increasing desire to climb new mountains and discover new worlds.

Of one thing I am certain: I will not stop. Out of frustration and out of desire come adventure, and fulfilment of a kind, even though there is always another horizon, and only ever a temporary haven. The world of tomorrow will change, and as if tomorrow were a foreign land, we must set out in search of it. The world of yesterday is written. We must read it. What was true in Burton's time is true in our own: no man is totally confined by his own time, and no man can move into the future without understanding the past. The future — as always — can only be grasped by those who are ready for it.

1885 cartoon of the ageing Richard Burton by "Ape" Carlo Pellegrini in Vanity Fair. *The editorial in the magazine reads: "As a bold astute traveller, courting danger, despite hardship, and compelling fortune, Captain Burton has few equals; as a Master of Oriental languages, manners, and customs he has none. He is still very young, very vigorous, very full of anecdote and playful humour, and, what is remarkable in a linguist, he has not disdained even his own mother tongue, which he handles with a precision and a power that few can approach."*

BIBLIOGRAPHY

Richard Burton wrote prodigiously and in his lifetime was written about by friend and foe alike. In the century that has passed since his death, critics, historians, biographers and devotees have added to the mass of information about him. In 1923, Norman Penzer wrote the most comprehensive Burton bibliography ever attempted. Today, scholars such as Jim Casada and Burke E. Casari are using modern bibliographical tools and techniques to classify and record not only printed material by and about Burton, but also extant manuscripts. My own efforts to locate Burton's original India letters gave me an understanding of the challenges involved in such work.

This bibliographical note offers a selection from among the many books by Burton and others that I found compelling and useful in researching Burton's India years and my journey in his footsteps.

Men of high rank, great wealth, or religious celebrity, are buried under domes of cut stone, some of them handsome and elaborately built, with arabesques and other ornaments. The tombstones of such worthies ... are always covered with richly-embroidered cloths, and their mausolea are closed by silver doors, sometimes with golden padlocks and keys.

SIR RICHARD F. BURTON, 1851
Sindh, and the Races That Inhabit the Valley of the Indus

BOOKS BY BURTON

- *The Book of the Sword*. London: Chatto and Windus, 1884. Reprinted with Note and slight alterations. New York: Dover Publications, Inc., 1987. Contains nearly 300 illustrations.

- *Falconry in the Valley of the Indus*. London: John Van Voorst, 1852. Reprinted with an introduction by Christopher Ondaatje. Karachi: Department of Culture and Tourism, Government of Sindh, 1995.

- *Goa, and the Blue Mountains; or, Six Months of Sick Leave*. London: Richard Bentley, 1851. Reprinted with an introduction by Dane Kennedy. Los Angeles: University of California Press, 1991.

- *Personal Narrative of a Pilgrimage to El- Medinah and Meccah*. London: Longman, Brown, Green, and Longmans, 1855, 1857.

- *A Plain and Literal Translation of the Arabian Nights' Entertainments, Now Entitulated The Book of the Thousand Nights and a Night With Introduction* [sic] *Explanatory Notes on the Manners and Customs of Moslem Men and a Terminal Essay upon the History of the Nights*. Benares: "Printed by the Kamashastra Society For Private Subscribers Only," 1885. Reprinted as *The Book of the Thousand Nights and a Night*. New York: The Heritage Press, *circa* 1940.

- *Scinde; or, the Unhappy Valley*. London: Richard Bentley, 1851.

- *Sind Revisited: with Notices of the Anglo-Indian Army; Railroads; Past, Present, and Future, etc*. London: Richard Bentley and Son, 1877. Reprinted with an introduction by Sirajul Haque. Karachi: Department of Culture and Tourism, Government of Sindh, 1993.

- *Sindh, and the Races That Inhabit the Valley of the Indus; with Notices of the Topography and History of the Province*. London: Wm. H. Allen & Co., 1851. Reprinted with an introduction by Mazhar Yusuf. Karachi: Indus Publications, 1988.

BIOGRAPHICAL WORKS

Blanch, Lesley. *The Wilder Shores of Love*. London: John Murray (Publishers) Ltd., 1954. Reprinted. London: Orion Books Limited, 1993. An incisive look at Isabel Burton's life and her relationship to her husband.

Brodie, Fawn. *The Devil Drives: A Life of Sir Richard Burton*. New York: W.W. Norton, 1967. Reprinted with biographical note. London: Eland, 1990. Contains map, illustrations, bibliography. Probably the most sensitive and psychologically penetrating biography of Burton.

Burton, Isabel. *The Life of Captain Sir Richd F. Burton, K.C.M.G., F.R.G.S.* London: Chapman & Hall, 1893. Isabel, above all others, was privy to the secrets of Richard Burton's life. Her work, though biased by her undying devotion, stands in a class by itself when it comes to bringing Burton alive for the reader. Isabel's biography contains autobiographical segments by Burton himself.

Farwell, Byron. *Burton: A Biography of Sir Richard Francis Burton*. New York: Holt, Rinehart and Winston, 1963.

Hastings, Michael. *Sir Richard Burton: A Biography*. London: Hodder and Stoughton, 1978.

McLynn, Frank. *Burton: Snow upon the Desert*. London: John Murray (Publishers) Ltd., 1990. Contains maps, illustrations, bibliography.

Rice, Edward. *Captain Sir Richard Francis Burton: The Secret Agent Who Made the Pilgrimage to Mecca, Discovered the Kama Sutra, and Brought the Arabian Nights to the West*. New York: Charles Scribner's Sons, 1990. Reprinted. New York: HarperCollins, 1991. Contains maps, illustrations and bibliography.

Stisted, Georgiana M. *The True Life of Capt. Sir Richard F. Burton K.C.M.G., F.R.G.S., Etc. Written by His Niece Georgiana M. Stisted with the Authority and Approval of the Burton Family*. London: H.S. Nichols, 1896. Reprinted. London: Darf Publishers Limited, 1985. This brief, readable biography is unique in its point of view.

BOOKS ON THE HISTORY AND CULTURE OF SINDH

Akhund, Abdul Hamid, ed. *Bhitai: The Message of the Master. An Anthology of Commentaries on the Poetry of Shah Abdul Latif*. Hyderabad, Pakistan: Shah Abdul Latif Bhitshah Cultural Centre Committee, 1993.

Andrew, W.P. *The Indus and Its Provinces, Their Political and Commercial Importance Considered in Connection with Improved Means of Communication*. Illustrated by Statistical Tables and Maps. *c.* 1857. Reprinted. Karachi: Indus Publications, 1986.

Bose, Mihir. *The Aga Khans*. Kingswood, Tadworth, Surrey: World's Work Ltd./The Windmill Press, 1984.

Daftary, Farhad. *The Ismailis: Their History and Doctrine*. Cambridge University Press, 1990.

Dumasia, Naoroji M. *Aga Khan and His Ancestors*. Bombay: The Times of India Press, 1939.

Eastwick, E.B. *Dry Leaves from Young Egypt. c.* 1849. Reprinted as *A Glance at Sind before Napier*, with Foreword by Riaz Siddiqi. Karachi: Indus Publications, 1989.

Kalichbeg, Mirza, trans. *History of Sind, Translated from Persian Books*. Karachi: The Commissioner's Press, 1902. Reprinted. Karachi: Scinde Classics, 1982.

Khuhro, Hamida. *The Making of Modern Sind: British Policy and Social Change in the Nineteenth Century*. Karachi: Indus Publications, 1978.

Khuhro, Hamida, ed. *Sind through the Centuries: Proceedings of an International Seminar Held in Karachi in Spring 1975 by the Department of Culture, Government of Sind*. Karachi: Oxford University Press, 1981.

Lambrick, H.T. *John Jacob of Jacobabad*. London: Cassell & Company Ltd., 1960. Reprinted with new preface by the author. Karachi: Oxford University Press, 1975.

Lari, Suhail Zaheer. *A History of Sindh*. Karachi: Oxford University Press, 1994.

Lari, Yasmeen. *Traditional Architecture of Thatta*. Karachi: The Heritage Foundation, 1989.

MacMunn, Lieut.-Gen. Sir George. *The Lure of the Indus: Being the Final Acquisition of India by the East India Company*. London: Jarrolds Publishers, 1934. Reprinted. Karachi: Allied Book Company, 1986.

The Memoirs of Aga Khan. Foreword by Somerset Maugham. London: Cassell and Co. Ltd., 1954.

Outram, Lieut.-Col. C.B. *The Conquest of Scinde: A Commentary. c.* 1843. Reprinted. Karachi: Indus Publications, 1978.

Postans, T. *Personal Observations on Sindh; the Manners and Customs of Its Inhabitants; and Its Productive Capabilities; with a Sketch of Its History, a Narrative of Recent Events, and an Account of the Connection of the British Government with That Country to the Present Period*. London: Longman, Brown, Green and Longmans, 1843. Reprinted. Karachi: Indus Publications, 1973.

Shah, Idries. *The Sufis*. New York: Doubleday, 1964. Reprinted. New York: Anchor Books/Doubleday, 1971.

Shaw, Isobel. *Pakistan Handbook*. London: John Murray (Publishers) Ltd., 1989. Reprinted. Chico, Calif.: Moon Publications, Inc., 1990.

Thomas, R. Hughes. *Memoirs on Sind, with an Introduction Entitled The Discovery of Sind, by Mahmudul Hasan Siddiqi*. Reprint of Selections from the Records of the Bombay Government, No. XVII. — New Series, originally published Bombay: Bombay Education Society's Press, 1855. Karachi: Allied Book Company, 1989. Fascinating selection of mid-nineteenth-century articles on Sindh.

Wolpert, Stanley. *Zulfi Bhutto of Pakistan: His Life and Times*. New York: Oxford University Press, 1993.

Yusuf, Zohra, ed. *Rhythms of the Lower Indus: Perspectives on the Music of Sindh*. Karachi: Department of Culture and Tourism, Government of Sindh, Pakistan, *c.* 1988. A series of essays.

Books on Goa, Bombay and British India

Assad, Thomas J. *Three Victorian Travellers: Burton, Blunt, Doughty*. London: Routledge & Kegan Paul, 1964.

Kaye, Myriam. *Bombay and Goa*. Lincolnwood, Ill.: Passport Books, 1990.

Leask, Nigel. *British Romantic Writers and the East: Anxieties of Empire*. Published by arrangement with Cambridge University Press. New Delhi: Foundation Books, 1993.

Morris, Jan. *Stones of Empire: The Buildings of British India*. Reprinted with new illustrations by the author. Harmondsworth, Middlesex: Penguin Books, 1994.

Panter-Downes, Mollie. *Ooty Preserved: A Victorian Hill Station in India*. New York: Farrar, Straus and Giroux, 1967.

Richards, J.M. *Goa*. Revised edition. New Delhi: Vikas Publishing House Pvt Ltd., 1993.

Tindall, Gillian. *City of Gold: The Biography of Bombay*. Reprinted with an introduction. Harmondsworth, Middlesex: Penguin Books, 1992.

BIBLIOGRAPHICAL AND OTHER

Davidson, James Dale, and Lord William Rees-Mogg. *The Great Reckoning:
Protect Yourself in the Coming Depression*. Revised and updated. New York:
Touchstone/Simon and Schuster Inc., 1994.

Jutzi, Alan H., ed. *In Search of Richard Burton: Papers from a Huntington
Library Symposium*. San Marino, Calif.: Huntington Library, 1993.
A collection of papers presenting the latest findings of a select group of
British, Canadian and American Burton scholars, collectors and devotees.

Penzer, Norman M. *An Annotated Bibliography of Sir Richard Francis Burton
K.C.M.G.* Preface by F. Grenfell Baker. London: A.M. Philpot Ltd., 1923.